D1826791

Political Campaigning and Communication

Series Editor
Darren G. Lilleker
Bournemouth University
Bournemouth, UK

The series explores themes relating to how political organisations promote themselves and how citizens interpret and respond to their tactics. Politics is here defined broadly as any activities designed to have impact on public policy. Therefore the scope of the series covers campaigns conducted by parties and candidates for election to legislatures, pressure group campaigns, lobbying, and campaigns instigated by social and citizen movements. Campaigning is an important interface between organisations and citizens, they present opportunities to study the latest strategies and tactics of political marketing as well as their impact in engaging, involving and mobilising citizens.

More information about this series at
http://www.palgrave.com/gp/series/14546

Dalia Elsheikh

Campaign Professionalism during Egypt's 2012 Presidential Election

palgrave
macmillan

Dalia Elsheikh
Bournemouth University
Bournemouth, UK

Political Campaigning and Communication
ISBN 978-3-319-75953-1   ISBN 978-3-319-75954-8   (eBook)
https://doi.org/10.1007/978-3-319-75954-8

Library of Congress Control Number: 2018935036

Cover illustration: ZUMA Press, Inc. / Alamy Stock Photo

Printed on acid-free paper

This Palgrave Macmillan imprint is published by the registered company Springer International Publishing AG part of Springer Nature
The registered company address is: Gewerbestrasse 11, 6330 Cham, Switzerland

To my family—my mother Nahla, my father Mahmoud, and my brother Mohamed—for their tremendous love, unconditional support, and patience, without which it would not have been possible to complete this work. Thank you for being proud of all that I do.

PREFACE

This book studies the first Egyptian presidential election campaigns after the 25th January 2011 revolution. It aims to answer two questions: to what extent this election was professionalised and to what extent the levels of professionalism impacted the democratisation process of Egypt. To answer these questions, the book analyses the top five presidential candidates' campaigns, applying the professionalisation index to them; this consists of two sub-indices that assess campaign structures and campaign strategies, offers insights into the organizational and tactical development of the campaigns and how they viewed the functions of campaigning in relation to this contest. The book does this through analytical qualitative research involving interviews with campaign staff and managers as well as analysis of secondary documents and contemporary media reports.

The book demonstrates the crucial role campaign professionalism played in the 2012 Egyptian presidential elections. The book infers that the professionalism of the 2012 elections campaigns might have been the main factor that led to the success of both Mohamed Morsi and Ahmed Shafiq in the first round of elections. The book also argues that the professionalism—as applied during this election through a "do anything to win" or a "win at all costs" approach—had negative implications on the democratization process of Egypt, as it hindered Egypt's transition to functional if thin democracy. On the contrary, it led Egypt to remain trapped in its transitional period.

ACKNOWLEDGEMENTS

My sincere thanks and appreciation are owed to several people without whom this book would not have been completed. Firstly, I would like to express my immense gratitude to Dr Darren Lilleker. I find myself speechless when presented with his unlimited and immediate support. Many thanks go to him not only for being an inspiration but also for providing me with the opportunity to learn from him. I would like to thank him for being in my life. I owe him a lot and I cannot find enough words to express my gratitude. I am deeply indebted to him for his kindness and generosity.

My sincere gratitude also goes to Professor Barry Richards for all his patience, guidance, and encouragement as well as for introducing me to a range of methodological approaches, which heavily influenced my research.

It was my great honour to have guidance from Professor Rachel Gibson who pioneered efforts to measure campaign professionalism. Her profound advice added immeasurable depth to this book.

The completion of this research would not have been possible without the support and constructive advice offered by the Bournemouth internal academic staff, especially Dr Daniel Jackson, Dr Anastasia Veneti, Dr Fiona Cownie, and Dr Pawel Surowiec. My sincere thanks also go to Jan Lewis for facilitating innumerable administrative tasks for me.

It is with extreme gratitude that I thank Dr Ali El Din Hilal, Emeritus Professor at Cairo University, for the gifts of his valuable time, advice, encouragement, and answers to my many questions, which he enthusiastically offered during our lengthy phone conversation.

I would be remiss if I failed to recognise the Palgrave team, especially Ambra Finotello and Imogen Gordon Clark, for their support in making this book into a reality; I appreciate their abundant assistance.

Notably, this book would not exist without the practitioners who were interviewed. I would like to thank them all for their input and valuable time.

I am also immensely grateful to all researchers in the field of election campaigning—especially Jens Tenscher (1969–2015)—whose work both informed and influenced this book.

Lastly, I thank my parents for their unwavering support over the past few years and for financially sponsoring this project. For their encouragement and belief in my work, I am eternally grateful.

London, UK   Dalia Elsheikh
2018

CONTENTS

LIST OF ABBREVIATIONS AND ACRONYMS

Al-Masry	Al-Masry Al-Youm newspaper
Brotherhood	Muslim Brotherhood
FJP	Freedom and Justice Party
NDP	National Democratic Party
PEC	Presidential Elections Committee
SCAF	The Supreme Council of the Armed Forces
SCC	Supreme Constitutional Court
Youm7	*Al-Youm Al-Sabaa* newspaper

LIST OF TABLES

CHAPTER 1

Introduction to Studying 2012 Egyptian Election

1.1 Overview

The year 2012 can be considered a watershed in Egypt's history as it came after a revolution that ended the rule of Hosni Mubarak, who had been in power for 30 years. For the first time in Egyptian history, not only in modern history, Egyptians were able to choose their ruler. There had been no form of presidential elections from the first ruler King Menes (3100 BC) taking power until the election of President Hosni Mubarak (2005) which did not follow the norms of democratic elections. Even after the 1952 revolution, Egyptians were not able to choose their president through multi-candidate elections. They were only able to do this through a referendum, where they had to say yes or no to one person, who always became the president.

In 2005, and after huge pressure from different powers in the country, President Mubarak changed article 76 in the constitution which allowed for a multi-candidate presidential election for the first time in Egyptian history. However, this election was widely seen as a façade, as it was already previously known that Mubarak was the one who was going to win. In 2011, the Egyptian revolution took place and for the first time in the history of the country, Egypt witnessed a real multi-candidate presidential election in 2012; where no one—even pollsters—was able to predict the winner.

© The Author(s) 2018   1
D. Elsheikh, *Campaign Professionalism during Egypt's 2012
Presidential Election*, Political Campaigning and Communication,
https://doi.org/10.1007/978-3-319-75954-8_1

The period prior to this election and the election result itself showed many surprises and unpredictable results. This indicates that this field still requires some attention by experts and scholars to know how elections work in a country in its transitional phase such as Egypt at that time. For instance, all polls conducted before the elections showed that the competition was mainly between two candidates, the first being Abdel Moneim Aboul Fotouh, who had previously been dismissed from the Muslim Brotherhood. The second frontrunner candidate was Amr Moussa who portrayed himself as a defector from the Mubarak regime. However, the actual results of the first round of the elections showed completely the opposite as the two winners were Ahmed Shafiq, the last prime minister during the Mubarak era, and Mohamed Morsi, the head of the Freedom and Justice Party, the political arm of the Muslim Brotherhood. Despite the role of the people in demanding change, the revolution's candidate Hamdeen Sabahi came third place. Another feature of the campaigning process is that many candidates refused to use some forms of campaigning. For example, all candidates except Moussa and Aboul Fotouh refused to participate in any form of debates.

Another controversial feature of this election was the winner: Mohamed Morsi, who entered the election by chance, became the president of Egypt. Was this the result Egyptians were looking for? What was the role of campaigning in this result? To what extent did the campaign conduct and its result impact upon the democratisation process in Egypt? These are some of the questions this book will answer.

1.2   RATIONALE FOR THE BOOK

This book presents the first analytical study of the levels of professionalism of campaigns in the 2012 Egyptian presidential elections. It provides the story of the five main campaigns by applying the professionalisation index to analyse their structures (hardware) and strategies (software). The book also provides an evaluation of the application of the professionalisation index to nascent democracies, and the impact of campaign professionalism on such democracies.

Due to the novelty of the whole topic, the results of this analysis add significantly to the understanding of campaigning and create an academic base for further studies within similar fragile democratic systems. Furthermore, it should offer campaigners practical guidance when approaching future elections.

This book aims to explore campaign professionalism in the 2012 presidential elections and to what extent this affected the democratisation process in Egypt. The book will focus on analysing the Egyptian case by answering these main research questions:

1. Using professionalisation theory, how was the 2012 presidential election campaigns organised and conducted?
2. To what extent did campaign professionalism determine the outcome of the first and second rounds of this election?
3. What were the implications of the election campaigns for the process of democratisation in Egypt?

To answer these questions, the book explores the possible implications of professionalism using literature which examines the relationships between professionalisation and democratisation. After that, it applies the professionalisation index to the five studied campaigns by analysing data from a set of semi-structured interviews with the campaign managers and officials which took place during the election in 2012, with some follow-up discussions taking place in 2017. The interviews were conducted with primary figure within each of the campaigns and then verified through interviews with other campaign team members and officials.

Through these interviews, the book explores how the campaigns were designed to raise voter awareness and participation, besides identifying what strategies were used to achieve the campaigns' aims. The interview questions depended on the professionalisation index, which measures both the strategies and structures of the campaigns. There were two sets of questions: the first set of questions focused on 'the campaign structure'. It consisted of questions covering size of campaign staff, management style, campaign premises, degrees of externalisation, the differentiation of internal communication structures, the nature and degree of feedback, the degree of opposition research, campaign budget, and the duration of the campaign. The second set of questions assessed the 'campaign strategy' and consisted of questions focusing on the degree of audience targeting, the degree of narrowcasting activities, the relevance of paid media, the relevance of free media, the relevance of talk shows, the relevance of the internet and social media, the relevance of debates, the degree of event and news management, and the degree of personalisation. The book also used descriptive, analytical, as well as comparative approaches when it came to comparing campaign strategies and structures and understanding campaign professionalism.

1.3   Book Structure

This chapter explains the importance of the 2012 Egyptian elections and gives an overview for the whole book. The chapter highlights why it's important to study campaigns in order to understand the outcome of the 2012 election as well as the longer-term political situation in Egypt. The chapter explains this by highlighting literature on campaign functions in elections and campaign professionalism (mainly what it means and how to measure it). In addition, it highlights the validity of using the professionalisation index in studying campaign professionalism. The chapter also discusses the relationship between professionalisation and democracy.

Chapter 2 sets the scene by describing the socio-political environment in which the 2012 Egyptian presidential elections took place. The chapter highlights the extent Egyptians were polarised by the time of election and argues that the confusion and mismanagement of the transitional period by all political forces led to flaws in the process of democratisation in Egypt making it difficult for first-time campaigners to work and mobilise voters.

Chapter 3 applies the professionalisation index to each of the five main campaigns separately and analyses their structures and strategies drawing on data from the series of interviews with campaign staff.

Based on that data, Chap. 4 analyses the five election campaigns by comparing and analysing their structures and strategies. By analysing the campaigns' professionalism, the chapter explores which campaigns were more professional and argues that there was a link between the professionalism of Morsi's and Shafiq's campaign and the results of the first round of elections, suggesting that professionalism played an important role in determining the results of the first round of elections. The chapter also explores the limitations of campaign effectiveness; finding levels of professionalism did not play the same role in determining the result of the second round of elections, as there were other determinant factors such as voters resorting to punitive voting.

The final chapter concludes the study by discussing the implications of the levels of professionalism on the democratisation process in Egypt. The chapter concludes that the professionalism—as applied by Morsi's campaign—had a negative impact on Egypt's democratic transition in general as it led Egypt to being trapped in its transitional period, rather than moving to a functional emergent but thin democracy. The chapter also provides an evaluation of the application of the professionalisation index to nascent democracies.

1.4   DEMOCRACY AND PROFESSIONALISATION: DEFINITIONS AND DEBATE

There are no studies to date on the 2012 Egyptian campaigns. This is the reason why this book depends on literature about campaigns and its relation to democracy from a wider perspective, so building a picture of campaigning in general and then applying that framework to the Egyptian case. This chapter argues that studying campaigns is essential to understanding elections and democracy. The chapter further argues that campaigns play a vital role in elections as they can influence both the process and the outcome of elections, thus influencing the quality of democracy in general. This is due to the functions campaigns play in the election process such as their role in informing, persuading, and mobilising voters (Norris 2002), making them a core feature of modern democracies. This chapter highlights campaign functions and relations to democracy and how campaigns can be studied academically by highlighting well-known frameworks used to examine the professionalism of campaigns. The chapter argues that literature on professionalism provides the most appropriate framework to study campaigns as it allows mapping how any specific campaign adheres to the core features of the postmodern era campaign. The chapter also argues that the professionalisation index, developed to compare campaigning over time and across nations, is the most appropriate framework to study campaigns as it deconstructs the campaign into structures (hardware) and strategies (software) which give an overall understanding of how the campaigns were planned and implemented. The chapter also highlights the main arguments regarding the relationship between campaign professionalism and democracy in order to test them on the Egyptian case in Chap. 5. The chapter will do this by reviewing literature on democracy, democratisation, elections, campaigns, and campaigns' professionalism.

1.4.1   On Democracy

There is agreement among scholars that democracy is the best type of governance tried so far. Despite having many flaws, no other system has ever been found to be better (Zihala 2003). For example, democracy is believed to protect and respect human rights (Poe and Tate 1994), reduce poverty (Sen 1999), and protect the environment (Quan Li and Rafael Reuveny 2006). Robert Dahl (1998) argues that democracy produces eight main desirable consequences which are avoiding tyranny, guaranteeing essential rights for its citizens, general freedom, self-determination, moral autonomy, human development, protecting essential personal interests, and political equality. He even argues that modern democracies produce more desirable consequences such as peace seeking and prosperity (Ibid.: 46–61). Despite the fact that some of these consequences have been criticised, no better alternative system of government has been provided rather than democracy.

Jean-Jacques Rousseau argued that 'citizens should be subordinate to the will of the whole', hence Rousseau's social contract argument created 'a collective body of the people who act as a whole for the good of the whole', what Zihala (2003) calls 'the greatest good for the greatest number'.

Wider definitions of democracy focus on elections, equality, individual rights, the rule of law, accountability, and participation. Joseph Schumpeter (1943: 271) defines democracy as 'free competition for free vote', thus highlighting the centrality of elections for democracy. Aristotle and Plato mentioned equality as a central aspect to the idea of democracy (Catt 1999). Juan Linz argued that without the rule of law, there is no democracy (Linz and Stephan 1996). A democratic government must also be accountable to its people (Przeworski 1999). Citizens' participation and engagement are also seen as crucial factors for democracy (e.g. Buss et al. 2006; Pateman 1970; Fishkin 1991; Gamson 2001; Dahlgren 2005). Dahl (1998: 37–38) highlights five criteria for a democratic process:

(1) Effective participation: all members must have equal and effective opportunities for making their views known.
(2) Voting equality: each member should have equal opportunity to express his vote.
(3) Inclusion of all adults: all adults must have their full rights of citizenship.
(4) Enlightened understanding: each member must have equal and effective opportunities to learn about relevant policy alternatives and their consequences.
(5) Control of the agenda: members must have exclusive opportunities to decide which subjects are placed on the agenda.

1.4.2   Measuring Democracy

There is no consensus on how to measure democracy. It can be measured by various means, depending on which definition of democracy is adopted. For instance, if the definition adopted is 'free competition for free vote' then elections and participation could be the main and only aspect in measuring democracy. On the other hand, wider definitions of democracy require wider means of measurement: what Bernhagen (2009) calls single and multi-dimensions of democracy or what Coppedge et al. (2011) calls 'thin' and 'thick' concepts of democracy.

Dahl's (1971) measurement of democracy depends on two variables: public contestation and citizens' participation, which he then highlights as the five criteria of democratic processes mentioned above. Michael Coppedge and Wolfgang H. Reinicke (1990) developed another method of measuring democracy based on Dahl's measurement known as the Polyarchy Scale, which measures the 'degree to which national political systems meet the minimum requirements of political democracy' (1990: 51). The Polyarchy Scale depends on six variables: free and fair elections, freedom of organisation, freedom of expression, media pluralism, availability of alternative sources of information, and finally the right to vote. Stressing the similarities between his variables and Dahl's variables, Tatu Vanhanen (2000, 2003) developed an index of democratisation that measures democracy according to two variables, which are competition and participation. According to Vanhanen, 'Competition and participation represent the most crucial aspects of democracy and therefore their combination may constitute the most realistic measure of democratization' (Vanhanen 2003: 55). For Gasiorowski (1996), measuring democracy depends on three variables: extensive competition at regular intervals without the use of force, inclusive level of political participation, and civil and political liberties.

Phillips Cutright (1963) developed an index of political development where he studied some socio-economic variables. Each country was given a score from zero to 63 points over the 21-year period of his study. Polity IV project, originally designed by Ted Gurr, depends on 'three principal characteristics: the recruitment of executive authority (i.e. how the chief executive gains office), executive constraints (i.e. checks and balances on executive action), and political competition (i.e. how public preferences are represented' (Marshall and Cole 2011).

Another famous index for measuring democracy is the Freedom House index, which depends on two dimensions: political rights and civil liberties. The rating process is based on a checklist of 10 political rights questions—which are grouped in three subcategories: electoral process, political pluralism, and participation—and 15 civil liberty questions, which are grouped in four subcategories: freedom of expression and belief, associational and organisational rights, rule of law, personal autonomy, and individual rights (Freedom House 2015). The Economist's intelligence unit's index of democracy is based on the rating of 60 indicators grouped in five categories: electoral process and pluralism, civil liberties, the functioning of government, political participation, and political culture (Kekic 2007).

Whether a thick or thin view of democracy is adopted, and thus a thick or thin means of measuring it, variables like elections and participation appear to be key components of democracy, though not the only ones, and could serve as a starting point towards democratisation.

1.4.3   Democratisation

Democratisation is not an alternative to democracy. Democracy is a political system that involves the values and criteria discussed above; democratisation is the process of establishing that democratic system (Paul Carnegie 2010: 14). According to Geddis, our understanding of democracy will determine how a political system can be democratised (Ibid.: 16). In general, democratisation can be understood as the process of replacing an undemocratic political system with a democratic one or the process of making a political system more democratic (Bernhagen 2009). A more comprehensive definition is provided by Laurence Whitehead (2002: 27) where he defines democratisation as a 'complex, long term, dynamic and open-ended process. It consists of progress towards a more rule based, more consensual and more participatory type of politics'.

Democratisation has been a dominant global trend, especially during the first half of 1990 where the number of democracies increased from 76 to 117 (Ibid.: 1). Francis Fukuyama (1992) described this triumph of democracy as the 'end of history'. Samuel Huntington (1991) also described it as 'one of the most important developments in the history of humankind'.

Huntington (Ibid.) also distinguishes three major waves of democratisation. The first waves started at 1828 and the latest wave started in 1974.

Renske Doorenspleet adds another fourth wave starting in 1989/1990 with the fall of the Berlin wall and the dissolution of the Soviet Union (Berg-Schlosser 2009: 42). This continuing eagerness towards democracy may be a further proof that democracy is the best model of governance so far, as explained previously.

However, that does not mean that the way is always paved towards reaching a democratic political system. Huntington explained two other stages of 'reverse' waves.

The democratisation process does not necessarily mean achieving the aspired democracy. Diamond and Myers (2001) show four categories a democratisation process could achieve. The first is when the democratisation process fully succeeds and reaches a liberal democratic political system. The second is a non-liberal democracy, where the country holds free and fair elections but has some constraints on individual freedoms or any other constraints on the process such as military interference or high levels of executive domination or judicial inefficacy. The third category is what is known as pseudo-democracies or hybrid regimes; such regimes offer some of the democratic practices such as elections and institutions but have one dominant political ruling party that hinders the process of free and fair elections, as well as citizens' participation and engagement. The fourth category is the authoritarian regime that does not allow formal political opposition, preventing the opposition from participating in the election process, as well as repressing individual rights.

Guillermo O'Donnell (1994) also speaks about 'delegative' democracies, where regular elections are taking place, but with less political participation for citizens, where politics is 'delegated' to ineffective leaders.

Arend Lijphart's (1999) patterns of democracies list main indicators according to which democracy can be classified. These include concentration versus sharing of executive power, the balance of power between the executive and legislature branch, the party system adopted, the type of government—whether it is unitary and centralised, or federal and decentralised, whether the legislative power is concentrated in a unicameral or bicameral legislature, the constitution flexibility or rigidity, judicial review, and finally whether the central bank is independent or controlled by the executive power.

There is no single explanation of why democratisation fails in specific countries, as every case differs. However, in general, many countries fail due to political leaders' reluctance to 'devolve power from the political centre to local authorities and groups in societies' (Diamond and Myers 2001: 5) or due to the unawareness of elites with the necessary 'values and beliefs needed to represent the citizen's interest' (Ibid.: 5). Other reasons include fraud and corruption in any aspect of the democratisation process, lack of power to those elected (Ibid.: 6), or inability to deal with ethnic or religious differences (Schlosser 2009).

1.4.4   Elections

Despite Aristotle's critique of elections being valid to an extent, he claimed it allows rule of all the people and not by the best people, elections are believed to be the prerequisite for democracy. Richard Katz (1997: 3) describes elections as the 'defining institutions of modern democracy' and 'the device that makes democracy possible'. Powell (2000) considers elections as the most crucial element of democracy, although not the only instrument of democracy. Rose and Mossawir (1967) describe voting through elections as a 'single act of political participation' (p. 173), which is a core aspect of democracy. Dennis F. Thompson (2002) also highlights that 'elections can occur without democracy, but democracy cannot endure without elections' (p. 1).

Whether adopting a thin view of democracy or a thick view, building a democracy should start by a process of free and fair elections. Democratisation via elections has been a common model of moving towards democracy, especially in the post-Cold War era or what is known as the third wave of democratisation, as it leads to peaceful transition towards democracy in many countries (Diamond 2009).

Richard Katz (1997) highlighted five main functions of elections in the democratisation process. The first function is to confer or confirm the legitimacy of the regime; without elections that are held with the view of democracy being adopted in the society, citizens will not have a chance to vote 'yes' and thus give legitimacy to the regime, or decide to vote no, or boycott, or spoil their votes, or vote for another candidate, thus conferring legitimacy from one side and giving it to another side. A second function is the installation of officials, as elections 'fill offices with people'. A third function is selection and choice, as without real selection and choice, the institutions of government could become authoritarian. A fourth function is to create representation, as elections are the institutions by which 'the represented authorise their representatives to act for them or in their place'. A fifth function of election is popular involvement, as elections drive citizens' involvements in politics and provide education about politics, mainly through election campaigns. Elections also ensure accountability and give voters some influence on the direction of the adopted policy. Rose and Mossawir (1967) highlight six main functions of elections. First, they solve the problem of leadership succession within a political system. Second, they control the policy decisions of government. Third, they influence the policy decisions of governments. Fourth, they legitimise the political regime. Fifth, elections may also lead to the repudiation of a regime, which can happen in extreme cases. Repudiation may take many forms, such as the refusal of a defeated candidate to leave office or the revolt of losers. Elections can also play an important role in authoritarian regimes, such as splitting oppositions into factions (Linz 1978), identifying and targeting opposition groups (Way 2005), and buying time for a later exit (Hermet et al. 1978). Those points may be an explanation of why authoritarian regimes tend to hold frequent elections, without the intention of democratisation, that is, elections without democracy.

For elections to play their role, they have to be free, fair, and regular. Robert Dahl described free elections as those where citizens can go to vote without fear, where coercion is not available. Dahl also defined fair 'when all votes are counted as equal'. Further international electoral guidelines added more specific criteria for free and fair elections. Such elections require a legislative framework, impartial practices by election administrations, media, and legislative and executive power. Fair and free elections should also allow monitoring of the voting and vote counting processes, transparent and well-known procedures for resolving election complaints and disputes, treating competing candidates as equal, guaranteeing freedom of speech and expression and campaigning, protecting the concept of a secret ballot, as well as administrating the whole process through an impartial committee, not controlled by the ruling party (Diamond and Myers 2001).

Despite the significant role elections play in democratisation, there is an academic debate around the idea of democratisation by elections (e.g. Lindberg 2009). The debate usually revolves around two issues: elections can lead to and enhance democracy or they can lead to enhancing autocracy, as is the case with the elections in the Arab world (e.g. Sadiki 2009; Lustokar 2009). This brings us to Diamond's (2009) conclusion that democratic transitions via elections do not happen in isolation but are affected by many criteria such as the degree of pluralism in a society, the strength of opposition, the ability to mobilise and monitor elections, the role of the international community, and the presence of international

observers. Pippa Norris (2004b) also argues that the design of the electoral system can also affect the election process and thus the democratisation process itself.

Despite the fact that elections can be deficient due to flaws within the
process itself or within the surrounding political environment, Lindberg
argues that even deficient elections are worth holding as they could lead
to democratic change later on, as elections 'provide a set of institutions,
rights, and processes stacking up incentives and costs in a way that tend to
further democratization' (2009: 17).

1.4.5   Campaigns and Democracy

Campaigns are seen as a core feature of democracy due to the important
role they play in enhancing democracy and elections, as will be explained
later. Campaigns are defined as organised communication efforts that seek
to influence the process of elections. Political campaigns are periods of
high-intensity information flows that reach broad cross-sections of the
general public, including many individuals who are typically inattentive to
politics (Cho et al. 2009). Thus campaigns are usually combined with
elections as they aim to influence the process and outcome of elections
(Farrell and Schmitt-Beck 2002: 3).

The role of campaigns has risen dramatically in modern democracies
due to three main reasons: (1) the decline in political parties as institutions
along with party dealignment made ordinary citizens, especially those not
affiliated to a specific party, rely more on campaigns in gathering information. (2) The growth of electronic media made it easier to communicate
campaign activities and messages, besides creating new opportunities for
campaign influence. (3) Constant use of public opinion ensures that voters
accept the final result.

Academic debate on campaigns used to revolve around whether they
matter or not (Farrell and Schmitt-Beck 2002). Traditional studies,
depending on the amount of voter persuasion, and voter turnout to assess
the importance of campaigns, used to claim that campaigns do not really
matter (Iyengar and Simon 2000). Other recent studies tend to prove that
campaigns have an important role in elections as they help in priming,
learning, education, political knowledge, civic engagement, and political
participation. Thus the debate has moved from whether campaigns matter
or not, to what effects campaigns have, and what sections of citizens they
affect: whether they have more influence on the politically aware citizens

or the less aware ones (Claassen 2011). This perspective thus supports the media mobilisation theories' perspective rather than media malaise theories, especially with campaigns being mediated. Campaigns are proven to be important in both established and new democracies. In a new democracy, there is a lack of resources in conveying the required messages. With the availability of public TV and social media for use by different candidates, besides the absence of established party loyalties, campaigns can play a role in shaping or influencing voters' decisions, mainly because of the information they provide (Popesco and Toka 2002). This is true whether voters are actively looking for information or whether the campaign itself is active and seeks to provide voters with information.

Pippa Norris (2002) argues that the organised efforts of campaigns revolve around three issues: inform, persuade, and mobilise, which can be understood as the main functions of campaigns. Campaigns play an important role in helping voters formulate their preferences and helping them make their voting decision according to the information they gain, as campaigns raise the voters' public awareness and knowledge about specific election-related issues or candidates. Campaigns also have a persuasion function in terms of reinforcing or changing public attitudes and decisions. They also have an effect upon mobilisation; one way of assessing this is by voters' participation and turnout. In order to reach the level of mobilising citizens to vote, campaigns serve other functions as well. Campaigns can also play an important role in the enlightenment process. They 'enlighten' voters about the interests and topics that are important to them. As a forum of debate and discussion, voters are more likely to learn something about the candidates and their positions as they follow the campaign (Holbrook 1996). The priming function of the campaign, along with enlightenment, helps citizens to be persuaded. Priming can make citizens change their minds by changing the relative weight of their opinions while taking their decisions (Gidengil et al. 2002). Thus campaigns can reinforce opinions and decisions made by citizens, create more voters from the non-voter pool, and influence the non-decided voters to support a specific candidate (Gronbeck 1978). Campaigns also promote citizens' participation, which is a core value in democracy, by different means. Perhaps the most notable form of participation is voter turnout, when campaigns encourage citizens to vote. However, there are many other forms of citizens' participation which a campaign can provide, such as financial support or volunteering support, besides participating in the wider topics and discussions within the campaign itself. Moreover, campaigns give all citizens—even outsiders—a platform to express their opinions and ideas, even if they are against the mainstream ideas. This gives the citizens the opportunity to control the agenda and express their views, a vital aspect in democracy (Medvic 2010). Campaigns also give citizens a chance for social interaction and a chance to engage in the democratic process by their participation in the public sphere (Gamson 2001), where citizens can use the topics and issues mentioned in campaigns in their informal talks, as well as giving the citizens a chance for self-reflection, where they have a chance to examine their opinions, preferences, and priorities (Gronbeck 1978). Moreover, campaigns do play a role in legitimising the regime or the political system, as they show that it is working and that the citizens accept its framework since they are still working within its rules.

Geer and Lau argue that campaigns are vital to the practice of democracy, not only because they affect 'the electoral choice that affects the course of government' but because they 'leave an indelible imprint on the process of democracy' (Pfau et al. 2005: 49). This brings us back to Dahl's criteria for democratic process. One can argue that campaigns do play an important role in the democratisation process itself as campaigns can fulfil the three main criteria of Dahl's. For instance, campaigns allow citizens to have equal and effective opportunities for making their own views and thus guaranteeing the effective participation condition. Campaigns also allow citizens to have equal and effective opportunities to learn about candidates and policies, along with the different consequences and alternatives, which is the enlightened understanding condition. Moreover, they allow citizens to control the agenda as they allow them to decide and amend the issues placed on the campaign and election agenda through their interaction and participation.

However, campaigns can be considered as a double-edged sword. Despite their significance in the process of elections, democracy, and democratisation, they can be a threat to them as well, depending on those who use them (Cwalina et al. 2011). People working on campaigns can make use of their important role and functions in providing false information and claims which may affect the whole process. However, with the availability of different sources of information and with the widespread use of media and communication mediums, especially the internet and social media, and with the awareness of citizens nowadays, false information and claims can be easily discovered, reported, and challenged.

1.4.6   Campaigns' Functions

1.4.6.1   Persuasion

One of the main functions of campaigns is to persuade the voter to vote for a specific candidate or party. Although this function is controversial among academics—as campaigns are not magic bullets that have an immediate, direct effect on voters, who are usually affected by many other things such as their backgrounds, internal differences, references groups, economic circumstances, level of knowledge, and their partisan resistance—campaigns can still play a role in persuasion, even if the voter's choice is not changed.

According to Bartels (1996), persuasion means 'any systematic change in prospective voters' electorally relevant attitudes and perceptions, over the course of the campaign'. According to this definition, campaigns can shift other sorts of voters' attitudes, such as their positions regarding some issues or policies and their evaluation of candidates' characteristics or the performance of the government, or by providing information that shows which candidate can move policies into their desired direction, or by providing information that can persuade voters to change their policy preferences (Erickson and Wlezien 2012). All these could lead to a probability that the voter will support a specific candidate or change their support from one candidate, party, or policy to another one, based on the new information given. Campaigns could also play a role in persuading undecided voters. They also account for pre-electoral vote swing between candidates.

The degree of persuasion, however, is determined by other criteria. Zaller (1992: 216) argues that 'citizens vary in their susceptibility to influence according to their general levels of political awareness and their predispositions to accept campaign messages they receive.' This brings us to what Claassen (2011) describes as the reception and resistance phases, where people receive new information and then decide whether or not they are going to accept it, based on many criteria such as their previous knowledge and background. Based on this, more aware citizens are more likely to resist the campaign messages as the content contradicts their previous beliefs and positions. On the contrary, resistance is lower among the less aware individuals, who are less able to filter out messages and who do not have prejudged stances.

Pippa Norris (2005) explained how campaigns can play a role in persuasion by giving the example of how labour supporters switched towards

Liberal Democrats after some British media heavily criticised the Labour government because of Britain's participation in the Iraq war.

1.4.6.2 Priming

Unlike persuasion, priming is 'any systematic change in the weights attached to prospective voters' attitudes and perceptions in the formulation of vote intentions over the course of the campaign' (Bartels 2006: 82), that is, giving more weight to some factors that may determine the voter's final decision, without changing their attitude. This process is strongly related to agenda setting effects where campaigns shift priorities among voters (Norris 2005). This leads to a change in the voter's final decision, by changing the standards people use to make their decisions, as the process assumes that people do not take into their consideration all they know for evaluating a complex political issue. On the contrary, people take into account those bits and pieces from their memories (Cwalina et al. 2011), and this brings us to the role of campaigns which can make voters give weight to issues they did not think about. Iyengar and Kinder (1987) give the example of the American 1980 presidential election, when the media reopened the issue of the Iranian hostages. This issue made voters consider the ability of candidates to counter terrorism when choosing between Jimmy Carter and Ronald Reagan, although terrorism was not on their agenda from the beginning of the campaigns.

According to issue ownership theory (Petrocik 1996), a campaign may be able to get the desired results if it is able to limit the debate to current issues facing the countries, which its candidate can tackle, and this can happen by giving these issues an extra weight in voters' minds. Vavreck (2000) believes that the issues candidates choose to emphasise can determine the election's outcome.

Priming can be seen as 'extension' of agenda setting. Priming occurs when extensive media coverage leads voters to attach more importance to a given consideration in deciding their votes. Priming can lead people to change their minds, not because they have changed their opinions of the candidate but because the relative weight of those opinions in their decisions has changed.

1.4.6.3 Participation

By participation, I mean participating internally within the campaign and externally within the public sphere. A good campaign should allow voters to participate and engage with the campaign itself and politically with the bigger society.

Participation is usually defined as the 'activity that has the intent or effect of influencing government action – either directly by affecting the making or implementation of public policy or indirectly by influencing the selection of people who make those policies' (Verba et al. 1995: 38). The same definition could be applied to participation within the campaign itself, that is, the activity that has the intent or effect of influencing campaigns' actions and decisions.

1.4.6.3.1   Political Participation Within the Public Sphere

With the excessive hypermedia (Howard 2006) use in election campaigns, there is a controversial debate between academics about the effect of campaigns' media (hypermedia) on voter's participation and engagement with political life. Some studies argue that campaigns' use of mass media had negative effects on citizens' participation and engagement within the political life or public sphere in general (Putnam 2000; Nie 2001; Ansolabehere and Iyengar 1995). Others argued that it can motivate political participation and promote civic engagement (Hendricks and Denton 2010; Norris 2001, 2002; Papacharissi 2002; Boulianne 2009). According to the second school, mediated campaigns allow normal citizens to have access to the information provided and, in some cases, create new public spheres such as the case with using the internet, which may act as a virtual public sphere. Based on the communication mediation model, a third school argues that mediated campaigns do actually have a positive effect on citizens' participation along with other factors such as interpersonal and background criteria, which can affect citizens, such as the message coming from the campaign (J. Cho et al. 2009). Moreover, the campaign can serve important functions in the public sphere, which can then be transmitted to the policy sphere by reaching decision makers and affecting them (Bennett and Entman 2001). This study argues that participation can be considered as an indication of the campaign's success as will be explained later.

1.4.6.3.2   Participation Within the Campaign

One of the main factors of a good campaign is to allow citizens to participate and engage with it. These engagements can alter the campaign's policies and plans through feedback and suggestions given by citizens. Citizens (voters) can participate in the campaign by various means such as participating in the campaign activities or by volunteering or working in the election campaign by attending rallies, meetings, contacting other voters, signing petitions, or even using social media outlets to support a specific candidate and promoting his or her stances by sharing it. Campaigns can also allow greater grassroots engagement (Gibson 2010). Volunteers can also fundraise on the candidate's behalf or send texts and emails to urge and remind voters to vote for their candidates. One of the famous examples that shows how campaigns can encourage citizens' participation is the Obama campaign in 2008 which established 'MyBarackObama.com' or the MyBO website in 2007 which introduced new techniques at that time to promote citizens' engagement and participation with the campaign. It allowed citizens to play an active role in the campaign. They were able to register and access the database, which allowed them to help the campaign in reaching other voters. Published figures showed how the campaign was able to engage citizens as over one million people signed up to the website, thousands of events were organised and held by volunteers, and around $35 million of donations were collected by supporters, which was around 6% of the final total raised (Gibson 2010). Many scholars argue that online participation with the campaign is the strongest indication of offline participation of citizens/ voters afterwards (Gil de Zúñiga et al. 2010; Dimitrova et al. 2014) which is another form of participation known as citizens' activism or citizens' campaigns (Green 2016).

1.4.7   Campaigns' Evolution

There is an agreement between scholars that the process of election campaigning has witnessed a series of transformations during the past years (Norris 2004a). These transformations created new terminologies in the political communications and campaign literature, such as the terms 'professionalisation' and 'Americanisation' of political campaigns. Moreover, these terms, with all their techniques, were implemented in various countries. Swanson and Mancini (1996) argue that there are four main characteristics for these changes which are the 'personalisation' of politics, the 'scientification' of the campaigning process, citizens' 'detachment' from parties, and the development of 'more autonomous structures of communications'. Pippa Norris (2004a) argues that these changes and transformations in election campaigning occurred due to the transformation and evolution of the 'modernisation' process itself, which lead to transformations within the party as an organisation, media, and electorate (p. 137). Based on this, Norris (2004a) divided campaigns' evolution into three main stages: pre-modern campaigns, modern campaigns, and post-modern campaigns. These stages explain the changes and development of campaigns (Norris 2004a: 137, 161).

1.4.7.1 Pre-modern Campaigns

They were developed in the nineteenth century and continued until at least the 1950s, with the emergence of televised campaigns and opinion polls which transformed the process. At that time, campaign organisation was based upon direct interpersonal communication between candidates and citizens. Campaign organisation depended on a party leader at the top, surrounded by close advisers, running a relatively short national campaign. They were mainly reaching the citizens through direct face-to-face communication. Media used by the campaigns were usually the partisan press, which acted as the main source of mediated information at that time. Further, the voters were characterised by their strong party loyalties, as if the main aim of the campaign and election was to reinforce party loyalties, rather than produce new alternatives (Lazarsfeld et al. 1944).

1.4.7.2 Modern Campaigns

Modern campaigns were developed from the early 1950s to mid-1980s, with the rise of television and the regular publications of opinion polling. The emergence of modern campaigns was a result of other main developments that occurred at that time such as: (1) the shift from partisan newspapers to national television, where it became the main source of campaigns news, replacing other media outlets. Thus those working in the campaign were keen to have their message broadcast on TV for the amount of coverage they could gain. (2) Parties started depending on politicians and paid professional consultants specialising in communications, marketing, polling, and campaign management, who start preparing for their campaign a long time before the official campaign starts. (3) Voters themselves became less attached to their parties, social classes, and religion. Moreover, they became more passive within the campaign as TV became their main source of information, and not the direct face-to-face communication which was one of the main characteristics of the pre-modern campaigns era. Thus they became more vulnerable to campaign messages.

With many campaigns occurring during this period, parties and specialists started adopting the techniques and practices that were proven to be successful in other campaigns. This established the main themes and methods that were used in campaigns at that time and created completely new 'jobs' with big markets, as those experts used to work on campaigns in different countries. This led to a dramatic change in the course of campaigns.

1.4.7.3 Postmodern Campaigns

Postmodern campaigns were developed mainly due to recent developments within communication outlets. The recent years have witnessed a revolutionary development in the field of media and communications. Unlike the pre-modern campaigns, which depended on face-to-face communications and newspapers, and unlike the modern campaigns, which depended mainly on television and polls, postmodern campaigns witnessed great developments in communication outlets with the development of existing outlets such as TV or emergence of new outlets such as the internet. In the era of modern campaigns, there were no more than two or three TV channels for voters or campaigners to depend on. Conversely, in the postmodern era, there are numerous TV channels, whether local or international. TV channels even became specialised: 24-hour rolling news channels and entertainment channels, besides many new programme formats that allowed interaction with audience such as talk shows. New technologies such as cable TV and satellite helped in having these diversities. The emergence of new outlets such as the internet introduced other new and complex outlets such as social media, YouTube, on-demand TV, podcasts, and so on where there is a great space for engagement between campaigns and voters. Unlike the modern campaigns, where voters used to become more passive within the campaign, in postmodern campaigns, voters can engage more within the campaign and can, in many cases, have an impact on the campaigns' strategies and policies through ideas and feedback they give or by being active on social media and the internet. Another aspect of postmodern campaigns is the role of professional consultants who became part and parcel of the campaigns and of equal importance with the politicians. Their role became essential in campaigning, and their influence on the campaign is equally effective as the politicians' influence. They also play a role as well in coordinating the campaigns' activities at grassroots. For the electorate, postmodern campaigns could have things in common with the pre-modern stage as new media allowed new forms of engagement and interactivity between voters and campaigners almost similar to the face-to-face communication which was available at the pre-modern stage. All these changes lead to changes of the communication process itself to the extent that the core concept of political marketing began to change from advertising or selling the political product and convincing voters with it to another concept that depends on putting the customer 'voters' first. This is done by studying the voters' needs and preferences and developing strategies that match these needs and preferences to get the maximum number of voters. In other words, trying to become adapted within the news environment rather than trying to be the main source that drives this environment. Having explained the main development in this stage, it is still unclear what other developments will appear in the future and to what extent they will have an impact on this stage, which remains under development.

However, according to Norris (2000: 151), the pace and development of the modernisation stages explained above are affected by four main mediating factors. These factors can determine to a great extent at which stage a specific country (specific elections) sits. These factors are the regulatory environment, the party system, the media system, and the electorate.

(i)   The regulatory environment: it includes the type of electoral system and its regulations, the type of the elections and their regulations, and the laws organising the campaigning process.
(ii)   The party system: this includes the party system within the country, its structure, its organisation, its membership, and how it is funded.
(iii) The media system: this includes the structure of news media within the country, whether it is privately owned or owned by the state, the consultancy industry in the country, and areas it serves.
(iv)   The electorate: this includes their voting behaviour, party loyalty, and access to media.

1.4.8   *The Professionalisation of Election Campaigns*

The term 'professionalisation' and its derivatives were excessively used by academics starting from the 1990s. They were usually coined within the postmodern campaigns. Professionalisation became widely used to describe recent changes that happened to campaigns in the postmodern era, that is, one word to describe postmodern campaigns. It was used to reflect all changes and characteristics of postmodern campaigns from employment of professional experts to making the campaign message more effective, the smart use of hypermedia, and the extent of citizens' interaction and engagement it allows.

There are several reasons behind the emergence of 'professionalism' as stated by some academics (Negrine et al. 2007; Norris 2004b; Farrell and Schmitt-Beck 2002) such as the influence of American campaigns and wide exposure of their consultants in other countries which is commonly known as the Americanisation process; conducting many elections in post-industrial democracies with party dealignment and having a bigger chance to influence the voter choice, especially with the increase of swing voters; and the globalisation era and new media and technologies which campaigns use methods of communicating its message to the voters.

Lilleker and Negrine (2002) concluded that the term is 'multifaceted and subjective' and cannot always describe the variation within political communications as it is used by many scholars as a direct opposite to amateurism, or used to describe the degree of specialisation. Strömbäck (2007) highlights many other words that are used by academics as a synonym for professionalisation, such as 'Americanisation', 'postmodern', 'phase 3', 'post-Fordist', and 'high tech'. Farrell (1996) argues that professionalised campaigns are characterised by the '3 Ts': technology, technocrats, and techniques. Scammell (1998) adds a fourth item to these elements which is 'the increasing centralization of political campaigns'.

Gibson and Römmele (2001: 33, 2009: 267) highlight four main areas for a campaign to be professionalised: (1) the adoption of new tools and tactics, (2) a change in the overall style of campaigning to be more capital-intensive, aggressive or attack-oriented, and continuous, (3) to be more interactive and targeting citizens, and (4) restructuring power relations within the party/campaign to be more centralised.

Lilleker and Negrine (2002) highlight the main definitions used in different academic fields such as: Gibson and Rommele's definition (2001) where they explain professionalism as giving campaigns' tasks to outside agencies and not to party members; or Mancini (1999), who sees professionalisation as in employing professional communicators; or political marketing literature, which combines specialised roles with effective delivery; or marketing literature, which argues that when campaigns become professionalised, those working in them will be professionals in their assigned tasks.

Strömbäck (2007) has a more comprehensive definition of a professional campaign where he mentions that it should be characterised by 'being permanent, central campaign headquarters being able to coordinate the messages and the management of the campaign; and using expertise in analyzing and reaching out to members, target groups and stakeholders, in analyzing its own and the competitors' weaknesses and strengths and making use of that knowledge, and in news management' (p. 54). This definition agrees with Lilleker and Negrine's (2002) conclusion that the term professionalisation is generally more used to 'describe degrees of specialization related to the development of new knowledge or new skills, the increased use of experts and the management or centralization of the campaign' (p. 100). This was developed later (Lilleker et al. 2015) where a professional campaign is described as the ability to 'mix strategic and structural components of different phases' which is defined as 'the degree of a party's adaptations to modernization-related transformations in the campaign environment, which contains a number of structural and strategic components' (p. 750). Thus, Lilleker et al. (2015) argues that the term 'professionalism' and its derivatives should not be limited to describing a specific period or era as was believed in the past, that is, being limited to the postmodern era, as explained above.

1.4.9   Measuring Professionalism

Many efforts have been made to measure the degree of professionalisation in campaigning. These efforts led to four main ways for measuring professionalism. From these measurements, we can identify two main approaches. The first is the approach that concentrates on measuring one dimension in the campaign such as the CAMPROF index, which was developed by Gibson and Römmele (2001), and adjusted later by Strömbäck (2009). The second approach is the professionalisation index introduced by Tenscher (2007) and Tenscher et al. (2012), which differentiates between two dimensions in the campaign: campaign structures (organisational adaptation or campaign hardware) and strategies (activities used by campaign known as campaign software). These two approaches can be summed up in these four methods of measurement: (1) party-centred theory of professionalised campaigning developed by Gibson and Römmele (2001), (2) CAMPROF index developed by Gibson and Römmele (2009), (3) developed CAMPROF index by Strömbäck (2009), (4) professionalisation index by Tenscher (2007, 2013).

(1) Party-Centred Theory of Professionalised Campaigning Developed by Gibson and Römmele (2001)
The theory argues that explaining the move towards professionalised campaigns depended on 'systemic-level factors' such as frequency of elections,

rules of political advertising and donations, and the level of party attachment to the voters. The theory argues that while these factors are very useful, they are not enough for explaining the process of professionalisation. The theory considers parties as significant actors in campaigning processes and argues that major changes happen in a party's campaigns when they realise that their goals are not achieved as a result of 'an interaction between certain external events or shocks and internal party traits' (Gibson and Römmele 2001: 36).

Based on this, the theory identifies indicators or variables for measuring professionalism. These variables are divided into independent variables and dependent variables, and each of these variables is measured by giving it a score. The results of the final scores identify the extent of campaign professionalism.

(a) For independent variables, the theory argues that seven criteria or variables should be taken into account while trying to understand the campaign's shift towards professionalism. These variables are divided into two sections: internal factors and external factors. The internal factors can be summed into:

   (1) Party goal: the theory argues that vote seeking should be regarded as the party's primary goal as this function will force the party into using new techniques and seeking the help of professional advisers.
   (2) Party ideology: the theory argues that having a strong ideological stance, such as right-wing ideology, will lead to the use of outside consultancy and marketing techniques, unlike socialist parties who are reluctant to use these types of business communications. Thus, a right-wing party is more likely to go towards professionalism.
   (3) Internal structure: the theory argues that parties with internal centralisation, with a more 'top-down' hierarchical structure culture, have also been regarded as more likely to professionalise, as they are able to engage with business media communications and using external expertise.
   (4) Party resources: the theory argues that parties with more resources can afford professionalised campaigning, since it is not cheap, thus only parties with large budget can go for it. The theory also adds another three external variables to be taken into account:

(5) Electoral shock: after heavy electoral defeat, a party would resort to new marketing techniques in order to get voters back.

(6) Leadership change/Internal event: when electoral shock leads to leadership change, the probability of changes within the party is greater, giving opportunities for changing the way the party campaigns, depending on more professionalisation strategies and techniques. To sum up, the theory argues that professional campaigns will occur in 'a well-funded, main stream, right-wing party with significant resources and a centralized internal power structure that has recently suffered a heavy electoral defeat and/or a loss of governing status' (Ibid. 2001: 37).

(b) For dependent variables, it mainly depends on assessing 'the tools and strategies used, and the nature of power associated' (Ibid. 2001: 39). To assess this, Gibson and Römmele suggest a Professional Campaign Index that is designed to measure 12 items: (1) use of telemarketing for contacting (a) own members and (b) outside market groups, (2) use of direct mail, (3) use of outside public relations/media consultants, (4) use of computerised databases, (5) use of opinion polls, (6) conducting opposition research, (7) presence of an internal/internet communication system, (8) email sign up, (9) outside campaign headquarters, and (10) continuous campaigning.

The results from measuring both dependent and independent variables should reflect the degree of campaign professionalism. One of the main criticisms of this theory is offered by Tenscher et al. (2012), where they argue that some factors such as the 'business-oriented', 'right-wing parties', or 'change of leadership' do not necessarily lead to professional campaigns.

(2) CAMPROF
Gibson and Römmele (2009) developed the party-centred theory into the CAMPROF index, where they measured 10 activities instead of 12, by consolidating the direct mailing and telemarketing so that each covers voters and members. They also grouped items according to whether they relied primarily on objective data or subjective assessment by coders. Each item of the ten items was placed on a score from 0 to 3, which

means that the maximum score of the index is 30. The score each campaign attains represents its degree of professionalism.
The objectively measured variables are six:

(1) Use of telemarketing,
(2) Use of direct mail,
(3) Internal/intranet communication system,
(4) E-mail subscription newsletter: the more widely and frequently these four variables are used, the more likely the campaign will be professional. These variables are measured according to the proportion of voters reached by campaign by using these methods.
(5) Outside campaign headquarters: this means having a separate management team that handles the campaign.
(6) Continuous campaigning: this variable is measured by both objective and subjective assessment to judge whether the party is engaged in an ongoing campaign, not depending only on 'hot' or high season campaign activities.

The subjective measured variables are four variables:

(7) PR/media consultants: the more the campaign depends on them, the more professional it is considered.
(8) Computerised databases: to what extent the party is on national and local databases to identify swing voters and tries to reach them.
(9) Opinion polling: whether the party has its own professional survey unit and to what extent it depends on it.
(10) Opposition research: whether the party has its own professional opposition unit that conducts research before and during the campaign and to what extent it depends on it. The more the party used and depended on these variables, the higher score it achieves and thus becomes more professional.

(3) The Amended CAMPROF by Strömbäck (2009)
Strömbäck has some reservations about the CAMPROF index, mainly with regard to the dependent variables and the way CAMPROF measures its scores. Strömbäck argues that the list of dependent variables suffers from 'a lack of focus on the expertise required in the use of the various campaign techniques' (p. 98) and that it does not measure some other

campaign practices such as focus groups and research of own party or campaign, thus not covering all aspects of professionalised campaigning. Strömbäck also criticises the manner of measuring the dependent variables by giving them only two numbers. He argues that this method of measurement can be applied in a country that has few parties, and not in multiparty systems. Thus, he slightly modified the original CAMPROF index by changing the way it calculates the scores. Furthermore, Strömbäck highlighted some shortcomings in the index such as not measuring the number of employees, that the measurement of the priming variables was not standardised and that it fails to elaborate whether some variables are more powerful than others.

Despite being widely applied and verified, the CAMPROF index, along with its new version, suffers from other limitations. First of all, it is a one-approach system, as it concentrates on measuring the campaign structures (hardware) without paying attention to what is done during the campaign period (software). Thus, it is limited by focusing on a certain range of functions only. Second, it is biased by 'new' media technologies, making it 'less applicable for longitudinal analyses' (Tenscher and Mykkänen 2014: 7). Last but not least, it concentrates on parties as the main actor in campaigning, neglecting the fact that in many countries, especially new democracies, candidates who run for elections are—in many cases—independent candidates, with no party supporting them. Add to these, that they 'restricted to single case studies and first-order national campaigns' (Tenscher et al. 2012).

(4) The Professionalisation Index by Tenscher et al. (2012)
To overcome the main deficits with party-centred theory and CAMPROF, Tenscher et al. developed a new index which consists of two sub-indices that measure both campaign structures and campaign strategies—unlike previous indices that used to measure only campaign structures. Both indices consist of numbers of variables, each variable take a score, and the degree of campaign professionalism is based upon the result of the final score.

The first sub-index which is 'the campaign structure' consists of eight items: the size of the election campaign budget, the size of the campaign staff, the degree of centralisation of the campaign organisation, the degree of externalisation, the differentiation of internal communication structures, the nature and degree of feedback, the degree of opposition research, and the duration of the campaign. The second sub-index, which is the 'campaign strategy', consists of seven items: the degree of audience targeting, the degree of narrowcasting activities, the relevance of paid media, the relevance of free media, the relevance of talk shows, the degree of event and news management, and the degree of personalisation. The maximum score for the campaign structure index is 24, and the maximum score for the campaign strategy index is 26. Thus, the maximum overall score of the whole professionalisation index is 50. The higher the overall score is, the more professional the campaign.

From this overview, it is clear that there are several attempts to try to find an efficient way of measuring professionalism. However, according to Tenscher et al. (2016), these attempts are either based on literature reviews or observations, and this does not take into account practitioners' perspectives which are involved with the practical part of the campaign. Thus, Lilleker et al. offer another dimension to add to the structure and strategies dimensions in assessing the degree of campaigns, that is, measuring practitioners' perspectives—along with structural and strategies dimensions—due to the important role they play in the campaign and their influence on it. Their perspectives can be measured by a set of closed questions which practitioners reply on. Lilleker suggested 32 items that can help in identifying the practitioners' perspectives and thus the overall degree of campaigns' professionalism. These items are '1) choice of right strategy, 2) negative campaigning, 3) willingness to attack the political opponent even 'below the belt', 4) clean (fair) campaigning, 5) choice of right issues, 6) the right top candidates, 7) willingness of the top candidates to reveal a little privacy, 8) good timing, 9) information on expectations and motivations of relevant groups of voters, 10) use of polls, 11) use of focus groups, 12) systematic observation of political opponents, 13) systematic press reviews and media content analyses, 14) having an impact on media's agenda 15) use of paid media such as TV spots, posters or advertisements, 16) TV spots on public channels, 17) TV spots on commercial channels, 18) radio spots on commercial channels, 19) radio spots on public channels, 20) advertisements in print media, 21) internet advertisements, 22) outdoor advertisements, 23) presence of party and top candidates on TV, 24) presence of party and top candidates on the internet, 25) communication with voters via telephone, 26) email, 27) Facebook, 28) Twitter, 29) YouTube, 30) other online media, 31) face to face, 32) canvassing.'

Although this method is still new and has been applied on a relatively limited sample, it can be a step towards a more comprehensive measurement of campaign professionalism as it combines both academic and practical perspectives. Nonetheless, perhaps a four-dimension measurement is needed, which takes into account the voters' perspective towards the campaign. However, this may be difficult because of voters' different backgrounds and personal differences, financial costs, and difficulty with getting a representative sample, but campaigns are a two-way process that contains several elements such as sender, medium used, and receiver. Each element should contribute towards better understanding of to what extent the campaign is professional.

Several concerns were raised regarding implementing the professionalisation index mainly for the following reasons: (a) it concentrates on communications practices without in-depth analysis of other criteria such as political, economic, social, and cultural content. (b) Variables are measured in a subjective way as it depends on researcher observation and assessment, rather than objective independent assessment. (c) It does not have a moral quality, as it fails to explain what is right or wrong, making the measurement itself 'more administrative than critical' (Herkman 2010), as if it is more concerned with ticking boxes rather than actual analysis. (d) It does not add weight to variables by explaining which variables are more important than others (Mykkänen and Tenscher 2014). (e) It tries to measure how practitioners from multiple countries have a general understanding of campaigns without trying to apply it to a single country with a more in-depth approach.

Despite these shortcomings, the professionalisation index still offers a better approach to studying campaigns, especially as it is the only approach that divides campaigns into two components: structures and strategies, offering a better comprehensive way in understanding and analysing how the campaigns are planned, managed, and implemented.

This book will use the professionalisation index as an interview guide while interviewing campaign managers in order to develop an in-depth understanding of campaign strategy, design, and execution. By using the professionalisation index as a framework for interviews, the book will figure out the campaigns' aims in terms of reaching and engaging voters, gaining support and mobilising them, and creating a vibrant political environment, reflecting on Dahl's features of the democratic process.

This book will overcome the professionalisation index's shortcomings by conducting in-depth analysis, depending on the professionalisation index only as an interview guide, taking into consideration other political and cultural contexts and trying to get answers to the main question: to what extent were the campaigns professionalised? And more importantly, trying to answer the question: did campaigns' professionalism positively impact Egypt? This question leads to the debate around the effect of campaigns' professionalism on democracy: does it enhance or weaken democracy?

1.4.10   Professionalism and Democracy

Despite the validity and recognition of professionalism, current literature on professionalism and democracy offers two conflicting trends (Rayner 2014). These two trends indicate that professionalised campaigns have clearer functions in thin democracies, but their applicability is more questionable in strong or thick democracies.

The first trend deals with professionalised campaigns in thin democracies. It believes that the professionalisation of election campaigns helps in enhancing democracy, as it helps candidates run effective, well-organised campaigns that are able to reach voters and convey information to them. It also helps candidates to communicate and engage with their audiences through interactive communication channels. It can also help in highlighting opponents' weaknesses by conducting opposition research and elaborating these weaknesses to voters (Rayner 2014: 342). The use of hypermedia in conveying messages by election campaigns acts as the main vehicle for mediating useful information to voters, helping them to be well-informed citizens, to build their decisions upon this information, and to interact with candidates or officials and in many cases helping in making candidates accountable in front of voters/citizens. The use of communication channels, especially social media, can play an important role in mobilising voters and urging them to participate. This mobilising role of social media was clear in cases like the eruption of the Arab Spring, especially in the Egyptian revolution where Facebook was the main vehicle for mobilising protesters and moving them to Tahrir Square (Elsheikh 2011), which can make it act as a new public sphere leading to a healthier democracy. The professionalisation of election campaigns led to other healthy consequences, which was clear in shifting voters' loyalty from parties to causes and opinion-led decisions that depend on several variables such as economic, political, and social variables (Koch 2011), meaning that voters' decisions can be changed and that they will vote for the better option for them, not what their party force them to vote for. Add to these that the use of marketing techniques in professionalised campaigns plays an important role in enhancing democracy (Koch 2011), as policies are adjusted according to voters' needs and not only top-down policies. The second trend raises more concerns about the role of professionalism in established democracies. It believes that professionalism does not help in enhancing democracy but offers a 'shallow campaign' that maximises and prioritises the use of 'dirty tricks and opponents' attacks' over content and political substances or real content which could lead to voters boycotting elections or at least withdrawing from the process (Rayner 2014: 342), which is the last thing a democracy wants. Advocates of this school argue that (1) professionalisation borrows some marketing techniques such as targeting voters into segments. These targeting processes make candidates concentrate more on voters and not on all citizens, forbidding all citizens from having equal access to information. According to this school, this can lead to segmentation of the public sphere and creating a knowledge and information gap between citizens in the same country, which leads to what Hamelink (2007: 182) calls 'democracy without citizens'. (2) Depending on mass communication media outlets in conveying the professionalised campaign messages, along with the rise of media logic, means that it could make candidates amend their stances or speeches to appeal to media coverage, which could lead to deceiving voters by using media to persuade them with policies against their will; thus it may manipulate and use citizens, instead of informing them. (3) Professionalised campaigns tend to maintain and improve the leadership's image. This could lead to strengthening 'totalitarian tendencies rather than contributing to development of open participatory and deliberative societies, since improving leadership image is usually related to authoritarian regimes' (Hamelink 2007: 183). (4) In many countries, people working in this field, 'the professionals', conduct their work without any ethical rules or associations that provide guidelines to their work, thus taking them away from public accountability (Hamelink 2007: 185) and perhaps providing them with an upper hand over the normal citizens away from rules and legislations in the country. (5) The use of negative campaigns and attacks may create a cycle of cynicism among citizens, making them lose trust in the whole process (Koch 2011). (6) Professionalism strengthens the role of citizens, not as active participants but as passive followers of those who represent them, as it deals with them as consumers when adopting marketing techniques or as spectators when adopting media techniques, but not as citizens (Koch 2011).

Although these two trends may appear contradictory, Rayner (2014) explains that they result from a different set of factors that are totally separate from the mechanism of campaigning itself, and that differentiate weak democracies from strong democracies, such as the nature of state, the legal framework, media organisation, and other cultural and institutional factors. This can take us to Cees Hamelink's conclusion that professionalised campaigns:

> fulfill clear functions within thin democracies. If, however, Societies decide for a strong model of democracy, they will need all the professionalism they can muster to engage in the grand scale teaching of democratic minds. (2007: 187)

Bearing in mind the above debate, this book will discuss to what extent were the 2012 Egyptian campaigns professionalised and to what extent this professionalism affected the outcome of the 2012 election and more importantly the democratisation of Egypt as a whole.

REFERENCES

Ansolabehere, S. and Iyengar, S., 1995. *Going negative: how political advertisements shrink and polarize the electorate*. New York: Free Press.

Bartels, L., 1996. Uninformed votes: information effects in presidential elections. *American Journal of Political Science*, 40, 194–230.

Bartels, L., 2006. Priming and persuasion in presidential campaigns. *In:* Brady, H. and Richard, J., eds. *Capturing campaign effects*. Ann Arbor: University of Michigan Press, 78–114.

Bennett, W. and Entman, R., eds., 2001. *Mediated politics: communication in the future of democracy*. Cambridge University Press.

Berg-Schlosser, D., 2009. Long waves and conjunctures of democratization. *In:* Haerpfer, C., Bernhagen, P., Inglehart, R. and Welzel, C., eds. *Democratization*. New York: Oxford University Press, 41–51.

Bernhagen, P., 2009. Measuring democracy and democratization. *In:* Haerpfer, C., Bernhagen, P., Inglehart, R. and Welzel, C., eds. *Democratization*. New York: Oxford University Press, 24–40.

Boulianne, S., 2009. Does internet use affect engagement? A meta-analysis of research. *Political Communication*, 26, 193–211.

Buss, T., Stevens Redburn, F. and Guo, K., eds., 2006. *Modernizing democracy: innovations in citizen participation (transformational trends in governance and democracy)*. Armonk: M. E. Sharpe.

Carnegie, P., 2010. *The road from authoritarianism to democratization in Indonesia.* New York: Palgrave Macmillan.

Catt, H., 1999. *Democracy in practice.* London: Routledge.

Cho, J., Shah, D., McLeod, J., McLeod, D., Scholl, R. and Gotlieb, M., 2009. Campaigns, reflection, and deliberation: advancing an O-S-R-O-R model of communication effects. *Communication Theory,* 19, 66–88.

Claassen, R., 2011. Political awareness and electoral campaigns: maximum effects for minimum citizens? *Political Behavior,* 33 (2), 203–223.

Coppedge, M. and Reinicke, W., 1990. Measuring polyarchy. *Studies in Comparative International Development,* 25 (1), 51–72.

Coppedge, M., Gerring, J., Altman, A., Bernhard, M., Fish, S., Hicken, A., Kroenig, M., Lindberg, S., McMann, K., Paxton, P., Semetko, H., Skaaning, S.-E., Staton, J. and Teorell, J., 2011. Conceptualizing and measuring democracy: a new approach. *Perspectives on Politics,* 9 (2), 247–267.

Cutright, P., 1963. National political development: measurement and analysis. *American Sociological Review* [online], 28 (2), 253–264.

Cwalina, W., Falkowski, A. and Newman, B., 2011. *Political marketing: theoretical and strategic foundations.* Armonk: M. E. Sharpe.

Dahl, R. A., 1998. *Democracy and its critics.* New Haven: Yale University Press.

Dahl, R., 1971. *Polyarchy: participation and opposition.* New Haven: Yale University Press.

Dahlgren, P., 2005. The internet, public spheres, and political communication: dispersion and deliberation. *Political Communication,* 22 (2), 147–162.

Diamond, L. 2009. Forward by Larry Diamond. *In:* Lindberg, S., ed. *Democratization by elections: a new mode of transition.* Baltimore: John Hopkins University Press, xiii–xix.

Diamond, L. and Myers, R., eds., 2001. *Elections and democracy in greater China.* Oxford University Press.

Dimitrova, D., Shehata, A., Strömback, J. and Nord, L., 2014. The effects of digital media on political knowledge and participation in election campaigns: evidence from panel data. *Communication Research,* 41 (1), 95–118.

Elsheikh, D., 2011. *New form of opposition in Egypt ... from movements to revolution.* Thesis (MA). SOAS, University of London, England.

Erickson, R. and Wlezien, C., 2012. *The timeline of presidential elections: how campaigns do and do not matter.* University of Chicago Press.

Farrell, D. and Schmitt-Beck, R., eds., 2002. *Do political campaigns matter?: campaign effects in elections and referendums.* London: Routledge.

Farrell, D., 1996. Campaign strategies and tactics. *In:* LeDuc, L., Niemi, R. and Norris, P., eds. *Comparing democracies: elections and voting in global perspective.* Thousand Oaks, CA: Sage, 160–183.

Fishkin, J., 1991. *Democracy and deliberation: new directions for democratic reform.* New Haven: Yale University Press.

Freedom House, 2015. Methodology. *Freedom in the World 2012* [online]. Washington, DC: Freedom House. Available from: https://freedomhouse. org/report/freedom-world-2012/methodology [Accessed 10 October 2016].

Fukuyama, F., 1992. *The end of history and the last man.* New York: Avon Books.

Gamson, W., 2001. Promoting political engagement. *In:* Bennett, W. and Entman, R., eds. *Mediated politics: communication in the future of democracy.* New York: Cambridge University Press, 56–74.

Gasiorowski, M., 1996. An overview of the political regime change dataset. *Comparative Political Studies*, 29 (4), 469–483.

Gibson, R. and Römmele, A., 2001. Changing campaign communications: a party-centered theory of professionalized campaigning. *Harvard International Journal of Press/Politics*, 6 (4), 31–43.

Gibson, R. and Römmele, A., 2009. Measuring the professionlisation of political campaigning. *Party Politics*, 15 (3), 321–339.

Gibson, R., 2010. 'Open source campaigning?': UK party organisations and the use of the new media in the 2010 general election [online]. *Annual Meeting of the American Political Science Association*, Washington, DC 2010. Available from: https://poseidon01.ssrn.com/delivery.php?ID=23612612610112409 40260261230920801260390410690770006006609108509710212211 00 05100095058000057047061023060098030109070087004124056073082 01107408009109408311908102709807305407912407010911700009208 09807007908800811009412301902712102908408808102708008 8089&EXT=pdf [Accessed 1 June 2016].

Gidengil, E., Blais, A., Nevitte, A. and Nadeau, R., 2002. Priming and campaign context: evidence from recent Canadian elections. *In:* Farrell, D. and Schmitt-Beck, R., eds. *Do political campaigns matter: campaign effects in elections and referendums.* New York: Routledge, 76–91.

Gil de Zúñiga, H., Veenstra, A., Vraga, E. and Shah, D., 2010. Digital democracy: reimagining pathways to political participation. *Journal of Information Technology & Politics*, 7 (1), 36–51.

Green, D., 2016. *Citizen activism and civil society. In how change happens.* Oxford University Press.

Gronbeck, B., 1978. The functions of presidential campaigning. *Communication Monographs*, 45 (4), 268.

Hamelink, C., 2007. The professionalisation of political communication: democracy at stake? *In:* Negrine, R., Mancini, P., Holtz-Bacha, C. and Pappathanassopoulos eds. *The professionalisation of political communication.* Bristol: Intellect, 179–188.

Hendricks, J. and Denton, R., 2010. *Communicator-in-chief: how Barack Obama used new media technology to win the White House.* Lanham, MD: Lexington.

Herkman, J., 2010. Re-evaluating the relationship between politics and popular media. *Media, Culture and Society*, 32 (4), 701–710.

Hermet, G., Rose, R. and Rouquie, A., eds., 1978. *Elections without choice.* London: Macmillan.

Holbrook, T., 1996. *Do campaigns matter?* Thousand Oaks, CA: Sage.

Howard, P., 2006. *New media campaigns and the managed citizen.* New York: Cambridge University Press.

Huntington, S., 1991. *The third wave: democratization in the late twentieth century.* Norman: University of Oklahoma Press.

Iyengar, S. and Kinder, D., 1987. *News that matters.* University of Chicago Press.

Iyengar, S. and Simon, A., 2000. New perspectives and evidence on political communication and campaign effects. *Annual Review of Psychology,* 51 (1), 149–169.

Katz, R., 1997. *Democracy and elections.* New York: Oxford University Press.

Kekic, L., 2007. The economist intelligence unit's index of democracy. *Democracy index 2007* [online]. Available from: http://www.economist.com/media/pdf/DEMOCRACY_INDEX_2007_v3.pdf [Accessed 10 September 2015].

Koch, T., 2011. The professionlisation of political marketing – a detriment to the democratic process? Department of Media and Communication, University of Leicester. *ResearchGate* [online]. Available from: https://www.researchgate.net/publication/215669646_The_Professionalisation_of_Political_Marketing_-_A_Detriment_to_the_Democratic_Process [Accessed 1 June 2016].

Lazarsfeld, P., Berelson, B. and Gaudet, H., 1944. *The people's choice: how the voter makes up his mind in a presidential campaign.* New York: Duell, Sloan, & Pearce.

Li, Q. and Reuveny, F., 2006. Democracy and environmental degradation. *International Studies Quarterly,* 50 (4), 935–956.

Lijphart, A., 1999. *Patterns of democracy: government forms and performance in thirty-six countries.* New Haven: Yale University Press.

Lilleker, D. G. and Negrine, R., 2002. Professionalisation: of what? Since when? By whom? *Harvard International Journal of Press/Politics,* 7 (4), 98–103.

Lilleker, D. G., Tenscher, J. and Stetka, V., 2015. Towards hypermedia campaigning? Perceptions of new media's importance for campaigning by party strategists in comparative perspective. *Information, Communication & Society,* 18 (7), 747–765.

Lindberg, S., 2009. *Democratization by elections: a new mode of transition.* Baltimore: John Hopkins University Press.

Linz, J., 1978. Non-competitive elections in Europe. *In:* Hermet, G., Rose, R. and Rouquie, A., eds. *Elections without choice.* New York: Wiley, 36–65.

Linz, Juan J., and Stepan, A. C., 1996. *Problems of democratic transition and consolidation: Southern Europe, South America, and post-communist Europe.* Baltimore, MD: Johns Hopkins University Press.

Lustokar, E., 2009. Reinforcing informal institutions through authoritarian elections: insights from Jordan. *Middle East Law and Governance,* 1 (1), 3–37. [Accessed 8 October 2015].

Mancini, P., 1999. New frontiers in political professionalism. *Political Communication*, 16 (3), 231–245.

Marshall, M. G. and Cole, B. R., 2011. *Global report 2011: conflict, governance, and state fragility* [online]. Vienna, VA: Center for Systematic Peace. Available from: http://www.systemicpeace.org/vlibrary/GlobalReport2011.pdf [Accessed 12 September 2014].

Medvic, S., 2010. *Campaigns and elections, players and processes*. Boston: Wadsworth.

Mykkänen, J. and Tenscher, J., 2014. Adding or weighting? Alternatives to measure parties' campaign professionalism [online]. *European Consortium for Political Research General Conference*, Glasgow 5 September 2014. Available from: https://ecpr.eu/Filestore/PaperProposal/7582fc4f-5b0a-48f8-83dc-5204237a7d16.pdf [Accessed 1 June 2016].

Negrine, R., Mancini, P., Holtz-Bacha, C. and Pappathanassopoulos eds., 2007. *The professionalisation of political communication*. Bristol: Intellect

Nie, N., 2001. Sociability, interpersonal relations, and the internet: reconciling conflicting findings. *American Behavioral Scientist*, 45, 420–435.

Norris, P., 2000. *A virtuous circle: political communications in postindustrial societies*. Cambridge University Press.

Norris, P., 2001. *Digital divide: civic engagement, information poverty and the internet worldwide*. Cambridge University Press.

Norris, P., 2002. *Democratic phoenix: reinventing political activism*. Cambridge University Press.

Norris, P., 2004a. The evolution of election campaigns: eroding political engagement? *Conference on Political Communications in the 21st Century*, University of Otago, New Zealand, January 2004.

Norris, P., 2004b. Political communications and democratic politics. *In*: Bartle, J. and Griffiths, D., eds. *Political communication transformed: from Morrison to Mandelson*. Basingstoke: Palgrave Macmillan UK, 163–180.

Norris, P., 2005. Did the media matter? Persuasion, priming and mobilization effects in the 2005 British general election campaign [online]. *Conference of the Elections, Parties and Public Opinion Group of the PSA (EPOP)*. University of Essex, September 2005. Available from: http://www.essex.ac.uk/bes/epop%202005/papers/epop%202005%20did%20the%20media%20matter.pdf [Accessed 12 October 2015].

O'Donnell, G., 1994. Delegative democracy. *Journal of Democracy*, 5 (1), 55–69.

Papacharissi, Z., 2002. The virtual sphere: the internet as a public sphere. *Online Media & Society*, 4 (1), 9–27.

Pateman, C., 1970. *Participation and the democratic theory*. Cambridge University Press.

Petrocik, J., 1996. Issue ownership in presidential elections with a 1980 case study. *American Journal of Political Science*, 40, 825–850.

Pfau, M., Houston, J. and Semmler, S., 2005. Presidential election campaigns and American democracy. *American Behavioural Scientist*, 49 (1), 48–62.

Poe, S. and Tate, C., 1994. Repression of human rights to personal integrity in the 1980s: a global analysis. *American Political Science Review*, 88 (4), 853–872.

Popesco, M. and Toka, G., 2002. Campaign effects and media monopoly: the 1994 and 1998 parliamentary elections in Hungary. *In:* Farrell, D. and Schmitt-Beck, R., eds. *Do political campaigns matter?: Campaign effects in elections and referendums*. London: Routledge, 58–75.

Powell, G., 2000. *Elections as instrument of democracy: majoritarian and proportional visions*. New Haven: Yale University Press.

Prezeworski, A., 1999. Minimalist conception of democracy: a defence. *In:* Shapiro, I. and Hacker Cordon, C., eds. *Democracy's value*. Cambridge University Press, 23–55.

Putnam, R., 2000. *Bowling alone: the collapse and revival of American community*. New York: Simon & Schuster.

Rayner, J., 2014, What about winning? Looking into the blind spot of the theory of campaign professionlisation. *Journal of Political Marketing*, 13 (4), 334–354.

Rose, R. and Mossawir, H., 1967. Voting and elections: a functional analysis. *Political Studies*, 15 (2), 173–201.

Sadiki, L., 2009. *Rethinking Arab democratization, democracy without elections*. Oxford University Press.

Scammell, M., 1998. The wisdom of the war room: US campaigning and Americanization. *Media, Culture and Society*, 20 (2), 251–275.

Sen, A., 1999. *Development as freedom*. Oxford University Press.

Schumpeter, J. A., 1943. *Capitalism, socialism and democracy*. London: George Allen and Unwin.

Strömbäck, J., 2007. Political marketing and professionalized campaigning: a conceptual analysis. *Journal of Political Marketing*, 6 (2–3), 49–67.

Strömbäck, J., 2009. Selective professionalisation of political campaigning. A test of the party-centered theory of professionalised campaigning in the context of the 2006 Swedish election. *Political Studies*, 57 (1), 95–116.

Swanson, D. and Mancini, P., 1996. *Politics, media, and modern democracy: an international study of innovations in electoral campaigning and their consequences*. Westport: Praeger.

Tenscher, J., 2013. First- and second-order campaigning: Evidence from Germany. *European Journal of Communication*, 28 (3), 241–258.

Tenscher, J. and Mykkänen, J., 2014. Two levels of campaigning: an empirical test of the party-centred theory of professionalisation. *Political Studies*, 62 (S1), 20–41.

Tenscher, J., 2007. Professionalisierung nach Wahl: Ein Vergleich der Parteienkampagnen im Rahmen der jüngsten Bundestags- und

Europawahlkämpfe in Deutschland. *In:* Brettschneider, F., Niedermayer, O. and Weßels, B., eds. *Die Bundestagswahl 2005: Analysen des Wahlkampfes und der Wahlergebnisse.* Wiesbaden: Verlag für Sozialwissenschaften, 65–95.

Tenscher, J., Koc-Michalska, K., Lilleker, D., Mykkänen, J., Walter, A., Findor, A., Jalali, C. and Róka, J., 2016. The professionals speak: practitioners' perspectives on professional election campaigning. *European Journal of Communication*, 31 (2), 95–119.

Tenscher, J., Mykkänen, J. and Moring, T., 2012. Modes of professional campaigning: a four-country comparison in the European parliamentary elections, 2009. *The International Journal of Press/Politics*, 17 (2), 145–168.

Thompson, D., 2002. *Just elections: creating a fair electoral process in the United States.* University of Chicago Press.

Vanhanen, T., 2000. A new data set for measuring democracy, 1810–1998. *Journal of Peace Research*, 37 (2), 251–265.

Vanhanen, T., 2003. *Democratisation: a comparative analysis of 170 countries.* London: Routledge.

Vavreck, L., 2000. How does it all 'turn out'? Exposure to attack advertising, campaign interest, and participation in American presidential elections. *In:* Bartels, L. and Vavreck, L., eds. *Campaign reform: insights and evidence.* Ann Arbor: University of Michigan Press, 79–105.

Verba, S., Schlozman, K. and Brady, H., 1995. *Voice and equality: civic volunteerism in American politics.* Cambridge: Harvard University Press.

Way, L., 2005. Ukraine's orange revolution: Kuchma's failed authoritarianism. *Journal of Democracy*, 16 (2), 131–145.

Whitehead, L., 2002. *Democratization: theory and experience.* Oxford University Press.

Zaller, J., 1992. *The nature and origins of mass opinion.* Cambridge University Press.

Zihala, M., ed., 2003. *Democracy: the greatest good for the greatest number.* Lanham, MD: University Press of America.

CHAPTER 2

The 2012 Presidential Election in Egypt

2.1 A Polarised Public Sphere

The idea of having a new president was ever-present since Mubarak left his post after the 25 January Revolution.[1] It became stronger during the transitional period, when the Supreme Council of the Armed Forces (SCAF) ruled the country. That is why Egyptians were very enthusiastic about this election: for the first time, they could choose their leader and the result was not known in advance. This enthusiasm was clear in the fact that the presidential election was the fourth and fifth times Egyptians went to vote in polling stations during the transitional period (Carter 2012).[2] Despite this enthusiasm, the presidential election on 23–24 May 2012 and the run-off on 16–17 June 2012 were both characterised by uncertainty regarding the future, mainly because the powers of the president were not clearly defined as there was no constitution in place (Hilal 2013; Carter 2012).

This uncertainty was clear enough in the controversial debates and incidents that took place during the transitional period before the election and which precipitated, to some extent, the shifting of the debate away from setting the presidential election's regulations and times.

These debates played an important role in polarising the Egyptian public and, in many cases, created tension. These debates included, but were not limited to, whether to follow the rule of law or of the revolution, especially regarding the trials of old regime figures, and which should

© The Author(s) 2018   39
D. Elsheikh, *Campaign Professionalism during Egypt's 2012 Presidential Election*, Political Campaigning and Communication, https://doi.org/10.1007/978-3-319-75954-8_2

precede the other in electing a president or drafting the constitution first, and whether to allow figures affiliated with the old regime to participate in the elections or to ban them.

The effect of these debates and incidents was not limited to the polarisation of the public sphere but also affected campaign work. For the campaigns that started during these times were involved in all of these incidents and debates; either by having an opinion, which affected them through gaining or losing voters, or by trying to keep a distance from being involved, which again had similar effects regarding voters, or even by participating in protests over these issues. This is especially the case as in the early stages after the revolution polarisation was issue-related, rather than group-related. These incidents, with all the debates and tensions taking place around them, used to lead, in many cases, to either protests or clashes between protestors or clashes between protestors and police forces. This affected the campaigns by delaying the election dates and the rules regulating it, causing the campaigns to work without any planned dates or laws. Moreover, most of the non-Islamic campaigns which started working at that time put their campaign work on hold to join these protests or clashes. For example, they would leave their campaign work and join a fight between police forces and football fans known as Ultras and similar incidents that took place at that time (Tadros 2012), entering into a continuous revolutionary mood, represented in the revolutionary forces' slogan 'the revolution continues'.

During this transitional period, the spirit of Egyptians was highly affected as well. The spirit of people after the revolution was very high. This spirit was manifested in many actions, such as the cleaning of Tahrir Square before leaving it or organising committees among the citizens in the streets to safeguard neighbourhoods and forming security checkpoints when the police structure collapsed and disappeared from the streets after the revolution. It was also shown when Muslims praying in Tahrir Square were surrounded by Christians protecting them. During this time, choosing a ruler for the country was one of the main issues. However, Egyptians, including candidates and politicians, were very much consumed by political battles that polarised the public sphere and ended the positive spirit Egyptians had after the revolution.

These clashes and political debates postponed the starting of the process of elections as there was no clear road map. It also reflected heavily on the candidates. By the time of elections, candidates, like all Egyptians, were classified to a certain degree according to their positions regarding these incidents that occupied the political and policy sphere during the transitional period.

Thus, the enthusiasm Egyptians had after the revolution was affected by political developments taking place at the time of the transitional period. In the end, this led to a polarised electorate, making the presidential election the result of a broader political transition taking place at that time. This section aims to describe and highlight some of these events and debates that took place during the transitional period in chronological order, to set the scene of the unclear and broader transition wherein the election took place and in which the campaigns were working.

2.2   Paving the Way Towards the Election

On 19 March 2011,[3] Egyptians voted in a referendum to amend nine articles of the suspended 1971 constitution in order to regulate and define the transitional period. The importance of this referendum was that it would act as a road map for the transitional period. Among the proposed changes was an amendment to Article 189, suggesting that a newly elected parliament would have six months to choose a constituent assembly that, in turn, would have an additional six months to draft Egypt's new constitution before it was put to a popular referendum. The amendments also suggested that the referendum on a new constitution would be held after a president was elected (Carter 2012).

At that time, most of the liberal, secular, leftist, and even the revolutionary forces campaigned strongly against the referendum. According to this group, the first element in this road map was to draft a new constitution before the elections, arguing that the elected officials could draft a constitution according to their own preferences. Thus, according to them, it was better to draft the new constitution before elections. For them, it would guarantee the inclusion and representation of all citizens if done beforehand.

On the other hand, military figures, including SCAF supporters, and the Islamist groups, including the Muslim Brotherhood, campaigned heavily in support of the referendum. They argued that a constitution-first approach would extend the time SCAF would be in power. For SCAF, it wanted to legitimise its role, and for the Muslim Brotherhood, they wanted to continue with elections as they knew they could win. In order to mobilise voters and make them vote yes, Islamist groups used Islam as their main way of campaigning, where sheikhs (Muslim clerics) at mosques would tell Muslims that it was a Muslim conquest at the ballot boxes: urging Muslims to vote yes as if it was a vote for Islam and for God (Said 2016). Videos of sheikhs in mosques describing the referendum as a Muslim conquest[4] were filmed by amateurs, who happened to be in mosques, and uploaded to social media and broadcast on television channels, mostly Islamist channels praising them and mobilising people through them and other non-Islamist channels using them to criticise such use of religion.

In the end, the nine amendments were approved by a majority of 77.2% of the voters who participated, which was also high: voter turnout at 41.19% was double the percentage in any previous referendum or election (Hilal 2013).

This referendum acted as a small test for all the political forces and their ability to campaign and mobilise voters, as it showed their actual weight in society. They were unable to achieve a majority of 'no' votes in any of the governorates (Hilal 2013). This illustrates the mobilising power of the Islamist forces compared with the revolutionary forces, and how they campaigned. It also acted as an indication for the presidential election result, but other campaigns did not pay close attention to it at this early stage. Even if they did pay attention, at such an early stage there was no Islamist presidential candidate to fear, given that the Muslim Brotherhood had announced that it would not nominate a presidential candidate.

The importance of this referendum does not lay in framing the transitional period only but in the way that it divided Egyptians into binaries such as religious versus civilian, civilian versus military, Islamist versus secular, or socialist versus liberal (Mogeeb 2013). These divisions increased the polarisation between each of these categories during the whole transitional period.

Despite these controversies, the referendum was still considered an indication of progress to democracy as it was the first step in determining a road map for the transitional period. However, on 30 March 2011, SCAF unilaterally issued a 63-article provisional constitution that acted as the replacement for the 1971 constitution (Hilal 2013). Moreover, the wording of some of the amendments voted upon on the 19 March referendum was changed, which made it unclear whether a new president would be elected or a new constitution would be written first (Carter 2012).

This wording created another controversial and polarised debate that caused a great deal of confusion in the Egyptian public sphere to the extent that those who wrote the wording were accused of favouring the Muslim Brotherhood and enabling them to hold parliamentary elections before forming the constitutional assembly; thus being able to control who participated in writing the new constitution (Al-Tahrir 26/6/2016; Sout Al-Ouma 23/11/2016).

Although the intention was to hold the presidential election before writing the constitution, the date for the election was not determined during this period (Carter 2012). Only on 1 January 2012 did the government announce its intention to hold the presidential election after drafting the constitution, stating that the official nominations for presidential candidacy would not begin until April 2012 (Ahram Online 1/01/2012). The announcement came amid activists' calls to hold an early presidential election in order to shorten the transitional period and end SCAF rule.[5]

After the conclusion of the parliamentary elections at the end of February, the political debate shifted towards electing the Constitutional Assembly to start drafting the constitution, paving the road towards the presidential elections.

The parliamentary election[6] in itself, for both the People's Assembly (lower house) and Shura Council (upper house), further acted as an early indication of what the presidential election might look like, as the majority of seats went to Islamist forces.[7] This again showed who had the real ability to mobilise and campaign in elections: the Islamist forces in opposition to revolutionary and other more liberal forces in society.

At the end of March 2012, the parliament met to elect the Constitutional Assembly. However, divisions emerged regarding whether to elect the Assembly from among the members of parliament or from outside. Parliament members wanted to elect all the 100 seats in the assembly within themselves only. The debate ended in a majority decision of the Islamist-dominated parliament, deciding that 50% of the Assembly should be chosen from members of parliament. In other words, members of parliament decided to elect themselves to write the constitution. This was opposed and criticised by all other non-Islamist political factions at the time, especially that many of the other 50 seats dedicated to figures from outside the parliament were also given to Islamic figures. This led to the fact that more than 65% of the assembly seats were given to members of Islamic parties; among the 100 elected figures, there were only six Christians and six women. All the others were Muslim and men (Hilal 2013). Moreover, this Constitutional Assembly refused all ideas presented by other political factions, such as guaranteeing representation for women and Christians. For these reasons, and others, many non-Islamist forces, along with Al-Azhar and church representatives, withdrew from the assembly because it did not represent all Egyptians and was not concerned with consensus (Hilal 2013).

Amid all these events, some citizens filed court cases against the assembly, resulting in the 10 April 2012 suspension of the 100-member Assembly that was drafting Egypt's new constitution (BBC 10/4/2012a, b). While all this was happening in the Egyptian political sphere, the preparation for the elections had started, with no idea of how or when the constitution might be finalised.

2.3   Preparing for Elections

Planning for the presidential election started in March 2012 with preparations for voter registration and candidate nomination. During the first days of candidate nominations, more than 1300 people went to the Presidential Elections Committee[8] (PEC) and collected the nomination applications, all announcing their intention to run for the presidency (Gaafar 2012). The process was very chaotic, as many people collecting applications were just ordinary citizens who wanted to be president. Among these people were cleaners, taxi drivers, and an ex-thief (Emarat Alyoum 14/3/2012). This large number of people queuing was filmed by television channels. It represented events in a way that undermined the process, such as interviewing a thief who would like to be president. This initiated a wave of anger from citizens who called in to condemn these incidents, denouncing the so-called democracy that would bring a thief and similar people to rule them; some even called for a return to Mubarak's days (Al Hayat TV 2012).

However, they were not able to fulfil PEC requirements to apply for candidacy. In order to be a candidate, the person must meet the criteria in Article 26 of the Constitutional Declaration: that the candidate has to be born in Egypt to Egyptian parents and cannot have dual nationality or be married to a foreigner, and their age must not be less than 40 years, and they must be able to practise their full civil and political rights (i.e. not be convicted of a crime and not be deemed insane). The candidate must be nominated through one of three ways: the applicant must gain the support of at least 30 members of the two houses of parliament or gain the support of a minimum of 30,000 voters from a minimum of 15 Egyptian governorates where the number of supporters from each governorate is not less than 1000, and where each voter could not support more than one candidate. A third way of entering the presidential race was through the support of a political party that held at least one seat from the previous elections of the People's Assembly or Shura Council.

The start of the nomination period witnessed a lot of other complicated circumstances that changed the calculations of many of the candidates who had already started their campaigns a year before the nominations opened. For example, the Muslim Brotherhood reversed its earlier decision not to nominate a candidate in the elections and nominated two candidates: Khairat Al-Shater, their deputy leader and mastermind, and Mohamed Morsi, the chairman of the Freedom and Justice Party. The decision to nominate two candidates was a clear indication of the Muslim Brotherhood's intention to be present in the presidential race if Khairat Al-Shater was disqualified from running, which was the case. In response to this, as described by many experts, Omar Suleiman, the former intelligence chief, joined the process as well. However, both Al-Shater and Suleiman were disqualified by the PEC. Al-Shater was disqualified for being in prison during the Mubarak era, while Suleiman was disqualified due to a mistake in the signatures he collected, which gave him 31 fewer signatures than required in the Asyut governorate.

Ayman Nour, Mubarak's rival in Egypt's first multi-candidate presidential elections in 2005, was also disqualified for being in prison during the Mubarak era. The Salafist leader, Hazem Salah Abu Ismail, was disqualified as his mother was a US citizen. The issue of disqualifying Abu Ismail contributed to further polarisation in Egypt. On 4 April 2012, the *New York Times* published an article stating that Abu Ismail's mother had US citizenship (Kirkpatrick 2012). Abu Ismail kept denying this until it was proven through citizenship documents. Amid these controversies, his supporters gathered in front of the PEC, protesting and occupying the streets in order to prevent any decision that would disqualify him (CNN Arabic 6/05/2012). Later on, Abu Ismail was charged with forging official documents during his application to run for president. He was also charged with inciting murder and defamation of police officers (Ahram Online 21/01/2014; Egypt Independent 22/04/2012). It may also be worth mentioning that Abu Ismail was the only candidate to present to the PEC both citizen signatures and parliamentary support. He applied for candidacy by providing proof of the support of 47 members of parliament and 152,835 citizens' signatures. The total number of his supporters exceeded what popular candidates such as Hamdeen Sabahi, Aboul Fotouh, or Amr Moussa received (Rabeea 2013).

The main implication of these incidents was the last-minute total change of the election map, which influenced in one way or another the other campaigns that were working hitherto, believing that there would not be a candidate from the Muslim Brotherhood or a candidate from the old regime. It also relieved other candidates from the pressure of having Abu Ismail with all his mobilising power in the presidential race.[9] It further shows the great deal of uncertainty and polarisation that was occurring at the time, especially from candidates' supporters who demonstrated, fought, and clashed in the streets. This diverted attention away from moving forward and continuing with the process and on to concentrating on each of these incidents and the ways to handle them. In the end, the PEC announced only 13 presidential candidates out of 23 citizens who were actually registered as candidates (Table 2.1).[10]

2.4   THE FIRST ROUND OF ELECTIONS: 23–24 MAY 2012

The first round of elections led to unpredictable results, with the top two candidates, Mohamed Morsi and Ahmed Shafiq, getting around 25% of the votes each and managing to make it to the second round. They were followed by the Nasserite revolutionary candidate Hamdeen Sabahi, who got 20% of the vote, then the former senior member of the Muslim Brotherhood Abdel Moneim Aboul Fotouh, who got 17%, and next the former Secretary-General of the League of Arab States, Amr Moussa, with 11% of the votes (Tables 2.2, 2.3 and 2.4).

Despite the fact that these results meant that the top winners came from the old regime and the Muslim Brotherhood, they also showed that 50% of those who voted did not choose to vote for either Morsi or Shafiq and decided to vote for other candidates from the remaining 11, who were either revolutionary or reformist candidates. The results also showed that if we added up the number of votes given to the three candidates who were considered revolutionary, they collectively got more than Mohamed Morsi, the top candidate. In other words, if there was a coalition between the revolutionary candidates to nominate one candidate on their behalf, the result might have been in the favour of this chosen candidate. This means that the results of the first round did not meet the expectations of the majority of eligible voters who voted in the election,[11] creating another level of polarisation in the Egyptian public sphere.

An example of this increased polarisation appeared after the three major revolutionary candidates, namely, Hamdeen Sabahi, Aboul Fotouh, and

Table 2.1 Presidential candidates

Name	Party	Method of candidacy	Job
1. Abul Ezz Hassan Ali Al Hariri	Socialist Popular Alliance Party	Party in parliament	Retired employee in textile company. Former member of parliament
2. Mohamed Fawzy Eissa	Generation democratic party	Party in parliament	Retired policeman
3. Ahmed Hossam Khairallah	Peace democratic party	Party in parliament	Former deputy of the Intelligence Agency; retired lieutenant-general in the Army
4. Amr Moussa	Independent	Supported by 43,906 signatures from voters	Former Secretary-General of the League of Arab States, Former minister of Foreign affairs
5. Abdel Moneim Aboul Fotouh	Independent	Supported by 43,066 signatures from voters	Former Muslim Brotherhood member
6. Hisham Al-Bastawisi	Al Tagammu Party	Party represented in the Parliament	Former vice head of the Court of Cassation
7. Mahmoud Hossam	Independent	Supported by 37,250 signatures from voters	Retired policeman
8. Mohamed Saleem Al Awa	Independent	Supported by 30 signatures from MPs	Lawyer and Islamic scholar
9. Ahmed Shafiq	Independent	Supported by 62,192 signatures from voters	Last prime minister appointed by Mubarak and former minister of civil aviation
10. Hamdeen Sabahi	Independent	Supported by 42,525 signatures from voters	Co-founder of Karama Party, Member of the parliament
11. Abdullah Al Ashaal	Al Assala Party	Party represented in the Parliament	Former assistant minister to the minister of foreign affairs
12. Khaled Ali	Independent	Supported by 30 signatures from MPs	Lawyer, human right activists
13. Mohamed Morsi	Freedom and Justice Party	Party represented in the Parliament	Chairman of the Freedom and Justice Party, the political arm of the Muslim Brotherhood group

Table 2.2   Statistical data on Egypt electorate

Data types	Number
Egypt's population	82,813,957[a]
Number of governorates	27
Number of registered voters	50,996,746[b]
Number of voters outside the country	586,803[b]
Number of candidates	13
Turnout for the first round	46.42%[b]

[a]Central Agency for Public Mobilization and Statistics website
[b]PEC website

Table 2.3   Top five candidates' results

Name of the candidates[a]	Number of votes
Mohamed Morsi	5,764,952
Ahmed Shafiq	5,505,327
Hamdeen Sabbahi	4,820,273
Abdel Moneim Aboul Fotouh	4,065,239
Amr Moussa	2,588,850

[a]PEC website

Table 2.4   Second round of elections' results

Name of the candidates[a]	Number of votes (%)
Mohamed Morsi	13,230,131 (51.73%)
Ahmed Shafiq	12,347,380 (48.27%)

[a]PEC press conference held on 24 June 2012

Khalid Ali, protested with their supporters, holding hands in rejection of the results and asking to apply the Political Exclusion Law, which excluded those who worked in a senior official position during the Mubarak era for a period of ten years. In this case, they were aiming to exclude Shafiq from continuing to the second round. This would have resulted in a run-off between Morsi and Sabahi. They also called for Egyptians to go into the streets and protest against the result of the election and called for the establishment of a civilian presidential council (Alyoum7 4/6/2012, 5/6/2012; Al-Masry 4/6/2012).

The implication of their gathering was not limited to fuelling and increasing the polarisation in society but raised concerns about the possibility of not accepting the results of the election, the first step towards the democratisation of Egypt and hence hindering the democratisation process as a whole, which could have made Egypt enter into a period of uncertainty with unknown consequences, at least at this stage. Whether it would have meant continuing the transitional period under SCAF rule, or having a leader or presidential council to rule the country against the election results and the official 'people's will', is unclear.

Their gathering and the demands they made also showed the lack of proper planning and the lack of experience between the three revolutionary candidates who refused to enter into a coalition or choose only one of them to be a presidential candidate that represented the revolution in the election, thus avoiding the fragmentation of votes that happened among those who supported the revolution.[12]

2.5   POLITICAL DEVELOPMENTS BETWEEN THE TWO ELECTORAL ROUNDS

In addition to the three failed candidates gathering in Tahrir Square, the period between the two rounds of the election witnessed two major political developments that increased dissatisfaction and uncertainty and also increased polarisation among voters.

The first development was SCAF initiating negotiations and mediating between Islamist and non-Islamist forces in order to reach an agreement on finalising the formation of a constitutional assembly. SCAF's step came amid the prediction of a Supreme Court ruling on the constitutionality of the Political Exclusion Law and the law under which the parliamentary elections were conducted. However, SCAF's efforts failed despite announcing that it might unilaterally amend the Constitutional Declaration in order to define the powers of the next president (Carter 2012). The main reason behind the failure of the mediation process was due to Islamist forces insisting on taking 50 seats, in addition to giving other seats, from the 50 seats that were supposed to be given to non-Islamists, to moderate Islamist parties and other religious institutions, rather than to liberal or other forces in society (Carter 2012; Hilal 2013).

The second development came on 14 June 2012, just two days before voting in the second round of the election, when the Supreme Court ruled that the Political Exclusion Law,[13] passed by parliament in May 2012 to exclude old regime officials from running in the presidential elections, was unconstitutional. This meant that Shafiq would continue in the presidential race in contrast to what the revolutionary candidates wanted, along with their supporters. The Supreme Court also ruled on the same day that the electoral law[14] that was used to elect a third of the parliament was unconstitutional, which meant dissolving the parliament.

These two incidents provoked anger and demonstrations in the streets that killed the last hopes for the revolutionary forces that Shafiq might be banned from continuing in the presidential race, and that the second round would be between Morsi and Sabahi, which would have meant that Sabahi would be the president.

Another reason for frustration was that by dissolving the parliament, the next president would have unimpeded powers with no clear responsibilities, especially given that there was no constitution as well. The dissolution of parliament led to various speculations, explanations, and comprehensions at the time. Each political force interpreted it as a conspiracy against their candidate. From these explanations, it was believed that parliament was mainly dissolved in order to limit presidential authority and weaken Morsi if he won; as the parliament was dominated by Islamist forces that would fully support him, or that it was dissolved as a way to bring back the old regime in case Shafiq won.

Fears of having the old regime back led to activists launching several campaigns, such as those calling for boycotting the second round of elections or campaigns calling people to vote for Morsi in opposition to Shafiq, so as not to get the old regime again, by launching a campaign known as 'squeezing the lime'. The name of the campaign came from a local expression that stems from the Egyptian practice of squeezing a lime or lemon onto food that does not taste good, is bitter, or is about to go bad: thus masking the bad taste and making it more palatable.

This campaign claimed that the blood of the protestors killed during the revolution was an obstacle between them and voting for Shafiq and that there was no such blood on the Muslim Brotherhood's hands at the time. They therefore urged Egyptians to 'squeeze the lime' and vote for Morsi, a bad candidate in the opinion of many. But just as squeezing a lime over bad food can make it sour, it is at least palatable, and thus so would Morsi be. There was mobilisation to vote for Morsi as a sort of punishment for the old regime that was represented by Shafiq.

2.6   THE SECOND ROUND OF ELECTIONS: 16–17 JUNE 2012

Despite all the uncertainty, polarisation, and protests in the streets, Egyptians went to the polling stations to choose a president who had no defined powers, and at the same time had unlimited powers due to the absence of a constitution and a parliament.

But another incident erupted that increased the polarisation and tension, as shortly after the polling stations closed on 17 June, SCAF issued an addendum to the 30 March Constitutional Declaration (Ahram online 18/6/2012). This addendum gave more authority to SCAF, eliminating some of the president's authority, such as not allowing the president to declare war without SCAF approval, giving SCAF leaders some immunities against removal until a new constitution was issued, and also giving SCAF the authority to appoint the new 100-member Constitutional Assembly if the new one failed to perform its duties. The addendum also stated that the president's oath would be taken in front of High Constitutional Court's general assembly, which would create another problem that will be discussed later.

The timing of the announcement of the new addendum was severely criticised. Egyptians were polarised once again around it. Opponents, mainly the Muslim Brotherhood, which was preparing itself for the presidency, described it as a 'constitutional coup', opposing the fact that their candidate might not have any powers and saying that SCAF had no authority to issue such an addendum, and thus act like the real ruler of the country, especially with no real public transparency regarding its working mechanisms.

Other political factions and presidential candidates were reluctant to announce their stance on it at the beginning but opposed it in the end, as it decreased the power of the president. Supporters, who were mainly opponents of the Muslim Brotherhood, said that this addendum was a practical solution to preserve Egypt until a new constitution was in place. Some felt secure that the new president, namely, Morsi, would not have supreme powers. This addendum increased the polarisation of the Egyptian public sphere while Egyptians were waiting for the result of the election.

Amid these controversies, the Muslim Brotherhood pre-empted the PEC and unilaterally announced that Morsi was the winner and thus the new president. His campaign even issued a book documenting his votes (Al-Masry 20/6/2012a, b). Moreover, some members of the Muslim

Brotherhood announced to their supporters who were demonstrating in various Egyptian squares and streets, and who were filmed by a journalist, that they would 'burn Egypt' if Shafiq won and that Egypt 'would not witness any other future presidential election' if Shafiq was announced the winner.

This led to Shafiq's campaign refusing Morsi's victory announcement and accusing the Morsi campaign of threatening the PEC. This polarisation was described in an *Al-Masry Al-Youm* newspaper headline on 20 June 2012 as a psychological war in the presidential elections and an uprising against the addendum (Al-Masry 20/6/2012b).

This incident again increased the polarisation and fears among Egyptians, with rumours spreading that the Muslim Brotherhood was putting pressure on the PEC to announce Morsi as the winner even if he did not win. This led to opposing statements between Morsi's campaign and Shafiq's campaign and to poisoning the public sphere with protests from both sides occupying the streets. This was accentuated by the delay of the PEC in announcing the result.

During this time, on 21 June 2012, representatives of various political currents, including liberal and revolutionary forces, such as Wael Ghoneim, the administrator of the 'We are all Khaled Said' Facebook page that called for the 25 January 2011 protests that led to the revolution, held a meeting with Morsi in the luxurious Fairmont hotel. This meeting was known as the Fairmont Meeting, where the revolutionary forces went to ask the Muslim Brotherhood candidate to withdraw and not compete for the presidency. However, after Morsi's refusal, these forces supported Morsi against Shafiq in order to end the transitional period and SCAF rule and what was described as a 'military plan to rig the election results', and in return Morsi agreed to their demands and promised to fulfil them during his term as president. Among these demands was that he be a president for all Egyptians and to not exclude others (Shukrallah 2013).

After revolutionary forces failed to cancel the election results by forming the Presidential Council or by convincing Morsi to withdraw, and amid protests from Morsi's supporters in Tahrir Square insisting he won, and other protests in Nasr City by Shafiq's supporters insisting he was the winner, the PEC finally announced the results on 24 June, one week after the end of voting, announcing that Morsi was the new president of Egypt, winning with 51.73% of the votes, and Shafiq gaining 48.27% of votes.

2.7   AFTER THE ELECTION

The controversies and polarisation continued as soon as Morsi was announced president. The first controversy was regarding where he would take the presidential oath. According to the 17 June addendum to the 30 March Constitutional Declaration, he should make it in front of the High Constitutional Court's General Assembly. However, since the Muslim Brotherhood and revolutionaries saw this as a constitutional coup, they wanted him to make the oath in Tahrir Square. To end this issue, Morsi made the oath three times in three different places (Al-Masry 30/6/2012 & 1/07/2012): in front of his supporters in Tahrir Square, in front of the High Constitutional Court's General Assembly, and at his inauguration party at Cairo University. Morsi's controversies were contained later on with his annulment of the 17 June addendum to the 30 March Constitutional Declaration and by installing members of the Muslim Brotherhood, or those affiliated with them, to public and official posts. This raised concerns about the future of democratisation in Egypt as well as the role of the rule of law in the coming period.

Another controversy was Shafiq's allegation that the election was fraudulent. An investigation was opened into this, especially after discovering ballot papers coming in from the governmental printer that were already signed. Furthermore, some Israeli reports talked about Shafiq winning (Beilin 2013), but Morsi claiming victory out of fear of unrest. However, the media was banned from publishing the story (Daily News 19/01/2016) until the ban was removed in January 2016 (Al-Watan 20/01/2016). Until now, the court has not ruled on this case. Shafiq's campaign still believes that Shafiq was the winner and SCAF interfered to announce Morsi's victory amid fears of turmoil and unrest in Egypt.

2.8   CONCLUSION

Although SCAF originally stated that it would hand over power to a civilian-elected president within six months, it stayed in power for more than a year. However, from the above overview, it appears that there was no clear plan for managing the prolonged transitional period which was characterised by confusion and a lack of clarity, both from the political forces present at the time and from SCAF itself.

This interim period was characterised by many matters that hardened the transition, such as the control of conflicts and divisions among political forces. These conflicts became more violent in many cases and were not solved through political competition or through legal institutions but rather through mobilising people to protest to force those responsible to implement their demands. This way of achieving demands by protest was not limited to political matters only, but extended to include any non-political, sectarian demands or work-related demands.

The transitional period also witnessed the emergence of new political forces that were not known before the revolution. Many of these forces were Islamist ones, such as the Salafist forces, with whom no one was familiar regarding their real position and intentions at such early stages. The main three powers present at that time also lacked full legitimacy (Mogeeb 2013). Firstly, SCAF derived its legitimacy from supporting the revolution, but it did not have popular support for its rule, which made the support it had change several times over the course of the transitional period. This appeared in the chants and slogans that were heard in the streets at that time, which changed from: 'the people and the army hand-in-hand' to 'down with the rule of the military'. Secondly, the revolutionary youth forces had the streets and the sympathy of the people, but they were split and without any legal or elected legitimacy and without a single leader to represent them. Thirdly, were the Islamist forces that had mobilisation capacity but were trying to exclude all other non-Islamist forces (Mogeeb 2013).

The relation between the three forces showed a distinct lack of trust between them, which was clear in failing to reach a deal or agreement in many incidents during the transitional period, one of which was the formation of the Constitutional Assembly. The result of all these factors led to a prolonged transitional period full of controversies that extended until after electing the president.

The same applied for presidential candidates as non-Islamist presidential candidates, along with their campaigns—especially those who belonged to the revolution—immersed themselves in the permanent continuous revolutionary status. They assumed people would be active enough and would support them as they did in the 25 January revolution. Apparently, however, people were fed up with the instability, deteriorated economic situation, job closure, and non-stop protests that used to block the roads making it difficult for many to commute. Liberals were ready to bear the price of this state of continuous instability and continuous revolution, aiming for a better future. Not all those who sympathised with them and supported them during the revolution were ready to sustain the same cost, especially with 19% of Egyptians living under two dollars a day during that time (Hellyer 2011).

On the contrary, the Muslim Brotherhood was the most organised political force present at that time, although it was more concerned with its own interest rather than Egypt's national interest (Hellyer 2011). It was able to concentrate on achieving its goals whatever they were, to the extent that it distanced itself from participating in numerous protests and events that other political forces, especially revolutionary ones, were participating in, such as protests asking for retribution for those killed by security forces amid the revolution or protests against SCAF or protests calling to end military trials of civilians (Selim 2015), the actions that were described by some as a deal or alliance between the Muslim Brotherhood and SCAF (Selim 2015).

The accumulation of all the political controversies explained in this chapter, along with the main themes that characterised the transitional period, led to a polarised society and polarised voters. It also participated in undermining the political transitional period and undermined the process of democratisation in Egypt in general.

According to Dahl (1998: 37–38), a democratic process should have five criteria. First: effective participation where all members must have equal and effective opportunities for making their views known. Second: voter equality, where each member should have equal opportunity to express their vote. Third: the inclusion of all adults, as all adults must have their full rights of citizenship. Fourth: an enlightened understanding where each member must have equal and effective opportunities to learn about relevant policy alternatives and their consequences. And fifth: control of the agenda where members must have exclusive opportunities to decide which subjects are placed on the agenda.

Although the five criteria mentioned above were fulfilled during the presidential election, not all of them were fulfilled during the transitional period that preceded the election, especially when viewing the controversial political incidents mentioned in this chapter from a wider perspective.

Despite the fact that the effective participation criterion was present in the election process itself, as all voters had an equal opportunity to vote in the elections, this criterion was not present in many of the events during the transitional period. This was clear, for example, in the controversies that surrounded forming the constitution and in not having a parliament that clearly reflected the different forces in society and that could make its views known. There was also no clear process or bodies to ensure the participation and transmission of public views in forms other than protest, which was the main form of expressing views at that time. The inclusion criterion was also not present in many incidents during this transitional period. The main example to prove this case was Islamists trying to exclude or limit non-Islamist political forces from participating in drafting the constitution and deciding on the future of their country.

Instead of encouraging a healthier debate and enlightening voters, each of these incidents provoked protests and in many cases protests that led to clashes, either between different protestors or between protesters and the army or police. The way Islamist forces used Islam to mobilise voters and direct them to vote in favour of the 19 March referendum, which framed the transitional period, also meant that not all citizens had equal and real opportunities to learn about the reasons why they should or should not support the referendum along with the alternatives and their consequences, meaning that the enlightened understanding criterion was not present either.

Further, Dahl's fifth criterion was not present in many cases during the transitional period, as most Egyptians' actions were reactions to sudden actions made by other political forces, mainly SCAF and the Muslim Brotherhood, meaning that they did not have exclusive opportunities to decide and control the political agenda. This was also clear in not having the chance to shorten SCAF ruling period or to set the election dates earlier.

Despite being an essential part of democracy, the rule of law (Rose 2004; Tamanha 2007, 2012) was not an agreed-upon element of democracy during this transitional period. It provoked several protests and demonstrations when applied during the transitional period. Examples of this vary from immediately after the revolution and the beginning of the trials of old regime figures, where some revolutionary forces did not want to prosecute them according to the existing law, but rather by creating new revolutionary laws, specially made for the transitional period, or to punish them directly since it was the 'age of revolution', leading to another level of polarisation. This polarisation surrounding the rule of law was clear as well when the parliament was elected, with some people still wanting to protest in Tahrir Square to communicate their demands. The polarisation was also clear in not accepting the Supreme Court ruling to dissolve the parliament or allow Shafiq to continue in the elections because the law was proven to be unconstitutional. It was also present immediately after the revolution by allowing SCAF to rule and manage the transitional period as this was against the law as well. According to the Egyptian Constitution of 1971 and all its amendments which was the one applicable during Mubarak's era, in case the presidential post became vacant, the post should go to the prime minister. If his post was vacant, it should go to the Head of Parliament, and if his post was vacant, it should go to the head of the supreme constitutional court. The debate around the rule of law extended till after Morsi was elected as president and was clear in the controversial debate which took place around where to swear the presidential oath, which he ended by saying three times to make everyone happy.

The confusion and mismanagement of the transitional period from all sides led to flaws in the process of democratisation in Egypt as explained above. This might have made it difficult for the election campaigns to work and mobilise voters. The following chapters will discuss how the first five main campaigns worked in this political environment by analysing their structures and strategies through a series of interviews with campaign staff.

Notes

1. The revolution was an unplanned one. It started with calls from youth online to protest in Tahrir Square on the 25 January—Egypt's National Police Day. Protests were initially calling for 'bread, freedom, and social justice'. Demands then escalated asking former president Mubarak to step down. Mubarak was forced to resign on 11 February 2011.
2. Egyptians voted in the constitution referendum and the elections of the Shura Council and People's Assembly with their two rounds.
3. On 11 February 2011, Mubarak left power, assigning SCAF to manage the country. On the same day, SCAF issued a statement where it promised to guarantee holding necessary legislative amendments and hold accordingly free and fair presidential elections. On 13 February, SCAF issued the first Constitutional Declaration, setting the general framework for the transitional period. The declaration included suspending the 1971 constitution and gave SCAF temporary executive and legislative authority for six months or until the election of a new parliament and president. It also called for the formation of a committee to amend the suspended constitution and for these amendments to be put to a referendum. (Hilal et al. 2013: 118). On 15 February, SCAF appointed a committee to propose amendments to the suspended 1971 constitution headed by Judge Tarek El-Bishry. The period from 15 February till 19 March was mainly about

the committee and the referendum. For more details about this committee, the legal and constitutional framework of the transitional period, see Hilal (2013: 111–204).

4. Famous video for cleric Muhammad Hussein Yacoub. See Said 2016.
5. After demonstrations against military rule, SCAF said that they would hand over power by the end of June. Different initiatives and proposals were prepared by activists to shorten this period, such as SCAF handing over power to parliament or creating a presidential council or conducting early presidential elections.
6. More than 50 political parties participated in these Parliamentary elections—which were the first after the revolution (Elsayyad and Hanafy 2014). Several explanations were given to Islamists dominating the results such as voters' illiteracy, conspiracy theory, money coming from Islamic gulf countries to support Islamic candidates, non-Islamic candidates unable to mobilise or reach voters and only using TV advertisements without reaching people, flaws within non-Islamic forces. See: (Elsayyad and Hanafy 2014; Tadros 2012).
7. Although the Muslim Brotherhood initially raised the slogan 'participation not domination', they entered the race for almost all seats, not concentrating on their strongholds. For more details, see Brown 2012. What Holtmann described as their sudden decision to 'have the whole cake and not sharing it with other parties' (Holtmann 2013: 198).
8. The PEC is the body responsible for managing and administrating the elections. It is chaired by the head of SCC and has other four judges. It has also a General Secretariat which is chaired by a secretary-general from the Judiciary and consists of 11 other judges. It issued a total of 21 regulatory decisions. According to Article 28 of the Constitutional Declaration, its decisions are immune and cannot be appealed against. For full details, see Rabeea 2013: 13–37.
9. During my interviews with Moussa's, Aboul Fotouh's, Shafiq's, and Sabahi's campaign staff, all considered Abu Ismail as the main popular candidate competing against them. This was mainly due to the mobilising power he had on his supporters and his campaign's spending which was clear in the unlimited posters all over Egypt including governorates, which was known at that time as Abu Ismail's poster phenomena.
10. For more info, see Rabeea 2013.
11. For detailed analysis of election's results, see Chap. 4.
12. Chapter 4 elaborates more on this point.
13. The Law on the Exercise of Political Rights, also known as the Political Exclusion Law, aimed to exclude those who had worked in a senior official position during the Mubarak era for a period of ten years (BBC News 2012 10/4/12). The debate surrounding this law started early after the

revolution, creating a great deal of polarisation. However, real steps towards enforcing this rule were only taken when General Omar Suleiman, the country's former intelligence chief, along with Ahmed Shafiq, the last Prime Minister of the Mubarak era, announced their intention to run for the presidency. The new law was tailored especially for them, as it stated clearly that it would apply only to those who held the office of president, vice-president, or prime minister. Ahmed Shafiq appealed to the Presidential Elections Committee (PEC) regarding the validity of this law, and the PEC presented the law to the Supreme Constitutional Court and, after a very long debate and much polarisation among the public, the Supreme Constitutional Court declared the law unconstitutional, allowing them (i.e. Shafiq) to run for the presidency (BBC News 12/4/2012a, b). This court ruling came only two days before the start of the second round of the election, which again increased the polarisation and confusion in the Egyptian public sphere.

14. Before the Parliamentary elections, non-Islamic forces insisted on changing the electoral system to be based on party lists and not individuals to end the role of local big families and what they called the remnants (*fulul*) of the old regime. To please everyone, SCAF chose a mixed system whereby two thirds of seats were chosen through party lists and one third in individual districts. This system led to many problems and affected the results as many families decided not to compete or competed against each other, leaving the place open for the Islamic forces (Tadros 2012).

REFERENCES

Ahram Online, 1/1/2012. Egypt constitution to be drafted before presidential elections: minister. *Ahram Online* [online], 1 January 2012. Available from: http://english.ahram.org.eg/News/30684.aspx [Accessed 28 January 2016].

Ahram Online, 18/6/2012. English text of SCAF amended Egypt constitutional declaration. *Ahram Online* [online], 18 June 2012. Available from: http://english.ahram.org.eg/NewsContent/1/64/45350/Egypt/Politics-/English-text-of-SCAF-amended-Egypt-Constitutional-.aspx [Accessed 28 January 2016].

Ahram Online, 21/1/2014. Salafist preacher Abu-Ismail jailed for insulting judiciary. *Ahram Online* [online], 21 January 2014. Available from: http://english.ahram.org.eg/NewsContent/1/64/92085/Egypt/Politics-/Salafist-preacher-AbuIsmail-jailed-for-insulting-j.aspx [Accessed 28 January 2016].

Al Hayat TV, 2012. *Talk show interview with ex-thief candidate for elections* [video, online]. YouTube. Available from: https://www.youtube.com/watch?v=BrwakPBEOc4 [Accessed 1 June 2016].

Al-Masry, 4/6/2012. *Aboul Fotouh, Sabahi and Aly in Tahrir Square* [video, online]. YouTube. Available from: https://www.youtube.com/watch?v=REi0LS_isJU [Accessed January 2016].

Al-Masry, 20/6/2012a. Morsi campaign confirms its candidates winning with a published book. *Al-Masry Al-Youm* [online], 20 June 2012. Available from: http://today.almasryalyoum.com/article2.aspx?ArticleID=343436&IssueID=2538 [Accessed 28 January 2016].

Al-Masry, 20/6/2012b. Psychological war in the presidential elections and an uprising against the addendum. Al-Masry Al-youm [online] 20 June 2012. Available from: http://today.almasryalyoum.com/default.aspx?IssueID=2538 [accessed 1 February 2017].

Al-Masry, 30/6/2012. The presidential oath in the square. *Al-Masry Al-Youm* [online], 30 June 2012. Available from: http://today.almasryalyoum.com/article2.aspx?ArticleID=344716 [Accessed 28 January 2016].

Al-Masry, 1/7/2012. Egypt says goodbye to 60 years of military rule. *Al-Masry Al-Youm* [online], 1 July 2012. Available from: http://today.almasryalyoum.com/article2.aspx?ArticleID=344826 [Accessed January 2016].

Al-Tahrir News, 26/6/2016. Tarik El Beshry, the founder of the crisis. *Al Tahrir News* [online], 26 June 2016. Available from: http://www.tahrirnews.com/posts/437458/القضاء+المصري+المجلس+العسكري+الأزهر+الشريف+التعديلات+الدستورية [Accessed 26 June 2016].

Al-Youm 7, 4/6/2012. Aboul Fotouh, Sabahi and Aly insist on forming a presidential council. *Al Youm 7* [online], 4 June 2012. Available from: http://www.youm7.com/story/2012/6/4/696640/بالفيديو-3مرشحى-رئاسة-سابقون-بالتحرير-صباحى-مصممون-على-تشكيل-مجلس [Accessed 1 January 2016].

Al-Youm 7, 5/6/2012. Aboul Fotouh, Sabahi and Aly march to Tahrir Square. *Al Youm 7* [online], 5 June 2012. Available from: http://www.youm7.com/story/2012/6/5/696795/اليوم-عصر-للتحرير-مسيرات-3يقودون-على-وصباحى-وأبو-الفتوح [Accessed 1 June 2016].

Alsyed, A., 23/11/2016. Profile on Tarik El Beshry. *Sout Al Omma*, [online], 23 November 2016. Available from: http://www.soutalomma.com/286888 [Accessed 1 January 2016].

BBC News, 10/4/2012. Egypt court suspends constitutional assembly. *BBC News* [online], 10 April 2012. Available from: http://www.bbc.co.uk/news/world-middle-east-17665048 [Accessed 28 January 2016].

BBC News, 12/4/2012a. Egypt court suspends constitutional assembly [online]. *BBC News* [online], 10 April 2012. Available from: http://www.bbc.com/news/world-middle-east-17665048 [Accessed 24 January 2016].

BBC News, 12/4/2012b. Egypt MPs bar ex-Mubarak presidential candidates. *BBC News* [online], 12 April 2012. Available from: http://www.bbc.co.uk/news/world-middle-east-17697246 [Accessed 28 January 2016].

Beilin, Y., 18/6/2013. Morsi did not win the elections. *Israel Hayom* [online], 18 June 2013. Available from: http://www.israelhayom.com/site/newsletter_opinion.php?id=5395 [Accessed 28 January 2016].

Brown, J., 2012. When victory becomes an option: Egypt's muslim brotherhood confronts success [online]. Washington, DC: Carnegie Endowment for International Peace. Available from: http://carnegieendowment.org/files/ brotherhood_success.pdf [Accessed 1 January 2017].

Carter Center, 2012. *Presidential election in Egypt, final report: May–June 2012* [online]. Atlanta, GA: The Carter Center. Available from: https://www.cartercenter.org/resources/pdfs/news/peace_publications/election_reports/ egypt-final-presidential-elections-2012.pdf [Accessed 28 January 2016].

Central Agency for Public Mobilization and Statistics website. Egypt [online]. Available from: http://www.capmas.gov.eg [Accessed 1 January 2014]

CNN Arabic, 6/5/2012. Abu Ismail's supporters besieging the PEC. *CNN Arabic* [online], 6 May 2012. Available from: http://archive.arabic.cnn. com/2012/egypt.elections/4/14/egypt.abuIsmail/index.html [Accessed 28 January 2016].

Dahl, R. A., 1998. *Democracy and its critics.* New Haven: Yale University Press.

Daily News Egypt, 19/1/2016. Media gag lifted in 2012 presidential elections forgery. *Daily News Egypt* [online], 19 January 2016. Available from: http:// www.dailynewsegypt.com/2016 January 19/media-gag-lifted-in-2012-presidential-elections-forgery/ [Accessed 28 January 2016].

Egypt Independent, 22/4/2012. Abu Ismail supporters continue sit-in for fourth day. *Egypt Independent* [online], 22 April 2012. Available from: http://www. egyptindependent.com/news/abu-ismail-supporters-continue-sit-fourth-day [Accessed 28 January 2016].

El-Watan News, 20/1/2016. *Al-Watan* publish investigation details of elections forgery. *El-Watan News* [online], 20 January 2016. Available from: http:// www.elwatannews.com/news/details/926974 [Accessed 28 January 2016].

Elsayyad, M. and Hanafy, S., 2014. Voting Islamist or voting secular? An empirical analysis of voting outcomes in Egypt's 'Arab Spring'. *Public Choice*, 160 (1/2), 109–130.

Emarat Al-Youm, 14/3/2012. A cleaner applies to be a presidential candidate. *Emarat Al-Youm* [online], 14 March 2012. Available from: http://www.emaratalyoum.com/politics/news/2012-03-14-1.468393 [Accessed 28 January 2016].

Gaafar, H., 2012. 1,305 applicants for presidency. *Masress* [online], 3 April 2012. Available from: http://www.masress.com/elwady/1707 [Accessed 28 January 2016].

Hellyer, H. A., 2011. The chance for change in the Arab world: Egypt's uprising. *International Affairs*, 87 (6), 1313–1322.

Hilal, A., 2013. Constitutional and legislative framework: drafting of the law under political pressure. *In:* Hilal, A., Hassan M. and Mogeeb, M., eds. *Egypt after the revolution: the struggle for a new political system.* Cairo: Al-Dar Al-Masriya Al-Libnaniya, 113–204.

Hilal, A., Hassan M. and Mogeeb, M., 2013. *Egypt after the revolution: the struggle for a new political system.* Cairo: Al-Dar Al-Masriya Al-Libnaniya.

Holtmann, P., 2013. After the fall: the Muslim Brotherhood's post-coup strategy. *Perspectives on terrorism* [online], 7 (5), 198–204. Available from: http:// www.terrorismanalysts.com/pt/index.php/pot/article/view/303/html [Accessed 1 June 2016].

Kirkpatrick, D. D., 2012. Anti-American Egyptian candidate may be tripped up by mother's U.S. ties. *New York Times* [online], 4 April 2012. Available from: http://www.nytimes.com/2012/04/05/world/middleeast/sheik-hazem-salah-abu-ismail-may-be-disqualified-from-egypt-presidential-race.html?_r=3 [Accessed 28 January 2016].

Mogeeb, M., 2013. The environment of transitional regime: searching for a road map. *In:* Hilal, A., Hassan M. and Mogeeb, M., eds. *Egypt after the revolution: the struggle for a new political system.* Cairo: Al-Dar Al-Masriya Al-Libnaniya, 63–110.

Rabeea, A. H., 2013. Constitutional and legal environment to 2012 presidential elections. *In:* Rabeea, A. H., ed. *Presidential election 2012.* Cairo: Al-Ahram Centre for Political and Strategic Studies, 11–48.

Rose, J., 2004. The rule of law in the western world: an overview, *Journal of Social Philosophy*, 35 (4), 457–470

Said, S., 2016. Five years on the 19th of March referendum. *Al-Badil* [online], 19 March 2016. Available from: http://elbadil.com/2016/03/5-سنوات-على-استفناء19-مارس-وغزوة-الصنادي/ [Accessed 1 January 2017].

Selim, G. M., 2015. Egypt under SCAF and the Muslim Brotherhood: The Triangle of Counter-Revolution. *Arab Studies Quarterly*, 37 (2), 177–199.

Shukrallah, S., 2013. Once election allies, Egypt's 'Fairmont' opposition turn against Morsi. *Ahram Online* [online], 27 June 2013. Available from: http:// english.ahram.org.eg/NewsContent/1/152/74485/Egypt/Morsi,-one-year-on/-Once-election-allies,-Egypts-Fairmont-opposition-.aspx [Accessed January 2016].

Tadros, S., 2012. Egypt's elections: why the Islamists won. *World Affairs* [online], March/April 29–36. Available from: http://www.worldaffairsjournal.org/article/egypt's-elections-why-islamists-won [Accessed 23 November 2016].

Tamanaha, B. Z., 2007. How an instrumental view of law corrodes the rule of law. *Depaul Law Review*, 56, 469

Tamanaha, B. Z., 2012. History and elements of the rule of law, The [article], *Singapore Journal of Legal Studies*, 2, 232

CHAPTER 3

Campaigns' Structures and Strategies

This chapter gives an overall understanding of how each of the five studied campaigns were planned and implemented. The chapter does this by deconstructing the campaigns into structures (hardware) and strategies (software) applying the professionalisation index as the main framework. By structures, the chapter gives an insight to campaigns' staff, management style, campaign's premises, and degree of externalisation, internal communication, feedback, opposition research, campaign duration, and budget. By strategies, the chapter gives an insight to each campaign's strategies regarding voters' targeting, narrowcasting activities, free media, paid media, debates, internet and social media, campaigns' activities, and degree of personalisation inside each campaign. The chapter will start by discussing the two top campaigns, those of Morsi and Shafiq; then Aboul Fotouh's and Moussa's campaigns which were expected from the public opinion polls to be the top two candidates, yet who were the last of the winners; and finally discussing Sabahi's campaign which was considered as the election surprise or the election's dark horse since he got the third rank although he was seen—especially at the beginning of his campaign—to have almost no chance (Tables 3.1 and 3.2).

© The Author(s) 2018   63
D. Elsheikh, *Campaign Professionalism during Egypt's 2012*
Presidential Election, Political Campaigning and Communication,
https://doi.org/10.1007/978-3-319-75954-8_3

Table 3.1 Top five candidates' results

Candidates	Number of votes[a]
Morsi	5,764,952
Shafiq	5,505,327
Sabahi	4,820,273
Aboul Fotouh	4,065,239
Moussa	2,588,850

[a]Number of votes in the first round of elections as appears on PEC website 2012

Table 3.2 Second round of elections' results

Candidates	Number of votes in the turn-off[a]
Morsi	13,230,131
Shafiq	12,347,380

[a]Number of votes in the second round of elections as appears on PEC website 2012

3.1   MOHAMED MORSI

3.1.1   *Mohamed Morsi: A Short Biography*

Dr Mohamed Morsi was the chairman of the Freedom and Justice Party and a former member of the Muslim Brotherhood's Guidance Bureau. He was the leader of the Muslim Brotherhood's parliamentary bloc at the People's Assembly between 2000 and 2005. He was also a professor and head of Materials Engineering in the Faculty of Engineering at Zagazig University (IkhwanWeb 7/5/2012).

During the presidential campaign, he was presented as an academic who studied in the United States and a former NASA engineer[1] (Black 2012). He was also positioned as a prominent opposition activist during Hosni Mubarak's presidency and was imprisoned several times as a result. Morsi's campaign gave examples of how he and his family suffered under Mubarak by highlighting the so-called injustice that his family suffered, as his son was arrested several times due to his father's political activities (IkhwanWeb 7/5/2012).

At the time of the 25 January Revolution Morsi was in prison, later leaving along with 129 other prisoners who escaped during the events of the revolution. He gave a telephone interview to the Al Jazeera TV channel at the time, with his campaign pointing to this phone conversation as proof that he was an imprisoned political opponent and as further proof that he did not break out but left the prison only when others entered and set him and his fellow inmates free (Ahram Online 23/6/2013).

Being the Muslim Brotherhood candidate, Morsi made religious appeals to calm the Christians who feared his rule, as well as many Muslims who feared his Islamist policies, by making statements like, 'there is no conflict between Islam and Christianity' (Al-Mehwar TV, May 2012), or 'Copts should have the right to build places of worship anywhere they want, just as Muslims do' (CBC TV, 10 May 2012). He also tried to allay fears regarding a strict application of Islamic Sharia and concerns over people changing their faith (Al-Nahar TV, May 2012).

During his campaign, he further relied on appeals of both a statistical and logical nature wherever possible during the election, mainly when talking about the election programme—Al-Nahda project. According to Hamed,[2] Morsi's campaign did not need to attack opponents during the first round of elections as they 'were too busy securing votes, especially due to the tight timeframe'. In the second round, however, the situation was different as they had to oppose Ahmed Shafiq. As Hamed describes the situation, in the second round of elections their opponent 'was well-known and the campaign did not waste time searching for any "scandals", as they were already known to us'. The campaign concentrated on emphasising that Shafiq represented Mubarak's regime and in contrast, Morsi represented the revolution; portraying the second round as an election between Mubarak's old regime and the revolution.

3.1.2   A Candidate by Accident

The Muslim Brotherhood had originally pledged not to seek presidency. On 10 February 2011, before Mubarak's abandoning power within one day, the Muslim Brotherhood's General Shura Committee voted not to run for presidential elections and not to approve any Brotherhood's members request to run for presidency (Habib 2013). This was an action that was described as a message of reassurance for both the international community and Egyptians that Mubarak's outset would not be replaced by Islamist domination (Trager 2016; Habib 2013). However, the Brotherhood reversed its decision as the election approached and decided to nominate the movement's deputy supreme guide, millionaire businessman Khairat Al-Shater for presidency.

Several explanations were given to explain this change in the Brotherhood's position, one of which was Abdel Moneim Aboul Fotouh's decision—the well-known Brotherhood's member—to run for presidency, an action that led the Brotherhood to dismiss him for opposing its decision in June 2011. According to ex-brotherhood leader Mohamed Habib (2013), Aboul Fotouh's decision was the main trigger for the Brotherhood leaders to reverse its decision since his winning would prove that the Brotherhood's initial decision was a wrong decision and would cause splits within the Brotherhood members (Habib 2013: 35). Other explanations revolve around (a) the strong appearance of other Islamist forces that would threaten the Muslim Brotherhood if they succeeded, (b) failed efforts from the Brotherhood to convince some characters to run for presidency with the Muslim Brotherhood's endorsement (Trager 2016),[3] (c) tactical manoeuver for dividing the Islamic votes to get other benefits from SCAF in return (El-Sherif 2012) or (d) a deal between SCAF and the Brotherhood as explained by Brotherhood member Kamal El-Helbawy who resigned from the Brotherhood because of this decision (CNN 1/5/2012), or (e) just an example of their inconsistent messages (El-Sherif 2012).

I would add as well that all the political developments taking place before the election period, as explained in Chap. 2, made the Brotherhood aware of its presence and mobilising ability especially in the March referendum and in the parliamentary elections, which would make it difficult for them to abandon and not to enter the presidential elections.

However, Al-Shater was later disqualified by the PEC due to a previous criminal conviction, making one of ten candidates who were dismissed as a result of their failure to meet candidacy requirements.[4] After being prevented from nominating its first candidate, the Brotherhood called on Mohamed Morsi, the head of its Freedom and Justice Party, to submit his nomination papers for the presidency in the last minute before the nomination door closed.[5]

Submitting his nomination papers in the last minute to be Al-Shater's replacement meant that the campaign which was originally established to work for Al-Shater had to convert its work and campaign for Morsi instead. It further meant that he was the last candidate to begin campaigning, as all other candidates started campaigning prior to the formal nominations.

3.1.3   Morsi's Campaign

Morsi's campaign—previously Al-Shater's campaign—had a major task in introducing Morsi to the public in a narrow timeframe, as he was less well-known and less charismatic than Al-Shater. This switch in the campaign's main candidate led to many jokes among Egyptians about Morsi, ridiculing him as a candidate by chance or giving him the nickname of 'spare tyre' ('estebn' in Arabic). Morsi was also rather boring to journalists as his speeches were too long and with few short quotable sentences for news clips.

Nonetheless, according to his campaign, not being as well-known as Al-Shater was not an obstacle due to 'the secured votes the Muslim Brotherhood could rely upon' (Hamed 2016)[6] which should be well-known for an organisation that had campaigned in elections before: a secured vote that would vote for the Brotherhood, no matter who the candidate was.

In the case of the Muslim Brotherhood, after the 25 January Revolution, they would refer to votes they were able to mobilise in the 19 March constitutional referendum and their votes in the parliamentary elections which were conducted six months before the presidential elections and dissolved two days before the presidential elections. Added to this is a history of elections recorded for more than 80 years, as the Brotherhood had participated in numerous elections previously, whether parliamentary, trade union, or even student union elections. All this information helped them to visualise what needed to be done and where.

Morsi's campaign was not different from other campaigns because of the starting time or the secured voters only but due to the availability of several bodies campaigning for him. As explained by Hamed, there were three bodies campaigning for Morsi: 'the official campaign, the Muslim Brotherhood, and the Freedom and Justice Party'. As Hamed elaborated, 'in reality, the whole party was converted into a campaigning organisation for its leader' (Hamed 2016).

El-Sharnouby[7]—ex-Muslim Brotherhood—elaborated more on the role of the Muslim Brotherhood as a group in campaigning for Morsi by referring to its organisational weapon[8] that is embedded in their numbers: total obedience[9] to their superiors through a top-down chain of commands, where each member campaigns for the candidate and their offices in both Egypt and outside Egypt. El-Sharnouby specifically refers to the Muslim Brotherhood London office by saying 'the headquarters of their international organisation in London[10] which acted as a main operation room during the presidential elections, and acted as a mini campaign for Morsi'. This does not deny that the three bodies—the group, the party, and the official campaign—were already organising with each other as they would all take general lines, if not orders, from the guidance office.

A main difference between the campaign and both the group and the party as Hamed explained was that 'the campaign was responsible only for the candidate, whereas the party was responsible for other issues including securing more votes'. Morsi would visit a governorate for one day, but he was not present for the rest of his campaign's work at that location. He was not available every day and thus he needed the party and the group to continue organising events and securing more votes, providing the promotion and campaigning necessary even in his absence.

For the sake of this study, the next section will apply the professionalisation index to Morsi's official campaign, deconstructing it into structures and strategies in order to understand how it was planned and implemented.

3.1.4   Campaign's Structure

3.1.4.1 Campaign Staff
As explained by Hamed, the campaign staff came from the Muslim Brotherhood, with the majority possessing previous experience in working on elections. The campaign staff was divided into ten committees or teams; each has main responsibilities that can be summarised in the following tasks.

3.1.4.1.1   Events and on-the-Ground Campaigning
This team was responsible for the candidate's agenda and for organising the campaign and the candidate's events in various governorates. Due to the short timeframe of the campaign, 'Morsi would visit two or three governorates in a single day' (Hamed 2016). The team managed and decided on where the candidate would go and what he would say in each of these places by providing him with the main issues and problems each of these places suffered from. Their large numbers and numerical advantage helped the team in achieving its goals.

3.1.4.1.2   Setting the Programme and Promises

This team was responsible for setting the programme and the election promises the candidate would make, that is, what he will do in his first 100 days in office and what his plans would be regarding all the various aspects and sectors in the country, whether they be agriculture, industry, healthcare, or otherwise. This team was already working during the original campaign of Al-Shater and the promises were already set. However, 'there were some alterations that were made when it converted to work for Morsi' (Hamed 2016). The efforts of this team led to the final election programme for Mohamed Morsi, which was known as the Al-Nahda (renaissance) project. According to Hamed, the programme was not presented as a separate Nahda project as media presented it,[11] but it was mainly the promises and projects from the FJP programme. This team was crucial to the campaign, as it provided materials and data for Morsi to talk about. According to Trager (2016: 134), Morsi did not depend on talking about himself or his vision but 'that he was the Brotherhood's candidate and as president would implement the Brotherhood Renaissance project, whatever that meant'; which explains the importance of this team in developing the content that Morsi depended on in his speeches and media interviews.

3.1.4.1.3   Advertisement and Branding Team

This team was responsible for the branding and the advertisements for the candidate, whether on traditional media like television or on social media. The campaign worked with a 'big company' in Egypt. However, campaign staff refused to disclose its name as it is still working in the country. They do not want the Egyptian security to be aware about it. Thus, it appears that they were working with a professional entity from day one. There was also a media office to deal with journalists.

3.1.4.1.4   Monitoring Team

This team was responsible for monitoring and observing everything taking place in the media about the elections. This included what the other candidates were saying and promising, how Morsi was framed in the media, and the reactions to what he said or did. In other words, it was responsible for getting feedback about their candidate's message and the campaign itself. They consulted professional advisors every time the candidate appeared and advised him regarding what was done wrong and what was done right.

3.1.4.1.5   Statistics Team

This team played a significant role in the campaign. It determined the areas and places where their candidate would win or get more votes based on public opinion polls conducted by a poll centre affiliated with the Muslim Brotherhood. Unlike other opinion polls carried out at that time by private polling bodies, which were proven to be inaccurate, Morsi's campaign trusted their polling centre as they had relied upon it many times before in previous elections. As Hamed explained, the campaign staff would sometimes challenge this team based on the campaign staff's judgements or observations, but the statistics team was proven to be accurate at the end. Hamed explained as well that the polls conducted by the Brotherhood's affiliated centre—through their statistics team—predicted that Morsi would win the final round with 52% of the vote, and the actual results came very close to their predictions.

3.1.4.1.6   Public Relations Team

This team was responsible for talking to specific different sectors in the community, such as the 'Arab Matrouh' and 'Arab Giza': large local tribes or communities of mixed origin somewhat similar to Bedouins, yet distinct from them, that show up to take part in elections. The public relations team differed from the other teams as it communicated with marginalised sectors and others deemed important in society, such as businessmen, industry, athletes, and artists who were active during the revolution. The real challenge for this team was during the second round of the elections where there were only two candidates and voter polarisation was very high. In addition to their role in securing the secured votes, they had to reach out and convince swing voters in each of these sectors to vote for Morsi.

3.1.4.1.7   Egyptians Abroad Team

This team was responsible for securing the votes of Egyptians abroad. They helped Morsi to communicate with Egyptians abroad in various countries via Skype and video conferences. The team even managed to arrange that one or two of their representatives were present on the day of elections at the various Egyptian embassies abroad where the voting took place. The campaign believed that Egyptians abroad played an important role, not just because of their numbers, but because of their 'psychological effect on the rest of voters, since their results used to appear earlier than the domestic votes' (Hamed 2016). This would be used as an indication to domestic voters regarding the overall result of the election.

3.1.4.1.8 Foreign Affairs Team

This team was tasked with communicating with any foreign state or any think-tank centre interested in understanding the candidate and his policies. The team used to deal with important high-profile bodies and people, whether state officials, embassies, non-governmental organisations, or think-tanks interested in studying the Arab Spring, elections, or the Middle East in general. It was thus different from the media and public relations team as it was only concerned with foreign affairs and foreign institutions and bodies. Most of the staff working there were from the Foreign Affairs Committee of the Freedom and Justice Party.

3.1.4.1.9 Spokespersons

The campaign had three spokespersons who were the officials assigned and authorised to speak on its behalf.

3.1.4.1.10 Executive Board

The executive board had one representative from each of the above teams in addition to the campaign's manager, who was Essam El-Haddad, a member of the Muslim Brotherhood's Guidance Bureau, which proves that the campaign was not working in isolation but co-ordinating with the Guidance Office (Maktab al-Irshad) which is the highest body in the Muslim Brotherhood group.[12]

3.1.4.2 Management Style

Despite the top-down hierarchical chain of commands inside the Muslim Brotherhood,[13] this hierarchy was simplified in the campaign 'to enable swifter actions' (Trager 2011: 136). As Hamed explained 'the campaign had a very flat organisational structure'. This was mainly due to the time restrictions, which made it difficult to create a strict or intricate structure. Hamed elaborated that the main tasks and responsibilities were agreed upon and there was cooperation between teams in the various fields to enhance each other's work. The executive board met daily to decide upon its agenda for the day and to make strategic decisions, necessitated by the rapid changes in the political sphere, such as political developments or even attacks by the media and others. The campaign was flexible enough to the extent 'that each team within the campaign, or a member of the party, could go and fill any vacant space they found' (Hamed 2016). This could be understood because of the rushed establishment of the campaign. It also shows the campaign was not working in isolation of the Brotherhood group and FJP, which indicated that there were two levels of hierarchy: a top-down chain of command between the Brotherhood Guidance Office—since the campaign manager was a member of it—and the campaign and another level of horizontal hierarchy inside the campaign.

3.1.4.3 Campaign Premises

The campaign was using all the premises of the FJP in all the governorates, as well as any other offices of the Muslim Brotherhood group. There was no need to open more offices, as 'the party converted all its offices for the sake of campaigning for Morsi, the party leader' (Hamed 2016). The campaign was managed centrally through two offices: the first one was the main office for the party in Al-Kasr El-Ainy, and the second was the previous headquarters of the FJP in El Manial.

3.1.4.4 Degree of Externalisation

The campaign referred to 'specialists from almost every field' (Hamed 2016). Most of the necessary specialisation was already available within the party or centres affiliated with it, such as its media production company or public opinion poll centre. Consequently, 'very little expertise' (Ibid.) needed to be brought in from outside the campaign.

3.1.4.5 Internal Campaign Communication Structures

As Hamed explained, the campaign utilised many types of communication 'depending on each situation'. There was no preferred method, although the most common method was the use of phone calls. In general, the communication means included: mailing lists, face-to-face meetings, video conferences, and Skype calls. Although El-Sharnouby was not part of the campaign, he stressed the importance of the Brotherhood's IT department in securing the process of internal communication, mainly between Brotherhood members. This securing process would include making sure emails and phone calls could not be hacked from the government or other entities.

3.1.4.6 Feedback

The campaign was able to receive detailed feedback mainly from (a) the monitoring team which was responsible for monitoring everything mentioned in the media about the elections, the candidate, and his opponents, (b) the statistics team which was conducting public opinion polls through the poll centre affiliated with the Muslim Brotherhood, and (c) the party branches in various governorates which were in direct contact with the voters in various cities and villages.

3.1.4.7 Opposition Research

This was done mainly through the monitoring team, which would monitor opponents as they appeared in the media. Hamed explained that 'there was also room for immediate interaction and responses'. The continual flow of information provided by the monitoring team meant that someone from the campaign or the party could go and provide immediate live participation or commentary in the media depending on the situation.

3.1.4.8 Campaign Duration

As explained, Morsi's campaign was the shortest campaign. The campaign initially started working for Khairat Al-Shater, but the subsequent one for Morsi began when he submitted his papers for the presidency shortly before the deadline, meaning that his campaign duration was around six weeks only.

Apparently, however, the relatively short time of Morsi's campaign was in his favour, as there was not enough time for others to investigate it and highlight the weakness of Morsi as a candidate, other than a few examples such as describing Morsi as 'the spare tyre'. There were some other rumours about his health which caused the campaign to publish his medical examination report.

However, after the campaign ended and Morsi was elected president, media and activists started revisiting what he did and what he promised during the campaign to find contradictions and deceptions in his messages, such as claiming to be a consultant to NASA which was proven to be false after a journalist contacted NASA to ask about this claim and after Morsi himself appeared on television confirming that he had worked for NASA for a long time, but then appeared on another Islamist programme denying that he had ever said so (Eissa 2013).

Another incident, which was also noted and highlighted after the campaign, relates to footage of Morsi talking to the public with the Supreme Guide of the Muslim Brotherhood, Mohammed Badie, standing nearby and who can be heard audibly instructing Morsi to use the word 'Al-Qassas' (Arabic for 'retribution') when referring to the deaths of those in Tahrir Square (Bassem Youssef 2013). The video had great impact as it portrayed him as a candidate that takes orders from the Muslim Brotherhood and as a candidate that used the deaths of protestors for propaganda. Also, after

Morsi became president, more details appeared on the electronic committees[14] which continued their work.

3.1.4.9 Campaign Budget

Officially, all campaigns including Morsi's campaign did not exceed the maximum amount of campaign spending which was set by the election as low as ten million Egyptian pounds (approximately around one million GDP[15]) for each candidate in the first round and two million Egyptian pounds (around 200 thousand GDP) for the second round. Each campaign had to submit financial documents to the PEC showing their campaign spending. In reality, all campaigns only included the liquid cash they spent. They did not include money that entered the campaign as 'in-kind contribution', which makes it difficult to assess the actual amount each campaign actually spent.

For Morsi's campaign, the budget in terms of liquid cash was mainly spent on media and advertisements. The campaign did not need to spend on infrastructure as the necessary offices and equipment were already provided by the party. Other tasks, such as transport used for advertisements in villages and printing brochures with subsequent distribution, were not calculated into the budget as they were usually paid for from the outside (i.e. by a volunteer or supporter) without any liquid cash entering the campaign's accounts.

However, after the election and Morsi's inauguration, Egyptian media reports revealed that the US Congress under the Obama administration had paid 50 million US dollars to support the Muslim Brotherhood's candidate (Abdelghany 2012). These reports claimed that Congressman Frank Wolf of Virginia had provided the US Congress with a legal document proving that the Obama administration had provided the Muslim Brotherhood with 50 million US dollars during the second round of Egypt's presidential elections (Abdelghany 2012). Although these allegations were widespread,[16] I found no basis for them. I contacted Congressman Frank Wolf of Virginia office to verify the story, who described it as a 'false claim'.[17] There are other widespread journalistic leaks about a secret agreement between the Obama administration and the Muslim Brotherhood (not the Egyptian government) to give 40% of the Sinai to allow Palestinians to settle there. The objective is to facilitate the conclusion of a comprehensive peace agreement between Israel and the Palestinians (Zane 2013). Other reports also revealed the role of the state of Qatar in funding the campaign (Ashour 2013).

It was difficult for me to verify these allegations, especially as after the ouster of President Morsi, the case was referred to the court to investigate the campaign finance and its sources of funding and whether these sources included foreign governments (Al-Hagag 2014). The court hasn't ruled yet in this case. However, according to Emad ElSayed[18]—current editor of the Daily News Egypt and former reporter on the judiciary and court cases during that time—these types of cases are usually put in 'the drawer' and 'will not be ruled at' for several reasons: there were many cases like this where an individual or lawyer raised it but do not follow it up or who just file this type of case to get media attention, and, more importantly, because the campaign had already ended by the time the case was filed, Morsi was no longer in office and was accused in more serious cases, thus nothing would change even if the court investigated it.

3.1.5   Campaign's Strategies

3.1.5.1   Voters' Targeting

According to Hamed, 'the campaign considered all voters important but there were priorities'. The first priority as explained by Hamed was to secure the Islamists' vote especially in the first round of elections, where not all the Islamist votes were guaranteed for their candidate due to the presence of other Islamist candidates in the election. Other important voters that the campaign targeted were the revolutionary youth, the 'sofa party', workers, and trade unions. There were other general priorities such as the larger governorates, which were more important than the smaller ones in terms of having a larger number of registered voters.

3.1.5.2   Narrowcasting Activities

The campaign conducted several face-to-face activities that mainly targeted the Islamist voters. These activities included door-to-door campaigning, which was especially successful in rural villages, cars equipped with speakers in village streets, SMS campaigns, face-to-face meetings, and Skype and video conference campaigns with Egyptians abroad. There was also a variety of meetings and electoral conferences in various governorates where Islamist supporters were invited to talk to the public in attendance and endorse the candidate. These conferences included some narrowcasted messages especially designed for the Islamist voters, as will be discussed in Chap. 7.

3.1.5.3 Free Media
The campaign divided free media outlets into three categories. The first was Egyptian media outlets. The second was those in the Arab world, and the third was media outlets in Western countries.

In Egypt, the campaign mainly depended on TV as the main communication medium. As Hamed explained, 'in Egypt, the campaign targeted all the television channels, as television remained the most popular medium'. This was done by the candidate's appearance, mainly in many talk show programmes. The campaign also used to secure a media environment for the candidate to express his point of view and opinions. The second medium that the campaign depended on in Egypt was the 'internet' which will be discussed in a separate section. For media outside Egypt, it was mainly done through interviews with foreign newspapers and foreign television programmes. These types of interviews were secured both by the media team and by the foreign affairs team.

3.1.5.4 Paid Media
In Morsi's campaign, the role of paid media was limited to advertisements. This included TV advertisements, billboard, and posters. His official TV advertisement mainly depended on showing ordinary citizens' endorsement for Morsi. The advertisement had the title of 'we need a president', then each of the citizens appearing would say a sentence describing what they need in their president. The advertisement was keen to show diversity in those endorsing Morsi. However, both the Christian religious man and unveiled girl did not appear talking like the rest of those who appeared in the advertisement. They only appeared in a collective scene at the end of the advertisement. The posters and billboards had the slogan 'renaissance is the will of the people' and did not use the normal colours that were generally used in the Brotherhood-printed brochures or advertisement which were green and yellow but employed a red background in an indication to the revolution.

3.1.5.5 Debates
As Hamed explained, the campaign 'made a strategic decision not to participate in debates', for the simple reason that they did not believe that debates would help their candidate in securing more votes. For them, the only presidential debate in that election, which was between Amr Moussa and Abdel Moneim Aboul Fotouh, was a clear example of how debates can affect both candidates badly.

The campaign goal was clear: it needed its candidate to win. Thus, it would only allow him to participate in activities that would bring him more votes. They would not participate in anything that might allow him to lose votes, whether it was common practice in democratic countries or even if it should have been introduced into Egypt regardless. For them, securing the vote was more important than putting on a show, or, in Hamed's own words:

> At the end, I have a candidate and I want him to win. This is my target and my criteria. Anything in the election process that would bring more votes will be done. Anything in the election process that would deduct from my votes will be left, even if it was applied in the United States as part of the political process, or even if it is new in Egypt.

3.1.5.6 Internet and Social Media

As explained by Morsi's campaign, the main aim of the online campaign was to influence the undecided voters, especially the younger ones. The social media team used to broadcast all his interviews and many other materials online. The candidate also used to dedicate specific special messages for YouTube and the online audience in general.

Regarding the so-called electronic committees,[19] the campaign denied usage of an army of fake social media accounts attacking supporters of other candidates and attempting to control the direction of what was said on social media. They responded by saying that their supporters were already large in number and that Muslim Brotherhood members may defend their candidate online as they wish. Thus, there was no need to resort to fake accounts to do this. However, the campaign's claim of not having these electronic committees was denied by ex-Muslim Brotherhood members, other campaigns, and by Egyptian social media experts.

Among those are El-Sharnouby who confirmed that the Muslim Brotherhood indeed operated these so-called electronic committees, by recruiting a group of people whose responsibility was to spread certain ideas and information in favour of the Muslim Brotherhood and making it appear as if public opinion supports these ideas or as if the public opinion is heading in a specific direction. In that way, they can affect the public as they often follow what they see as the majority point of view. The role of these committees also included insulting and destroying opposition figures through fake social media accounts. El-Sharnouby also confirmed that these electronic committees used to work under the direct supervision of Al-Shater and that they were working under an open budget. Accordingly, not all of those working on the campaign or the party were aware of the details. El-Sharnouby adds that the committee used to access Facebook pages and websites via fake accounts, denying any link or responsibility thereto, and would attack and distort the opposition by spreading rumours and also attacking journalists critical of the Muslim Brotherhood or its candidate.

In another project, as revealed by a report for Al-Watan newspaper,[20] the Brotherhood worked on establishing a news agency that was not known to be affiliated to them. The aim of this project was to feed newspapers and media all over the world with stories from the Brotherhood's perspective. The Muslim Brotherhood had already trained 140 youths among its members to work as journalists in this field (Hamed 2013).

From the above, the role of social media was not limited to positive or direct campaigning but extended to what is known as astroturfing, which will be explained in detail in the following chapter.

3.1.5.7 Campaign Activities

The campaign used a wide range of activities to reach voters and to urge the media to cover them. The main three distinguished activities for Morsi's campaign were the human chains which were mainly aimed at media coverage. The campaign also depended on face-to-face communication which was mainly used in the form of door knocking or electoral conferences attended by both voters and media representative. The campaign also depended on the Muslim Brotherhood's female members for face-to-face campaigning with other women in areas the Muslim Brotherhood are not popular in or areas in which they do not have a base (Shoman and Saleh 2013).

3.1.5.8 Degree of Personalisation

According to Hamed, there were different types of news that the campaign needed to pass on to the media or that they tried to focus media attention upon. This mainly depended on the timing: at the start of the campaign, there was a need for personal information-related news to introduce Morsi as a candidate to the public. He was not famous like Al-Shater, and he also lacked Al-Shater's charisma. Therefore, the campaign highlighted his education and other qualifications to the public, mainly through the media. At a later stage, when the candidate was better-known, the campaign started highlighting his political career. They needed the voters to know that he was not new to politics and that he had parliamentary experience when he was head of the Muslim Brotherhood bloc during the rule of Mubarak. After that, they reiterated his political views and stances by highlighting what he said in the campaign and the election promises he was giving. According to the campaign, Morsi himself did not mind being asked about either personal or general issues.

3.1.6   Did the Campaign Matter?

Morsi's campaign had advantages over other campaigns which helped their candidate to win around 5.7 million votes in the first round of elections and enter the run-off against Ahmed Shafiq. One of these advantages was the secured votes comprised mainly of the Muslim Brotherhood membership and its supporters, a support base built up over 80 years of political activity in Egypt.

Another advantage was access to professional and mostly accurate opinion polls, as the campaign described them. This luxury was not available to other candidates. As explained by Morsi's campaign, there are few public opinion poll centres in Egypt, and very few entities can carry out polls in a narrow timeframe. The available centres in Egypt capable of carrying out polling can mostly only do so on other issues that are not politically sensitive—that is, not the elections—and even then, it will take them a long time. They have small teams and can only work and move between five and six governorates. As Hamed described, to move between all the governorates, to take large samples, and to do so in two stages of an election that were very close to each other required significant presence on the national level, adequate resources, and experience. These resources were available to both the state and the Muslim Brotherhood, but not to the relatively new private centres.

A third advantage of the campaign was the presence of the FJP with all its logistical expertise and resources, such as head offices and computers. Thus, the campaign did not have to consume time or money in building up the necessary infrastructure, unlike other campaigns which were managed centrally and used to go and open branches in various governorates.

A fourth asset to Morsi's campaign was its foreign affairs committee, which helped in enhancing and improving his image both abroad and domestically, as Egyptian media would often translate and present what was said and written in Western media about Egypt, its elections, and candidates. Most Western newspapers, for example, did not realise that, during the time of the campaign, Morsi was not working for NASA and even wrote it as one of his jobs in their biography of him in such reputable papers as *The Guardian*, which described him as 'the former NASA engineer' (Black 2012). This was echoed in Egypt and taken as a matter of fact not doubted by Egyptians.

The Muslim Brotherhood's electronic committees helped their candidate, especially in the short term and more so in the run-off by framing and convincing public opinion and voters that they were essentially choosing between Mubarak's National Democratic Party and the Revolution. However, the role of the aptly named 'squeezing the lime' campaign was perhaps the main reason behind Morsi winning the second round of elections. The name of the campaign came from a local expression that stems from the Egyptian practice of squeezing a lime or lemon onto food that does not taste good, is bitter, or is about to go bad, thus, masking the bad taste and making it more palatable. This campaign was run by some activists, one of whom was Alaa Al-Aswany, the writer who was the reason behind Ahmed Shafiq's resignation from his post as prime minister after appearing with him on the ONTV television channel.

The 'squeezing the lime' campaign claimed that the blood of the protestors killed during the revolution was an obstacle between them and voting for Shafiq and that there was no such blood on the Muslim Brotherhood's hands at the time. They therefore urged Egyptians to 'squeeze the lime' and vote for Morsi, a bad candidate in the opinion of many, but just as squeezing a lime over bad food can make it sour, it is at least palatable. Thus the 'lime squeezers' in Egypt refers to all those who voted for Morsi only because his opponent, Shafiq, had been a prominent figure in the Mubarak regime, even though they did not want Morsi either. All these assets and factors will be explained in detail in the following chapter while discussing campaigns' impact on election results. The next section in this chapter will discuss Ahmed Shafiq's campaign, Morsi's main rival.

But did the campaign really matter for Morsi in this election? This question was asked of Hamed to get a practitioner's evaluation of the campaign after it had already ended. Morsi's winning was usually reported as only due to the Brotherhood's organisational strength, as if he would not do the same without having a campaign. So according to those who worked in his campaign, did his campaign really matter? In other words, did it help Morsi to win?

According to Hamed, 'campaigns do matter. They form part and parcel of the election process, and are the main method of securing votes'. However, Hamed clarified that 'the candidate's situation before the election cannot be separated from the situation during and after'. This means that a campaign could carry out its duties to the maximum and still not succeed. This would happen if it failed to address its candidate's political presence before the campaign, during the revolution, or during the run-up to elections. Hamed continues:

> If the candidate does not have a secured and loyal voter-base built up over years, or if rural and poor voters do not know of the candidate, the campaign cannot help him win. If the candidate has never visited remote places like Nubia or Sinai, does not know their problems, and has no actual presence there, the campaign will not be able to secure him these votes. The candidate can be methodical and hire the best professionals, but if he does not have a presence in society, he cannot win however competent his campaign staff are.

Although Hamed believes that the campaign succeeded in securing enough votes for Morsi, allowing him to win, he also believes that the campaign's biggest mistake was 'raising people's expectation'. He continues that if the election was to be repeated, they would have reduced expectations and not given as many promises. According to Hamed, the promises they gave were based on their expectations and vision of how to run the state, but when they entered government they found that their expectations and the reality of governing were very different.[21]

3.2   AHMED SHAFIQ

3.2.1   Ahmed Shafiq: Short Biography

Ahmed Shafiq was the last prime minister in Mubarak's era. Amid the 25 January Revolution and during the last days of Mubarak's presidency, Mubarak implemented some changes to calm protestors, one of which was Shafiq's appointment as the prime minister on 29 January 2011.

Despite speculation years before the revolution that Shafiq could be a possible successor to Mubarak, before being overshadowed by the inheritance scenario,[22] Shafiq's relationship with the protesters had soured quickly after being appointed as prime minister: he was believed to have ignored some of the protestors' demands, offering to send them sweets ('Bonbon' in particular) and suggesting removing the protesters' campsite in Tahrir Square to Hyde Park's Speakers' Corner. Shafiq was also in charge when armed thugs on camels attacked protesters in Tahrir on 2 February 2011, which was known as the Battle of the Camel.

Shafiq resigned on 3 March, a day after appearing in a talk show on ONTV private channel where he was accused and critically undermined by the famous author and opposition figure, Alaa Al-Aswany. The talk show represented one of the rare examples—if not the first—of televised criticism of a high-ranking government official in Egyptian history.

During his time as a prime minister, many jokes erupted about him such as 'Shafiq bonbon', referring to his sweets offer to the protesters, and 'Shafiq pullover' referring to his trademark blue jumper, to the extent that there were Facebook pages called by these nicknames.

After keeping a low profile for several months, Shafiq re-entered the public arena when he announced in December 2011 his intention to run for the presidency.

3.2.1.1 Early Career

Shafiq was born in 1941 in Cairo. He graduated from the Air Force Academy in 1961 and has a master's degree in military sciences and a PhD in military strategy. He fought in three wars including the 1973 Arab-Israeli war as a senior fighter pilot under the command of Mubarak, the commander of the air force at the time, and is said to have downed two Israeli warplanes. He served as the military attaché in the Egyptian embassy in Rome between 1984 and 1986, then as Air Force Chief of Staff between 1991 and 1996, and later became commander of the Egyptian Air Force between 1996 and 2002 (Fathi 2012). Prior to the revolution, the public had started to become more familiar with Shafiq during his years of tenure as civil aviation minister from 2002 to 2011.

His role as an aviation minister raised speculation that he could be a possible successor to Mubarak, but this was soon overshadowed by the inheritance scenario. Shafiq's name was mentioned along with other possibilities such as Amr Moussa, the former Foreign Minister and the General Secretary of the League of Arab States, and Omar Suleiman, the former head of intelligence.[23]

As aviation minister, he aimed to transform Egypt Air, the government-owned main airline, into a more competitive, international carrier (Knell 2012c). He successfully lobbied the World Bank to finance air transport projects in Egypt for the first time and thus gained the funding for a new terminal at Cairo International Airport and renovated the other terminals, giving a boost to tourism. He also secured the membership of Egypt Air in the elite Star Alliance international courier constellation in 2008. He was positioned as a hard-working and efficient minister (Fathi 2012).

However, after the revolution, a number of lawsuits had been filed against him, mainly around corruption allegations. Shafiq repeatedly denied these allegations, insisting that he did not participate in any wrong-doing and expressing that his records were free from any violations.

A new legislation called the Political Exclusion Law was passed by the parliament in order to hinder Ahmed Shafiq from running for presidency. According to this law, senior officials from former President Hosni Mubarak's regime were banned from standing for office. After the law was passed by the parliament, the election commission announced Shafiq was barred from continuing in the presidential race. Then the Supreme Court decided that he could continue to run for president by rejecting the unconstitutional exclusion law that would have barred him from standing only two days before the election date.

3.2.1.2 Political Positioning

During his presidential campaign, Shafiq portrayed himself as the strong state person who could lead and implement projects, referring to his era as an aviation minister. He promised to bring safety and security back to the street, to stop chaos, and to sustain productivity, especially after job losses and closures following the revolution. He portrayed himself as the only presidential candidate who had both the civilian and military exper-tise needed for Egypt's gradual shift to purely civilian rule (Knell 2012c). In an interview with Reuters (Awad 16/2/2012), he warned of the con-sequences of assigning the presidency, who is also tasked with being the supreme commander of the armed forces, to someone who has no knowl-edge of Egyptian military life, as any Egyptian president would have to deal with the army. He was promising a 'smooth handover' to civilian rule and changing the way the army works in Egypt which was described by some activists as a state inside the state, promising to make it pay taxes on its businesses. He also promised to reform the presidential institution. He tried to reflect his position as a statesman on his campaign's colours as well, as he chose navy and dark blue which are the official formal colours.

During his campaign, Shafiq and his staff concentrated on some main messages and appeals to preserve his picture as a strong statesman, which was the main brand associated with him, aiming to maintain his secured votes and influence swing voters. This was clear in the usage of the following appeals:

a. **Fear:** One of the main messages the campaign played on was fear. The fear of Egypt's situation at that time, the fear of the future of Egypt and the future of the revolution as well if the president who was elected was inexperienced and unable to adapt; as Ibrahim[24] explained, the fear from the uncalculated risk if Egyptians voted for a candidate who did not know how to run the country. Fear was also used when Shafiq mentioned that the 'Abassyia is just a rehearsal' when he commented on violence in the streets and the possibility of using force in the future to stop violent demonstrations. This was one of the times where his 'positioning' appeared clear to his supporters, who needed a strong man. As Ibrahim commented, 'a strong man who can use force to protect his citizens and restore order'.

b. **Emotions:** The campaign wanted Shafiq to appear as a strong man, not emotional. Thus, according to Ibrahim, 'emotions were used with limit in some circumstances as when his photos with disabled people in one of the conferences were published'. Emotions also appeared when his wife died at the middle of his campaign, although this was not planned.

c. **Logic:** Logic and numbers were used in addressing topics such as education, health, and other issues addressed in his programme/vision. Unlike other candidates, he did not write a full programme. They were 'sure that Egyptians would not vote according to it' (Ibrahim 2016[25]). He wrote a vision that was published to the public three days before the election, as he did not want other candidates to steal his ideas. The campaign claimed that many of his ideas were stolen by other candidates such as the exemption for farmers' loans.

d. **Religion:** Shafiq was presenting himself as a conservative Sufi Muslim. He was also presenting himself as the prophet's descendant (known as Al-Ashraf in Arabic). However, he did not volunteer and enter discussions about religion unless he was asked or when he tried to get the support of Sufi groups in Egypt who were against both Salafists and the Muslim Brotherhood. His point of view on Shari'ah Law was that 'The application of Shari'ah [Islamic] law is complicated... Civil law is the best choice for Egypt' (CBC TV, 1 May 2012)[26].

e. **Attack and negativity:** The campaign attacked other candidates using fake social media accounts.[27] For example, the campaign was the first to highlight the fact that Hazem Abu Ismail's mother was American. As Ibrahim explained, they saw the news at the beginning and it was not highlighted. They passed it on to social media without verifying it, creating a controversial debate that was passed to traditional media, then to the authorities, leading to the prevention of Abu Ismail from entering the presidential race. The campaign used to attack its main opponent Amr Moussa through fake accounts as well. They were the ones who highlighted the issue of Moussa's daughter helping him in the campaign and compared it to Gamal Mubarak's son helping his father along with the inheritance scenario. They also used to publish photos of him smoking cigars with Zakaria Azmi, the former chief of presidential staff during Mubarak's era. The aim of publishing this photo was to show him as a friend of the old regime and living a luxury life by smoking expensive cigars. The campaign additionally highlighted that Shafiq has physical achievements in Egypt and that his name is written on several buildings that perpetuated his name, unlike Moussa. They also used to discuss other issues about candidates such as disclosing articles about Aboul Foutouh as a part of the Muslim Brotherhood and previously Al-Gama'a Al-Islamiyya, a fact he did not want the media to concentrate on.

f. **Attacking Shafiq's campaign:** As a result, Shafiq's campaign was highly attacked as well, from opening Facebook pages mocking him and describing him as the 'pullover' or 'Mubarak's man' or the 'Bonbon man', to the setting of his campaign headquarters on fire.[28] He was especially attacked about wasting public money and the camel field, but the campaign was utilising these allegations on the website with his own replies. At the time of the isolation law, they published his photo with his lawyers to reassure his supporters. When his wife was in a hospital in Paris before her death, he used to travel to see her at weekends. Every time he travelled, the media said he had escaped and had left the country. During his interview with a Christian channel, he spoke about substituting religious subjects with ethics subjects. The Muslim Brotherhood interpreted this, claiming that he wanted to cancel religion from schools. Media and opponents were also claiming that the Egyptian intelligence service along with the army and state were helping Shafiq to win.

3.2.2   Campaign Structure

3.2.2.1   Campaign Staff

A main feature of Shafiq's campaign was that staff working on it were divided into two categories: staff acting as the mastermind of the campaign who were working secretly with the candidate and staff known to the public who were responsible for specific tasks such as media and advertisements.

As Ibrahim explained,[29] the campaign did not concentrate on giving official job titles to those working on it. Many of its staff were working secretly. 'There were no contracts, only word of mouth'. Most of the staff were working as volunteers; thus, there was no structural organisation as such, but 'it was understood between people working there of the duties of each other'.

Influential people who worked on the campaign were working secretly as the campaign depended mainly on staff who worked in previous elections with the National Democratic Party, the ruling party in Mubarak's era. The main reason for resorting to these people was 'their experience in elections and the data they had', which they were willing to give to Shafiq due to previous ties and as they were not approached by others.

The campaign had some people who were working in front of the public, such as its manager, General Ibrahim Manaa, a former aviation minister and Shafiq's friend. He was dealing mainly with the budget and managerial administrative issues. The media office was led by Shafiq's media officer when he was aviation minister, Yousryia Ragab. There were two spokespersons for the campaign. The media interviews and appearance team was led by one of the well-known producers, Mahmoud Baraka, who had his own production company. The advertisement team was led by Tarek Nour, one of Egypt's tycoons in the field of advertising and a TV channel owner. These were almost the only people known to the public.

However, the cornerstone of this campaign and its actual manager who was involved in the day-to-day work was the journalist Abdallah Kamal, who was well-known for his strong support of Mubarak's regime when he was an editor-in-chief to a newspaper owned by the government. Abdallah Kamal was also a friend of Shafiq. Abdallah Kamal, as stated by Ibrahim, 'acted as the real manager and the real engineer for this campaign'. Abdallah's position remained secret from the public until a mistake revealed his role to journalists. This mistake was that the media officer forwarded one of the press releases Abdallah had written for the campaigns to the journalists' mailing lists, which showed his email address and signatures instead of copying and pasting it. In a previous TV interview before the election, Shafiq was asked if Abdallah Kamal was part of the campaign and Shafiq said no. This was a clear indication to the public that people affiliated to Mubarak's regime were working on the campaign, something the campaign was trying to hide.

Another key figure in the campaign who acted as an advisor was Mohamed Kamal, senior figure in the NDP and close friend to Gamal, Mubarak's son. As Ibrahim explained, 'he helped in the strategic political thinking of the campaign'.

The governorates team, known as the 'organisation', was the team responsible for dealing with the governorates. It had around 5000 representatives covering all Egypt's governorates of which there are 28. This team was led by staff who used to work closely with Ahmed Ezz, the national organiser of Mubarak's National Democratic Party (NDP) before its disbandment following the 25 January 2011 uprising. They were highly trained abroad on elections and campaigning and participated in both parliamentary and presidential elections. Their work in the NDP allowed them to have access to a lot of data such as the voter registration database (an old version as it was renewed after the revolution) and key figures in different villages and cities who had the ability to mobilise people to vote, known in the Egyptian culture as elections' brokers, such as influential families, reference groups, ex-MPs, ex-council members, and the like.

A major event that took place at the beginning of the campaign was Shafiq meeting with 5000 people from different governorates. As Ibrahim explained, no one then noticed the importance of this meeting to the campaign; the media at that time wrote the news 'as if Shafiq was meeting with his supporters, but they were his representatives in the governorates'. Those 5000 played a very important part in the campaign in general and the elections specifically.

The reason for keeping these people working in the shadows, as explained by Ibrahim, was that 'it would divert the discussion and could be another door for attacking the campaign'. This attack could make the campaign lose the undecided voters. It was part of the political harmonisation process the campaign had to play especially after rumours spread that the intelligence service and Ahmed Ezz himself—who was in prison at that time—were funding and participating in the campaign. For those working in the campaign, they knew that Egyptians outside the capital, especially in villages, would not go to vote unless mobilised. They sought the help of few professionals who were working in elections in the NDP and were not owned by Ahmed Ezz, even if they were helping him because of his title at the NDP. They needed that data to help them to gain votes.

Staff working under these teams comprised around 150–200 staff members in the campaign's head office in Cairo alone. There was also a social media team, which will be highlighted in detail in the social media section. It was also led by Mahmoud Ibrahim, former member of the NDP. There was no role for Shafiq's family in this campaign.

3.2.2.2 Management Style

The campaign had two levels of management style. There was a horizontal management style at the management level beneath the candidate and campaign manager but a centralised vertical management style at the top level. This can be explained as follows:

There was a daily meeting each morning with key figures in the campaign to decide on campaign developments and daily issues. They would pass what is necessary to lower level teams who were working horizontally. Daily decisions with regard to daily work in various departments had to be taken by each department. Strategic decisions or formal decisions had to be approved by the Abdallah Kamal.

For the organisation team dealing with the governorates, there was an internal call centre. Its phone numbers were not published to the public but were provided to the 5000 representatives. Each day there was a so-called communication wave to follow up on current statuses. The 5000 representatives did not have direct access to the campaign manager, Abdallah Kamal, nor Ibrahim Manaa. The team leader was responsible in managing the 5000 representatives via direct communication through the call centre.

One of the main aims of this hybrid way of management—as explained by Ibrahim—was that the campaign 'did not want crowds around the candidate and others speaking on his behalf'. Sometimes, a list of the 5000 representatives was given to the candidate using which he phoned them personally just to give support or thanks.

3.2.2.3 Campaign Premises

The headquarters was located in Dokki and was rented to Mahmoud Baraka, the campaign's media producer. It was intended to be a headquarters for his production company, but he gave it to the campaign. In the governorates, campaign offices and premises were mainly managed and paid for by the 5000 representatives. After the headquarters was burned and damaged by protestors who threw Molotovs on it when the results of the first round were announced, it was left as a place for volunteers and journalists, but actual work was not done from there. The daily morning meeting used to take place in hotels or in Shafiq's house. In other words, the main work was done away from the campaign's main official premises.

3.2.2.4 Degree of Externalisation

According to Ibrahim, choosing the staff depended on 'their specialization and political position'. The campaign hired outside agencies such as the Tarek Nour communication and advertisement company to manage the campaign's advertisements, Baraka Media Production for managing the candidate and campaign media, Mahmoud Ibrahim for social media, and Abdallah Kamal and Mohamed Kamal for political advice. Some youths who were working previously in the NDP were directed to manage and deal with elections in the governorates and the representatives there. The campaign also resorted to around 20 specialised experts in various fields in dealing with what was known as the candidate's vision for the country which was his equivalent to his election programme.

3.2.2.5 Internal Communication

Communication inside the campaign was mainly by face-to-face meetings between key figures in daily meetings. There was also a WhatsApp group exchange between small teams and texts and calls between Abdallah Kamal and various team leaders. In addition there were phone calls known as the 'communication wave' between the headquarters and the 5000 representatives in the governorates.

3.2.2.6 Feedback and Opposition Research[30]

There was not a specific department for feedback or opposition research, but feedback was mainly gathered through three departments. The first was the 'organisation' department responsible for getting feedback from various governorates. As Ibrahim explained, 'this determined voters' needs that were not addressed by the media or by other candidates'. The campaign used to amend its messages depending on this feedback which represented public opinion direction in these governorates. Some messages were added depending on this feedback, such as exempting farmers from their agricultural loans. Such a problem would not appear in the city. A second way of getting feedback was via the social media team who used to monitor everything mentioned about Shafiq using the 'TweetDeck' programme. This was a free software that allowed them to keep updated with everything written on Shafiq on Twitter. The third source for monitoring and getting feedback was Abdallah Kamal himself, through his monitoring and analysis of the media and of opponents' various activities. The campaign did not depend on public opinion polls or media as a form of accurate feedback but maintained an awareness of them without relying upon them as it was known from experience that they lacked the resources to represent the real situations in Egypt.

3.2.2.7 *Campaign Duration*
The campaign started working with the candidate from February/March 2012 till the election date in June 2012. Before that time the candidate was preparing to take the decision to enter the presidential race, not preparing for his campaign. This means that Shafiq's campaign was the second shortest campaign in terms of its duration.[31]

3.2.2.8 *Campaign Budget*
As explained previously, the official maximum limit allowed by law for the campaign to spend was ten million Egyptian pounds in the first round of elections. Such as in any other campaign, the money was spent mainly on logistics and production. However, there were a lot of items that were not included in the budget—again like other campaigns—such as offices, computers, cars, and so on. Volunteers used to bring and provide these for the campaign, without involving the campaign budget, as it was not paid for by this. Some of the campaign staff who were not volunteers were paid by an accountant from one of the small businessmen who wanted to help in the campaign.[32] The day-to-day budget was managed by Abdallah Kamal, while the overall budget was managed by General Manaa and the candidate himself. There were allegations that the campaign received funds from outside countries such as the United Arab Emirates, but, apparently, it was not proven and the campaign denied it several times.[33] There were also allegations that specific businessmen related to Mubarak and the NDP were funding the campaign secretly. However, these allegations were apparently unfounded as most of them were in prison and their

assets were frozen. The campaign denied taking money from these parties but clarified that it had used manpower utilised by the NDP in previous elections.

3.2.3   Campaign Strategies

3.2.3.1   Voters' Targeting

The campaign was aware that it would not be able to get votes from those against Shafiq, either from the revolutionist sectors or the Islamists. It was aware that it would not be able to change attitudes and behaviours. Thus it targeted and segmented its potential voters which Ibrahim summarised in the following ten categories:

1. The traditional conservative power in the community. This included those with conservative ideas and resistance to change or those who did not participate in the revolution on either side.
2. The sofa party, which is a term widely used in Egyptian politics referring to millions of Egyptians who avoid participating in protests and have no political affiliation. They are inclined to participate in anything in favour of sitting comfortably at home.
3. Senior families and reference groups outside Cairo and Alexandria, mainly in villages, urban, and semiurban governorates.
4. Christians, who were afraid of the Muslim Brotherhood ruling Egypt in the future.
5. Women who saw Shafiq as elegant and polite. (As Ibrahim explained, they knew this from the comments they received after a photo session for Shafiq.)
6. Any sectors in the Egyptian society who were upset about the standstill situation Egypt was suffering from after the revolution.
7. Any sector who wanted safety and security.
8. Undecided voters who were choosing between him and his opponent, Amr Moussa.
9. Sufism groups and Sufism Muslims. They were not politicised and against the Muslim Brotherhood.[34]
10. Those against the Muslim Brotherhood.

The campaign's general message and the candidate's political positioning were able to steer in this direction. According to Ibrahim:

the campaign was not against the revolution publicly but it was focusing on a position that the past was past and Egypt needed to move forward, and that the next stage had to be led and managed by an experienced statesman without removing gains people got from the revolution by giving Egypt to people who didn't understand the Egyptian state or how to run it.

In addition to this general message that the campaign was keen to highlight, it also developed specific messages for each group on the potential voter list mentioned above.

3.2.3.2 Narrowcasting Activities

Various activities were conducted depending on each sector of the targeted voters. The main method used for narrowcasting was face-to-face communication. This included various forms like visits to certain sectors such as visiting churches in villages to support Christians or visiting families and senior figures in their homes in villages. As Ibrahim explained, visiting families and senior figures gave these influential figures prestige and reassurance that they were close to the candidate and that they would not be forgotten in the future.

The 5000 representatives in the governorates played an important role in conducting narrowcasting face-to-face activities in various governorates as well as amending the campaign's messages. In their narrowcasting activities, they would be alerted to the main problems that their potential voters suffered from or asked about, so they advised the campaign to add specific messages for them. For example, they alerted the campaign that the farmers took loans for seeds and other supplies and because of the economic problems, they were not able to sell their crops and were thus unable to pay their loans back therefore prompting the need for exemptions. This was adopted by the campaign, as the candidate promised to exempt farmers from paying the debts if he became president. Another message that was amended was the white taxi drivers' loans. They were affected by the security after the revolution and the protests everywhere. Thus, they were not able to pay their taxi's instalments/loans, and the campaign suggested a flexible plan for them to repay their debts if Shafiq was elected. As Ibrahim explained, the taxi message was a complex message, as it highlighted the importance of a having a strong man who can restore security: 'Shafiq would return the security for them, so they would be able to work again and he restructured their debts.'

3.2.3.3 Free Media

Shafiq's relationship with the media was not good, especially after his experience with the ONTV talk show where he resigned from his job as prime minister a day after appearing in it. He continued to have some problems with media after that. Opponents used to take clips from what he said and mock him about it. Amid the campaign, his media producer, Mahmoud Baraka, confiscated tapes from a BBC Arabic interview after he was questioned about the future of the head of the military council, Field Marshal Hussein Tantawi (BBC Arabic 22/1/2012). At the time, Baraka claimed that the technique used in filming was not satisfactory for him and that it would affect his candidate's professional appearance. After interviewing his campaign staff, it became clear that this was because Shafiq had attacked Tantawi and the campaign did not want problems with SCAF. Ibrahim said that in contrast to the popular assumption, SCAF was not supporting Shafiq. Shafiq continued to appear in TV interviews and talk shows conducted for the elections by various channels except Islamic channels, and of course, ONTV, where he had his bad experience. He also appeared on Christian channels.

After starting the campaign, Shafiq's appearance on media was managed by Baraka Media Production with 300 people dedicated to the campaign. As Baraka explained, they made 150 short films for the campaign including songs. Some of them were used as advertisements. They had channels' and programmes' ratings, beside distribution numbers of newspapers. Due to their connection with the media, they were able to decide when they should appear on each channel and at what time, to deliver particular messages.

3.2.3.4 Paid Media

Just like the rest of the campaigns, the role of paid media was limited to advertising. This included TV advertisements, billboard, and posters. However, the most important feature of Shafiq's campaign advertising was a series of mysterious blue billboards around Cairo reading 'The President' in both Arabic and English. For months, no one knew what they were for until Ahmed Shafiq's name was revealed on them on the first day of the official election campaigning, after months of speculation over who was behind this mysterious campaign.

The main colour used in Shafiq's advertisement was navy blue. As Ibrahim explained, it was chosen as it was an official colour used in official documents, thus, again stressing the idea of the 'statesman'. He was also wearing his trademark pullover in all the photos. This was an action that was interpreted by many as a way of challenging his opponents who used to mock him for wearing pullovers and not a full suit (Shoman and Saleh 2013). However, as Ibrahim explained, Shafiq was a practical man. His previous work was not an office job, but a practical job that required his presence in working locations and sites. He was keen to appear as himself: a practical man who would not stay in an office isolated from his people's problems. This was the main theme of the animated song that urged people they should vote for Shafiq.

Shafiq had several TV advertisements that were rebroadcast on other outlets such as online and radio. In the first one he appeared talking to the Egyptian people on the importance of taking correct decisions. He explained why any decision should be taken seriously and why it is important and highlighted all the important decisions he took, including his decision to run for the presidency. He then talked to each sector in Egypt such as Muslims, Christians, church, Al-Azhar, media, parliament, judge, police, and so on. Another advertisement showing the importance of the future and not being immersed in the past asked Egyptians critical questions such as whether they would like to protect Al-Azhar or follow what he called the general guide's state, in clear reference to the Muslim Brotherhood candidate. He also had other advertisements highlighting his past achievements as a statesperson and his future plans for Egypt. All the campaign's advertising carried its main logo 'deeds not words', again to reflect that he was a practical man, implementing his words into actions and deeds as he did before and not a man who would give promises and not fulfil them.

3.2.3.5 Debates

Shafiq did not participate in any debates. There was only one debate between two presidential candidates, and it badly affected both candidates who participated in it. Shafiq's campaign believed that the idea of debates does not suit Egypt and that it would make a candidate more likely to lose. As Ibrahim elaborated:

> Egyptians would prefer to see their president as a strong man, not attacked or questioned by another candidate or presenter. No president in Egypt's history – including Mubarak – has participated in any debates. Thus, there was no reason for him to participate in such activity. It will not bring more votes. And at the end, I need my candidate to win.

3.2.3.6 Internet and Social Media

The online platform was a different arena. As Ibrahim explained, the campaign knew that they would not get votes from it, but they were trying 'to neutralise it'. Ibrahim explained four main roles for social media in Shafiq's campaign: (1) to discredit other campaigns. This role was clear, especially in dealing with their opponent Amr Moussa. The campaign highlighted the role of Moussa's daughter in his campaign and described it as inheritance in Moussa's campaign. They used to do this away from their official page or account, through other people's accounts who were working on the campaign unknown to the public or social media users. A second role of the team was (2) to stop rumours about Shafiq by replying quickly to prevent further repetition. A third campaign role was (3) to consume the time of opponents' campaign staff, knowing that other campaigns had a shortage of staff. They would discuss with the administration of another campaign a single point for more than 3 hours as if they were members of the public in order to consume their time, thus not allowing them to do other important tasks in their campaigns. (4) A fourth role was to strengthen and support Shafiq's supporters online. During that time, Shafiq supporters were attacked when they supported him online. Therefore, the social media team used to encourage anyone who supported Shafiq online through accounts of unknown members of the campaigns or through fake social media accounts.

As Ibrahim elaborated, the social media team consisted of a team leader and 24 staff members. They worked 3 eight-hour shifts in a 24-hour period with eight people on each shift. Each staff member on the team had 20 fake accounts on Twitter to manage and administrate, in addition to other fake accounts on Facebook. These 480 fake Twitter accounts played an important role in passing campaign messages covertly. The campaign used to concentrate more on Twitter as it demonstrated a greater potential for dissemination of ideas to a larger sharing population.

News websites were also applied to this social media strategy. Staff members had to enter comments on any news published about Shafiq and attack other opponents in news stories that were published as well.

The team used to give indirect messages through commenting on social media and created debate that would support their candidate. For example, when Shafiq spoke on TV, someone from the campaign would comment on social media about being bored with long commercial breaks. A reply that commercials are long because the man is strong and people were watching him so the channel would make profits would be added by another staff member.

The social media team's role extended to cover voting in online surveys. Two people from the team were dedicated to this task. With the help of IT, they were able to remove cookies and vote again every 25 seconds, filling the survey box and manipulating the survey.

Despite the team activity in other outlets, they did not concentrate on their own campaign website. They made a simple official campaign website for their candidate that contained basic information. It only cost them ten thousand Egyptian pounds and was hacked twice. Once, the campaign was able to restore the news bar and wrote a sentence to the hackers saying that they would catch them. As Ibrahim explained, this was to avoid media coverage claiming that the candidate who had promised security had his own website stolen without them noticing. The campaign was not keen on developing the website or having strong security for it due to a shortage of funds. They always wanted the money for manpower and did not want to work with non-trusted companies.

On the contrary, the campaign created another website known as 'presidential elections' website, where it used to appear as if it was collecting all candidates' news from all newspapers and from their own websites. At the time, the website appeared to be a good source of information about all other candidates. However, as explained by Ibrahim, they were highlighting controversial news about candidates, for example, if two candidates were attacking each other or show a torn candidate poster on the floor with a title referring to a collapse in this candidate's campaign. They would highlight news that could create an image and help in getting the hesitant voters to support Shafiq. The website appeared to have been managed by a group of journalists, but no one—at the time of the campaign—doubted that it was managed by senior figures in Shafiq's campaign.

3.2.3.7   Campaign Activities

Various activities were conducted depending on each sector of the targeted voters. Occasionally, one activity would include messages to all these sectors such as TV programmes or conferences. Other activities would include narrowcasting as explained before. Sometimes Shafiq used to enter villages with what is known in the Egyptian culture as *zaffa baladi* where he entered on a horse with drums, a tradition associated with welcoming heroes, an action that would attract the attention of both those living in the area and the media.

A big part of the campaign's activities was conducted in the governorates which was mainly the responsibility of the 5000 representatives. They kept the head office updated about various campaign activities such as conferences, advertisement cars with microphones running in the villages, or door knocking in villages and handing out brochures. They were campaigning for the candidate and convincing people locally in the governorates to vote for him.

Each of the 5000 representatives was responsible to the central campaign for bringing a variable number of voters in on the day of the election. The number of voters estimated to be mobilised and transported by each of the 5000 was one thousand each. Thus, in total, the 5000 representatives were expected to bring five million voters. They used to provide cars or buses to collect and return voters back on the day of the elections. Either they did this with cars from their own money or they asked the head office to provide them.

3.2.3.8 Degree of Personalisation

Due to the semi-secret nature of the campaign's staff, the campaign was only keen on covering news about its own candidate. They were not interested in media coverage about the team working on the campaign. Most influential figures were working in secret without contracts or official titles. As explained by Ibrahim, the real manager himself, Abdallah Kamal, would not enter the campaign headquarters from the main door. In a talk show, Shafiq even denied that Abdallah Kamal was part of his campaign, until the previously mentioned email revelation.

Personal stories were also not a priority for the campaign. A lot of personal events happened during the campaign that they did not use or highlight, including the death of Shafiq's wife. The campaign did not use or publish the incident on their own resources, and this was only done by other media.

Shafiq refused to publish or announce to the public his tax return documents. He believed that it was confidential information and that it should not have to be shared with the public but only be given to the correct authority. According to Ibrahim, 'publishing it would imply that he was accused and was trying to defend himself. This would destroy the image of the strong statesman.'

3.2.4   Did the Campaign Matter?

Shafiq's campaign was characterised by three main assets that distinguished it from the majority of other campaigns. These assets are its 5000 representatives in the governorates, experienced staff who had previous experience with campaigns and election employment in Egypt, and finally, the social media team. But did the campaign really matter in this election? This question was addressed to Ibrahim in order to get a sense of the staff evaluation of the campaign, especially amid accusations from other campaigns that Shafiq won because of state support.

According to Ibrahim, 'campaigns are essential to the Egyptian elections'. Ibrahim believes that, 'without the campaign, Shafiq wouldn't have won against his main opponent Amr Moussa and be able to continue to round two'. He also believes that those who say that campaigns are not important 'are those who failed in it'. He elaborated that some campaigns concentrated on the media, on the offices, and creating shows around the candidates but neglected to consider 'how will they mobilise voters who rarely access TV or who can't read a newspaper?'

That is why the campaign emphasised the role of the 5000 representatives. As Ibrahim explained, from day one, the campaign was aiming to get five million votes in the first round which is why they were concentrating on the five thousand representatives and their roles in securing the five million votes. Their main internal slogan was '5 thousand equals 5 million'. As Ibrahim elaborates, 'people outside the capital don't feel the momentum of general elections, unlike Cairo'. That is why too many efforts needed to be concentrated on mobilising them as no one would leave his home easily and vote without being urged and mobilised to do so. Ibrahim denied the accusations of using money or the state infrastructure to secure Shafiq's votes by saying:

> People / senior families prefer prestige over money. They want to enter council or parliamentary elections, or have a relationship with those who are in power, and it was the role of the campaign to understand and make use of these people to help their candidates get votes.

Ibrahim explained that in the first round of elections, the 5000 representatives and the social media were perhaps the two pillars that helped Shafiq secure the votes that he did. The campaign resorted to using staff that had experience in previous elections—even if they have it from the NDP—and gave them privileges on other campaigns as they were capable of reaching people who could mobilise voters. It helped them as well in not believing media and public opinion poll estimations or even social media predictions. Their social media team helped in supporting Shafiq's supporters and not making them feel alone or attacked.

However, as Ibrahim continues, the situation was different in the second round of elections. According to Ibrahim, 'they were mistaken'. They were not able to manage the campaign to the extent they would have loved to during the second-round due:

> to the severity of the attacks, especially from the Muslim Brotherhood. The headquarters was burned and damaged. Candidates who lost in the first round went to Tahrir Square, united in solidarity to lead more attacks on Shafiq. He was not able to do visits or conferences freely lest opponents should send someone to attack him, which would be highlighted and over-analysed in the media. In round two, he did two conferences in hotels that were to be secured and people who attended were chosen carefully.

Another dimension the campaign regretted ignoring—according to Ibrahim—was that they did not pay attention to foreign media. For example, famous writers from famous foreign newspapers came to Egypt and wanted to meet Shafiq, but they were very busy campaigning and trying to secure votes, thus foreign media was not on their agenda as a priority, and they did not meet these journalists. Thus, these writers returned to their country and either wrote about Morsi instead or wrote negatively on Shafiq.

Another mistake the campaign made—that Ibrahim highlighted—was that many of the staff, including himself, left the office and went on holiday after the voting in round two had ended. They did not predict that a problem would erupt with regard to the results, such as Morsi's campaign and the Muslim Brotherhood announcing the election result before it was announced officially. Ibrahim believed that this was their biggest mistake, especially as the campaign believed until then that Shafiq was the winner, which is why they should have waited until the results were announced officially.

In contrast to what was believed in respect that the state was not with Shafiq in supporting him, Ibrahim said that 'the state was afraid to deal with Shafiq so as not to be criticised at this sensitive time.' And regarding allegations that the intelligence service was creating fake social media accounts or 'electronic committees' to help Shafiq, Ibrahim replied that they 'find it unfair that all their work would be credited to the state or the security services that did not help them'.

For Shafiq's campaign, campaigns in Egypt are no different from any other campaigns in the world. The only difference is the cultural one. Or using Ibrahim own words:

> In other countries, the campaigns will send emails, but in Egypt they have to knock on doors in villages and explain their candidate's positions and even bring them buses to go to the polls and vote on Election Day.

3.3   AMR MOUSSA

3.3.1   Amr Moussa: Short Biography

Amr Moussa is a former Egyptian foreign minister and was the head of the League of Arab States until he stepped down in mid-2011 to run for the presidency.

When he left his job as Egyptian Foreign Minister, it was believed at the time that President Mubarak had removed him from his post and sent him to the Arab League to place some distance between him and the public due to his popularity amid the inheritance scenario. The latter refers to speculation that Gamal Mubarak was going to succeed his father as president, and Moussa was seen by many during that time as a viable successor to Mubarak.

His popularity even led a popular singer called Shaaban Abdel Rahim to sing a song for him: 'I hate Israel but I love Amr Moussa.' During his time as Foreign Minister and Secretary-General of the Arab League, he made several statements supporting the Palestinian cause and attacking Israel and spoke strongly against the 2003 US-led invasion of Iraq. All of these statements added to his popularity.

3.3.2   Political Positioning

Moussa positioned himself as a reconciliatory presidential candidate with a reconciliatory message for Egyptian society and as a secular presidential candidate with an international profile. His advantage, as he presented it, was that since he had served Egypt on the international stage and as head of the Arab League that he would like to serve it once again as president. He also positioned himself as a supporter of the revolution and had joined the crowds in Tahrir Square on 4 February 2011: a week before Mubarak stepped down.

He also mentioned that he if succeeded, he would be in office for just one term because of his old age. He stressed that his economic reforms policy as president would deal with the poor before the rich, given that more than 50% of Egypt's population is near or under the poverty line (Knell 2012a, b, c). This also addressed one of the demands of the 25 January Revolution, which called for 'bread', in addition to the other two demands for freedom and social justice, by promising to rebuild Egypt 'on the principles of democracy, reform and development' (Knell 2012a). Moussa further believed that Egypt had a significant role in promoting democracy in the Arab world and in the Middle East and that he would be able to perform this role given his diplomatic experience and relations with world leaders.

In order to maintain this political positioning, Moussa's campaign restored some appeals and abandoned others as follows:

(a) **Emotions and logical appeals:** the general theme of the campaign revolved around a solid thoughtful speech, 'preferring to rely on logical and practical appeals' (Khalaf 2016).[35] However, the campaign did resort to emotional appeals or commented on some emotional events. It was therefore 'more of a reaction than a deliberate or pre-planned act' (Khalaf 2016). Such events necessitating an emotional response included violent events leading to deaths and injuries, such as the Port Said stadium incident where 72 people were killed during a match at the stadium, and other similarly unfortunate incidents. The candidate held a press conference to comment on the issue amid widespread mourning over the incident.

(b) **Attacks:** According to both Shafiq's and Moussa's campaigns, Moussa was attacked a lot mainly by Shafiq's campaign. For Shafiq's campaign, Moussa was their main rival in the first round of elections. Shafiq's campaign knew that it would not get votes from potential voters of other candidates apart from Moussa's potential voters as they targeted almost the same voters. Khalaf highlighted some examples where they were affected badly by attacks. According to Khalaf, Shafiq sent an SMS message on the second day of voting saying that there were indications that Shafiq was about to win and Moussa was failing. Other such tactics included the publishing of a torn photo of Moussa, saying it was the collapse of his campaign, or spreading rumours that Moussa was against SCAF. According to Khalaf, the Muslim Brotherhood used to attack him by pointing out that he drank wine and portraying him as a heavy drinker. Despite being harmed by the attacks, the campaign used to rise above it and not counterattack. Kotb[36] explained that they received photos of Shafiq's daughter that could harm Shafiq's campaign if published, but Moussa refused to use them. According to Kotb, both the campaign and the candidate believed in democratic values, ethics, and the need to maintain good values among Egyptians.

(c) **Religion:** the campaign did not employ or play on religious appeals, but they were speaking to those who saw them as an important aspect of the election. Sometimes they would quote Quranic verses or poetry when it was relevant to the topic at hand, which is a practice common among Egyptians.[37]

3.3.3   Moussa's Campaign

Those working on Moussa's campaign believed that their campaign was more advanced and professional than other campaigns. Khalaf stressed their adoption of what she called the 'Obama campaign model'. As both Khalaf and Kamel[38] explained, there was a separation between the role of the candidate and the management of the campaign itself. There were some strategic decisions that were agreed upon with the candidate, but in general there were no separate individual decisions from Moussa, except in special circumstances such as the decision to participate in the debate. The next section will address the campaign's structures and strategies as follows.

3.3.3.1 Campaign's Structures

3.3.3.1.1 Campaign's Staff
The campaign was divided into ten teams, including a campaign manager who acted as a co-ordinator, as follows:

1. Campaign manager and political liaison: Former ambassador Hesham Youssef, who was the director of Moussa's office when he was the Secretary-General of the League of Arab States. He worked closely with the candidate and co-coordinated various campaign departments. As Khalaf and Kamel explained, he acted as the link between the candidate and others, as the campaign did not want their candidate to be overwhelmed by details from many people which could lead to his time being unnecessarily consumed. He was

also tasked with co-ordinating political meetings with various political and societal forces and community leaders at the time, such as those among the Bedouin tribes and in the areas of Nubia, Halayib, and Shalateen.

2. Governorates co-ordinator and field manager: General Said Zaatar. Khalaf described him as the campaign's 'executive arm'. He was supposed to manage the campaign in the field in the various governorates. He was responsible for the local headquarters, conferences, events, the candidate's visits to these governorates and other such events. He was also responsible for the governorates on the days of elections. He was responsible for getting endorsements and lobbying the big families in the governorates, as well as the sectors affecting voters in each governorate or city, such as traders, fishermen, peasants, and other such categories. He also chose representatives for the campaign in each governorate.

3. Programme co-ordinator: the main role of the programme co-ordinator was to develop and compile the candidate's programme for the election. The team dealt with many advisors from different fields to develop Moussa's final election programme. The programme was also translated and published into English, which shows that the campaign was keen on its image abroad.

4. Finance department: this team was responsible for the budget, fundraising, and donations.

5. IT team: this team was responsible for all the IT needed for the campaign. The team was also responsible for social media, wherein it used to campaign for the candidate and for managing the campaign's official pages.

6. Secretarial team: this team was responsible for managing and amending the candidate's schedule. Hania Moussa, the candidate's daughter, oversaw this team. As Khalaf explained, if there was a conflict in the candidate's schedule between high-profile figures, she would call and amend it. If the campaign needed money, she would make calls and bring in donations as she was well-connected with her father's contacts. All of these things are responsibilities Moussa would not have had time to attend to himself.

7. Marketing and advertisement team: this team was responsible for the campaign and candidate's photos, colours, slogans, and their testing on focus groups before adoption.

8. Egyptians abroad and communities' team: this team was responsible for campaigning outside of Egypt and for reaching Egyptians abroad. The team's role was facilitated by Moussa's connections with Egyptian diplomats abroad, whom he came to know during his work as Egyptian Foreign Minister or later as the Secretary-General of the League of Arab States.

9. Media and PR team: responsible for content development, Egyptian media, and international and Arab media. This team previously worked and managed the campaign of Amr Hamzawy in the parliamentary elections. This was why they were contacted by candidates to work during the presidential elections, due to their previous experience in the parliamentary elections.[39]

10. Advisory board: this consisted of public figures who were not working on the campaign on a daily basis but who endorsed the candidate and acted as an advisory board for him.

3.3.3.1.2 Management Style

Khalaf and Kamel explained the management style as a horizontal one that did not require the approval of the candidate on all decisions. According to them, 'the campaign was managing the candidate rather than the reverse', but there were 'some strategic decisions taken by the candidate, and his input was clear'.

However, as they elaborated, almost all decisions were based on discussions, except decisions related to politics and dealing with political entities such as the Supreme Council of Armed Forces (SCAF) or other political parties or foreign countries that the candidate would deal with using his experience and personal evaluation of the situation. Additionally, there were a few decisions taken by the candidate despite the campaign's refusal, such as the decision to participate in a debate or the decision to reply to nonsensical and provocative questions in social media events, as will be explained later in this chapter.

This indicates that there were two levels of management style in the campaign: a vertical one in political decisions and a horizontal one between different departments and with regard to daily work.

3.3.3.1.3 Campaign's Premises

The main headquarters of the campaign was in Dokki, Cairo, where they rented a villa for this purpose. The campaign paid a lot of attention to media and the image of their candidate. There was a photo booth with the campaign logo in the background so that anyone who visited the campaign office could take a photo with the candidate shown as a backdrop. There was also a special office dedicated to and equipped for journalists. The campaign was keen that journalists had an appropriate place lest they go wandering about the building and hear conversations or arguments that the campaign wished to keep private. This reflected their understanding of journalists and the media environment in Egypt and reflected the sorts of places the candidate worked in before. Both the Egyptian Ministry of Foreign Affairs and the League of Arab States had such dedicated places for journalists.

The campaign's other offices in the various governorates were either places given to the campaign by volunteers or strategic locations rented by the campaign for the duration of the elections. In every office in these governorates, there was usually a journalist who supported the candidate and volunteered as a local media officer and who knew and had connections with other local journalists, to whom they could distribute press releases and other news from the campaign. As explained by Khalaf, this journalist would also write about internal campaign events in the governorate and send them to the central media office in the campaign headquarters.

The relations between the campaign headquarters and the other premises in the governorates were managed through the governorates co-coordinator and field manager. There was a central email sent everyday containing daily reports, in addition to communications throughout the day via various means to deal with any updates or questions that arose. The central media team updated the governorates with the content and media information they needed through the governorates co-ordinator and field manager. There was also daily communication between journalists in the governorates and the campaign's central media office, which was keen on feeding journalists in the governorates with news about the candidate and the campaign in order to discourage them from inventing any fictional stories in the absence of real material, Khalaf explained.

3.3.3.1.4 Degree of Externalisation
The campaign relied upon several specialisations, such as media and public relations, marketing, and advertising companies. They also acquired relevant information from research centres, in addition to the experts and specialists who helped in writing the campaign's election programme. The campaign staff also turned to their friends working abroad, either as diplomats or journalists, to reach Egyptians in other countries.

3.3.3.1.5   Internal Communication

Almost all types of communication were used by the campaign, including but not limited to phone calls, emails, WhatsApp, BBM, SMS, video messages, messages on Twitter and Facebook, uploading videos on YouTube for others to see, uploading downloadable files elsewhere online, and video streaming.

The campaign also used walkie-talkies after an incident when the campaign travelled to an isolated area called *Wadi Feran* (Feran Valley). As Kamel explained, that place had not been entered before except by President Sadat and Amr Moussa. They were escorted by Bedouins as police do not enter the area. On the bus, some journalists who were accompanying the campaign fell asleep and nobody noticed them; they were not able to use their mobile phones as there was no coverage in the area. After the bus doors were closed, they went unnoticed until they were about to be die of suffocation, when, luckily, they were seen by one of the bus drivers who happened to pass by at the time. After that, the campaign staff used to travel with walkie-talkies and three phones with three SIM cards from the three mobile companies in Egypt in case of a network coverage problem in the areas they visited.

3.3.3.1.6   Feedback

The campaign did not have a specific department for feedback. As Kamel and Khalaf explained, they received feedback from social media, traditional media, and reports from the governorates and public figures that used to call the candidate. The campaign also assigned an expert in media and public opinions who used to get feedback from focus groups in addition to feedback the campaign received from journalists and the public.

Khalaf gave an example of a journalist who told Moussa about an old lady in one of the villages who admired him. The campaign asked for her contact and invited her to come and meet the candidate. Later on, this lady acted as a campaigner for Moussa in her village and used to call them to provide feedback from her observations as well.

3.3.3.1.7   Opposition Research

The campaign did not have a separate department for opposition research. As Khalaf explained, the role was embedded with other departments such as the media unit which analysed all opponents with their strengths and points of weakness. There was a daily analysis of the media outlets that also covered everything related to the other candidates.

3.3.3.1.8 Campaign's Duration

The campaign staff explained that they started in two phases. The first phase was from April 2011 to December 2011, when Moussa took the decision to run for the presidency and began visiting the governorates and meeting people. This was the phase where the programme was researched and started to be written.

The second phase lasted from January 2012 to May 2012, when the campaign was working intensively on all aspects, with special attention on the media, both local and foreign. However, the campaign believes—as explained by Khalaf—that this was 'a strategic mistake as this extended their candidate's exposure time', unlike other candidates who entered the presidential race at almost the last minute. The campaign believes that it was a mistake that he worked on the ground in the first six months, 'as raising his exposure increased the attacks against him' and was generally not a good move in Egypt's political climate at the time, with its many political developments taking place daily and because of other candidates resorting to attacking their opponents. As Khalaf explained:

> Public Figure candidates generally have already built up their support among the public, and cannot go much higher than that. On the contrary, the candidate may lose votes if he starts his campaign too early. This contrasts with those who announce their intention to run for president later and start their campaign later, thus minimising the chances of losing votes.

3.3.3.1.9 Campaign's Budget

Unlike information acquired from other campaigns, Moussa's campaign says that the money spent on media and advertisements was less than the money they spent at the time of the election itself.

As Khalaf explained, the campaign was divided into two parts: the campaigning period and voting week. During the voting week, the campaign spent two thirds of its budget on what they called 'expenses prior to election'. This money was spent on hiring buses to bring people to voting stations, and living and accommodation expenses for the campaign's representatives in the polling stations all over Egypt, including meals served twice daily, as these people were working from 9 a.m. to 9 p.m. There were also lawyers hired to pass by the polling stations to make sure there were no violations. As Khalaf explained, as a campaign, they could not depend on volunteers to do these jobs, as a volunteer can easily call in sick on the day.

Khalaf elaborated further that the campaign faced shortages of money during the voting period. They had to call fundraisers and businessmen asking for donations. This was the role played by Hania Moussa, as she was well-connected to people known to her father who could donate and who might become embarrassed when she called, compared with any other member of the campaign calling.

The campaign also explained that before the official start of campaigning for the 2012 elections, which only took place after the candidates submitted their papers to the PEC, the candidate used to work through what was known as 'the popular campaign'.[40] This meant that money spent during this period was not calculated in the official budget as it was either for the popular campaign or was in the form of goods, products, or logistics that were needed and paid for by volunteers for the formal campaign.

Another problem that they faced in their budget towards the end of the elections was billboards. There were some people who acquired permission from councils for strategic places to put up posters and then sold them to others at higher prices, making a business out of it and becoming known as a result as the 'brokers of elections and billboards'.

3.3.3.2 Campaign's Strategies

3.3.3.2.1 Voters' Targeting

The campaign was aware that it was not going to be able to convince the already-polarised or decided voters and thus aimed at all the undecided voters. According to Khalaf, they mainly targeted:

1. The 'sofa party' that was looking for stability and someone they could trust to lead the country
2. Those who dreamt in the past, when Moussa was foreign minister, that he would succeed Mubarak and who believed he was moved to the Arab League to be away from the Egyptian political arena

These two categories would come to include many other groups such as housewives, those who are settled and have stable jobs, old people on pensions, and the football fans known as 'Ultras'.

As Khalaf explained, in order for them to reach the undecided voters, the campaign, with the help of experts, created 'something like a map', based on the parliamentary election results which took place around six months before the presidential elections, showing the political inclinations of the various areas as well as the more prominent families.

They received endorsements from the big families in the governorates who were not affiliated with political groups or already decided. However, they later discovered, when the votes were counted, that these people are ineffective as not all of them would vote, and they also would not mobilise others in their areas to go and vote on Election Day. As Khalaf explained:

> They would come to campaign rallies in large numbers, sometimes more than 22,000 of them, to attend an event for the candidate, but they would not vote, attending the events largely out of curiosity.

According to Khalaf, the campaign also received the endorsement of Egypt's Coptic Christian Pope Shenouda III just prior to his death in March 2012.[41] Khalaf said that during a phone conversation between Moussa and Shenouda, 'the latter told Moussa that he would get the Christian votes'. It was believed that the pope would mobilise and direct the vote of Christians and it was agreed—according to Khalaf—that the votes would go for Moussa.[42] But as Khalaf explained, during other campaigns' attacks against Moussa, a message was circulated with the content that Moussa would reconcile with the Islamists and that he was opposed to SCAF. Khalaf elaborated that this message raised fears among Christians—who were afraid of Islamist rule and wanted the protection of SCAF. That is why the campaign believes that the Christian vote did not go to Moussa and instead went to his opponent, Ahmed Shafiq, who was seen as a clear opponent to the Islamist forces and part of the military.

3.3.3.2.2 Narrowcasting Activities
These activities varied depending on the audience. For example, the campaign depended on door-to-door campaigning, especially in villages. They also organised several electoral conferences. The campaign considered its official launch as one of its most important activities. The campaign was launched from *Ezbet El Nakhl*, a poor slum area, in contrast to the more affluent locations of other campaigns, which gave a clear message that, as a president, Moussa would deal with the poor before the rich and that he would protect those below the poverty line. The campaign had also targeted SMS campaigns through mobile phone companies whereby they sent messages to specific areas at a specific time (the place could be a church address and the time could be a time of a prayer when Christians would be there and receive the message), face-to-face meetings, and visits

to governorates and to Egyptians abroad, in addition to media campaigns on television, radio, the internet, and social media, along with another campaign in the international and Arab media.

3.3.3.2.3 Free Media

The campaign's media team was the team responsible for content development for the campaign and would provide media outlets with stories. The campaign divided media intro three categories: Egyptian media, Arab media, and international (Western) media. There was a person dedicated to each of the three categories. Moussa had an advantage over the other candidates as he already had access to Arab and Western media due to his previous positions.

For the campaign, media was a vehicle to address public opinion across the world. As Khalaf explained, Moussa realised that Egypt cannot be without friends or survive on its own. Thus he tried to address public opinion across the world for support so that when he won and took office, he would find international support. According to Khalaf, 'he was thinking of his post-electoral position'.

In the international media, foreign journalists asking to visit the campaign or to interview Moussa were offered the chance to accompany him on his campaign visits and rallies in the villages in various governorates, instead of undertaking the interviews at the campaign office. He would hold press conferences and sessions with foreign journalists. His language and previous experience in dealing with the media helped him in this regard, as he did not need any training on how to deal with them. As Kamel explained, he was also well aware of the informal rule of the Egyptian media: 'get published outside of Egypt, and all the Egyptian media outlets will re-publish it'. For the Arab media, he already had a team of journalists working therein that covered the news of the League of Arab States. The campaign used to pass on topics related to the Arab world and feed them to journalists. The campaign also used to organise round-table sessions with high-profile journalists, writers, and editors-in-chief, where they could come together and ask the candidate all the questions they wanted, which was reflected in their writings later on.

Due to the reconciliatory nature of Moussa's political positioning, he used to appear on most television channels. As Khalaf explained, 'the campaign believed that every programme, even if unpopular, has its audience'. At the start of the campaign, new channels opened whose ideologies or bias were not yet clear. Thus, the campaign used to appear on almost everything, so as not to run the risk of overlooking one sector of society in favour of another. The campaign also provided Egyptian media with stories about the candidate and the campaign. This included giving them the contacts of his hairdresser, old friends, and so on.

Khalaf explained, from their experience working with the media in Egypt, the campaign divided each outlet and staff according to their ideology and political inclinations, in addition to dividing them according to their target audiences, whether they be the elite, businessmen, youth, housewives, retirees, or otherwise. The campaign also used to develop a specific message for each of these categories. They did not ignore any voters but concentrated on their target audience and expected voters. This is why the candidate appeared on Muslim channels to reassure them that he was not secular and was not a heavy drinker or smoker.

They also appeared on other media such as sports channels on television to reach the 'Ultras' youth, which was a group of militant Egyptian football fans and one of the country's largest civilian groups (Dorsey 2012).[43] According to Khalaf, the campaign believed that the revolution had divided people within the family. This is why it chose to appear on several outlets to reach different people with the aim of reassuring all voters, even if they were not all going to vote for Moussa. The campaign wanted to 'reassure them so that when Moussa became president, they would not be afraid or go out and protest'.

The campaign appeared on 25 January in Channel Al Jazeera (which was loosely, but unofficially, affiliated with the Muslim Brotherhood) and in Al-Anaadool, Turkish news agency, which were all supporting the Muslim Brotherhood. According to Khalaf, 'the campaign did not want to give them the chance to say that Moussa refused to appear or speak with them'.

However, he did not appear on entertainment programmes as they do not suit his character, such as cooking programmes, for example, but he did, nonetheless, show his sense of humour on other programmes. The campaign also helped him to reach this type of voter by producing short films or personal interviews where he highlighted the personal aspects of his life.

3.3.3.2.4 Paid Media
This mainly involved advertisements on radio, television, and newspapers, along with the targeted SMS campaigns and billboards and posters in the streets.

For posters and billboards, the campaign had three main designs (Shoman and Saleh 2013). One was used in street advisements and the other two for social media. The poster was in grey with the background showing Cairo and had either the campaign slogan 'we are able to challenge' (Ad Al-Tahady in Arabic) or the wording 'Amr Moussa, president for Egypt'. As Khalaf explained, the posters were not good, 'he appeared much older and it used the grey colour' which the campaign was doing its best not be associated with: opponents used to describe him as going to grey areas, an idiom meaning that he does not take clear—black or white—decisions but goes to the grey area.

The TV advertisement had the same colour and slogan themes, with Moussa appearing stating his promises along with ordinary citizens endorsing him. It had the same problems as his posters and billboard advertising. According to Khalaf, the reason was mainly that the campaign started these advertisements too early and resorted to a marketing company that had 'some problems'. They did not have the time or resources to repeat them.

For televised advertisements, they paid only for the production costs. They would strike a deal with channels whereby Moussa would appear on their programmes and waive his fee, and in return the channel would play his campaign advertisement for free.

3.3.3.2.5   Debates

The debate between Moussa and Aboul Fotouh was the first ever presidential debate in Egypt and in the Arab world. However, the campaign believed that it should not have agreed to a debate, as it harmed both of the candidates who participated. The campaign explains that the debate should have been between all the initial top candidates, according to public opinion polls published at the time. The campaign agreed to participate based on the participation of other candidates.

As Kamel explained, when the campaign discovered that the other candidates refused to attend, Moussa's campaign refused as well. However, Naguib Sawiris, the businessman who owned the channel, then called the candidate directly and agreed with him to appear. Moussa agreed, reasoning that it would be good for the democratic process. As Kamel quoted Moussa:

> Moussa further argued that Egyptians had never seen such debates before, and that it was their right to see one after the revolution, and that Egypt had to be an example of democracy in front of the Arab world.

The campaign explained that their political communications team was afraid that the popularity of Aboul Fotouh could increase because of his appearance in the debate. However, as Kamel explained, this did not happen in the end, as 'Moussa managed to highlight his opponent's relation to the Muslim Brotherhood, as well as other things Aboul Fotouh tried to conceal'. According to Kamel, 'the debate may have harmed Moussa, but it ruined Aboul Fotouh'.

Khalaf elaborates that as far as the campaign was concerned, the debate mainly harmed Moussa as it cost him the undecided and non-aligned voters due to successful attacks made by Aboul Fotouh. He also lost the supporters of the former NDP, 'as the party was attacked by his opponent and Moussa did not defend it'.

3.3.3.2.6   Internet and Social Media

Both the internet and social media were managed by one team within the campaign which was the IT team. It was managed by Moataz Kotb who was specialised in digital marketing.

For the internet—as Khalaf and Kamel explained—the campaign website was delayed because one of Moussa's fans had acquired the domain with his name and would not give it to the campaign unless she could manage his campaign website. The campaign explains that this was one of the things they suffered from. Everyone was sure that Moussa would win, thus they started making a business out of it. This fan made a website with his name (www.amrmoussa.com), expecting that he would become president and that she would be able to sell the domain name for a large amount of money. This incident delayed the launch of the campaign website as they were consumed in negotiations with this volunteer until they resorted to another domain name: AmrMoussaForEgypt.com. The campaign added that this volunteer gave Moussa the domain name as a gift after he lost the election.

According to the IT manager, Moataz Kotb, in a phone interview in September 2016, the website they made had international technical standards. It was plain and simple, artistic and white. However, they found that the traffic was not as expected. They went to a local company that makes website designs in Egypt. The company told them that Egyptians like crowded websites where everything is on the front page. The company changed the website as advised. As a result, the website was down for three hours due to traffic. They exceeded its traffic limit at 1.5 million visits per hour. Unlike Shafiq, Moussa's campaign ensured security and a firewall for their website, so as not to be hacked.

The campaign also developed an iPhone application for the candidate with basic information about him. They also used to do search engine optimisation (SEO) to counter attacks from other campaigns that would cut and edit his speeches and publish them out of context. During the last two months, they paid money for 'boosting posts' on Facebook, in addition to some advertisements on newspaper websites. On social media, there were many fake accounts in his name. The campaign had to report all of these which was very time-consuming as Khalaf explained. Thus, they were often on the defensive. There were also many fan pages that had no relation to the campaign. The campaign used to feed these with news and content to publish about Moussa.

The candidate himself did not appear a lot on social media unless there was a major event that he had to comment on or a specific message he wanted to send. The social media team used to take the content from the media department and publish it on Facebook and Twitter.

Kotb explained the role of social media by saying, 'it was an ethically-run campaign; we did not aim to attack or create fake accounts'. Kotb demonstrated this by referring to an incident that happened after Shafiq's campaign attacked Moussa's daughter, as some of Moussa's fans sent the campaign inappropriate photos of Shafiq's daughter. However, the candidate and the campaign refused to use these images.

According to Kotb, their real victory on the social media front was the fact that 'their fans were increasing on Moussa's page even after the campaign had ended'. Nonetheless, the campaign did speak of problems regarding their candidate's attitude towards social media. Although he was aware of all such technological developments, he had some problems dealing with a social media audience. Khalaf gave the example of a live Twitter event they held, where Moussa proved to be keen on answering every single question, even mocking impolite ones, rather than ignoring them. One such question referred to the wife of famous person, and Moussa insisted on replying that this was rude. According to Khalaf, the social media audience did not take kindly to this as he appeared to be reprimanding them.

3.3.3.2.7 Campaign's Activities

The campaign used a variety of activities depending on the audience targeted. In addition to the narrowcasting activities—which were often covered by the media—the campaign had some other activities such as a branded bus moving in the streets; a call centre with general numbers for voters to call the campaign and ask questions; planned events, including the campaign official launch and face-to-face meetings; and visits to governorates and to Egyptians abroad, in addition to media campaigns on television, radio, the internet, and social media, along with another campaign in the international and Arab media.[44]

3.3.3.2.8 Degree of Personalisation

As Khalaf explained, the campaign divided the content it provided to the media into the following categories:

a) Popular topics: Because of his work as a diplomat, Moussa would hitherto usually appear in a suit and holding a cigar. However, the campaign needed to highlight the other more popular side of his character. Thus the campaign used to feed the media with photos of his visits to the villages, eating food with his hands among the peasants, or with the people they visited. They also highlighted his visits to urban slums and other such poverty-stricken areas.

b) Political topics and political speeches designed for officials, the interim government, and SCAF.

c) Topics for general voters: the campaign was also keen on passing certain types of stories to the media which included:

i. News about the daily activities of the campaign and candidate, whether in Cairo or the other governorates.

ii. They also made announcements regarding his upcoming media appearances, including which programme and at what time.

iii. Reports about the Arab League or issues related to the Arab world, where he could express his views.

iv. Highlighting the campaign team itself as well, allowing the team to speak about themselves to show that Moussa employed professionals. Thus he could be expected to do the same when he became president.

v. The campaign would remind Moussa about personal stories in his life to mention to the media, as he generally only remembered to tell stories about negotiations and disputes from his previous work.

vi. The campaign created a list of all his friends, former neighbours, schoolmates, and his old porter in order to ask them about personal stories related to the candidate. Then they would then pass these on to the media without the media noticing that they were being dictated the news topics.

However, as Khalaf explained, 'the candidate did not like involving his family and personal life in the campaign'. She gave an example of when a television crew wanted to go to his house in a gated compound and film there, the campaign refused. For the campaign and the candidate, they wanted to 'present Moussa's professional experience more than his personal life'. Khalaf gave another example: when his son got married during the campaign, they had a small wedding ceremony and did not tell the media. This was 'to avoid the event being used in the election', especially given that the media might have assumed that all those attending were endorsing or voting for Moussa. 'He also did not want to embarrass his guests, some of whom may not be voting for him', Khalaf added.

3.3.3.3 Did the Campaign Matter?

Moussa resorted to those who campaigned for Amr Hamzawy in the parliamentary elections. This act demonstrated a need for those with election experience in Egypt, of whom there were not many. However, in a country with weak and divided political parties, experience in elections and how they are managed, as well as the ability to secure votes (especially outside Cairo), were competencies only found in the Muslim Brotherhood and the former NDP because of their experience in parliamentary elections, student unions, trade unions, and so on.

Moussa's campaign was working for the period after the election as well, as if their candidate had already won. This is why they attended to many details that other campaigns overlooked, such as the location, photo booth, and separate rooms in the campaign headquarters for journalists equipped with computers, fax, and internet or the targeting of world leaders and global public opinion for the sake of international connections after the election.

The campaign had advantages over the other campaigns on the media front, but it was not that active in the field and in the governorates, mainly due to a lack of experience in elections, particularly those outside of Cairo. They also did not resort to those who possess the necessary field experience for political reasons, as those people who had the experience were either from the former NDP or the Muslim Brotherhood.

The role of the media team was to help the governorates' co-ordinator and field manager in building up the image of the candidate, creating his branding and the visual work, but both the field manager and communication with various political forces had to bring in the actual votes.

The campaign only started working with representatives and the so-called brokers of elections and billboards after other candidates had done so already: in other words, at a later stage in comparison with other campaigns. This meant that they were not aware of the real business of campaigning on the ground. In most cases, they were not able to monitor those representatives or brokers they had agreed with, unlike Shafiq's campaign. This led to some of these 'brokers' taking money from Moussa's campaign and not doing the job required of them.

Furthermore, choosing an ethical campaigning approach and reconciliatory message, in contrast to the polarising speeches that were common at the time—such as old regime speeches, revolutionary speeches, or Islamist speeches—caused the campaign to lose the polarised voters. Added to this is the fact that it was negatively affected by the attacks from other campaigns, notably Shafiq's campaign. Its reconciliatory message was understood or advertised by opponents as insubstantial and aimed at pleasing everyone, whether supporters of the old regime, revolutionaries, or Islamists, just to get more votes.

The campaign also mentioned that one of its security team, who loved and supported Moussa, did not vote for him on the day of the election[45] He apparently believed that the candidate was good enough to win without needing his vote, especially given that the media and public opinion polls in the country had him as the favourite to win. He therefore voted for Shafiq, for which he was greatly criticised. This is an example that shows the difficulty in predicting voters' behaviour.

All these combined factors contributed to the final result, with Moussa losing the election in the first round, despite speculation during the campaigning period that he was the favourite to win. But how did his campaign's staff evaluate the role of their campaign in the 2012 elections?

Moussa's campaign was divided on the question of whether campaigns were important or not. Khalaf (2016) believed that campaigns were important as they made everyone aware of the candidate. For her, elections are like football matches: 'it is not important to manoeuver with the ball during the match, but to score goals, even if only through penalties.'

In other words, although the campaign kept its integrity and its values by not participating in attacks and negativity, or resorted to people from the former NDP, it lost. Thus, according to Khalaf:

> It might have been wiser to resort to the help of those who were aware of the rules of the game to win the election, and to play on polarisation at least behind closed doors, or to attack instead of consuming time replying to rumours, especially given that traditional Egyptian media presents what is written on social media as if it is the truth or what the public wants. This caused ordinary people to follow or believe these things as truth.

Khalaf added, 'once elected, the candidate can adhere to his own rules and values once again, instead of losing at everything'. However—as Khalaf explained—it is because the candidate played according to his own values and kept his integrity during the campaign that he is still respected in Egyptian society now. He still had a role in the political arena after the election, such as his role as the head of the 'Committee of 50' which was assigned to set up the new Egyptian Constitution after the ouster of Morsi. For her, at least, these values and ethical rules made Egyptians regret not voting for him after Morsi's winning.

However, according to Kotb (who decided to quit campaigning work after participating in another two parliamentary elections) campaigns were not a decisive factor in the 2012 presidential elections. Kotb explained:

> Votes in the villages were in the hands of a relatively small number of people. A senior family leader can bring a candidate 30,000 votes if he has an agreement with the candidate or was promised a future position. However, if he did not have such an agreement, he could be the person behind these 30,000 people protesting against the candidate, or even ruin an event organised for the candidate in front of the media.

Kotb disagreed with Khalaf's arguments that they should have played the game as it is—without ethics—and later on adhered to the candidate's own rules if he became president. According to Khalaf, a candidate who played by these rules would not be able to withdraw his promises afterwards and attempt to apply the demands of the revolution or even just democratic values. As he further explains:

> The candidate would have to pay back his debt, finding himself in a situation similar to that of a policeman who wants to catch a prostitution ring, and instead finds himself involved in it not only as a pimp but as a prostitute.

3.4   ABDEL MONEIM ABOUL FOTOUH

3.4.1   Aboul Fotouh: Short Biography

Aboul Fotouh was a prominent figure in the Muslim Brotherhood group. He was dismissed from the group after announcing his intention to run for president in May 2011, contrary to the group's decision not to nominate any of its members (Al-Jazeera 19/6/2011). He was one of the 16-member Guidance Bureau of the Brotherhood from 1987 to 2009. He was, however, from the reformist wing of the Muslim Brotherhood. During his campaign, he attracted the support of many Muslim Brotherhood youths who were in support of change within the organisation. Some of them were also dismissed from the group and worked with him on his campaign.

He had a long career in doctors' unions and relief organisations and as the head of the Arab Medical Union, as well as his role on the emergency and relief committee of the union, which played an important part in relief efforts during the Second Palestinian Intifada in 2000 and anti-war efforts against the US invasion of Iraq in 2003 (El-Gundi 2012). Aboul Fotouh's opinions changed significantly over the previous years. He was a co-founder of the first cell of the Islamic Group (Al-Gama'a Al-Islamiyya) and he believed that violence was allowed to spread the message of Islam and establish an Islamic state. However, he later came to condemn all these views (Knell 2012b).

He was imprisoned three times due to his political activities (El-Gundi 2012). In 1977, when he was the leader of Cairo University's Student Union and he confronted President Anwar Sadat in a public debate where he told Sadat to his face that he was surrounded by hypocrites and raised issues around the restrictions Sadat placed on political Islamic activities. He was jailed along with hundreds of other opponents just a month before Sadat was assassinated in 1981. He was imprisoned again by President Hosni Mubarak from 1996 to 2001 after being sentenced by a military court for belonging to a banned group seeking to overthrow the regime in 1996–2001 and again for five months in 2009. While serving a prison term under Mubarak between 1996 and 2001, Aboul Fotouh obtained a bachelor's degree in law from Cairo University (El-Gundi 2012). Aboul Fotouh supported the 25 January Revolution. He helped in establishing field hospitals in Tahrir Square to provide first aid to injured protestors.

3.4.2   Political Positioning

Aboul Fotouh positioned himself as a consensual politician who could gain the popular support of people who come from different backgrounds. As El-Shahawy, his campaign manager, describes it, he 'opposed the use of religion for the sake of appearances', and positioned himself as a moderate and civilised reformist Islamist. He also highlighted his role in relief work and his opposition to both Mubarak and Sadat. However, he was keen to distance himself from the Muslim Brotherhood, and his campaign did not like media interviews highlighting or questioning his relations with the Muslim Brotherhood.

In his promises, he highlighted that Egypt was an impoverished country rather than a poor one. He argued that with the use of the available resources at the time, he could fight corruption and make Egypt a stronger country. This was reflected in the campaign's main slogan: 'Egypt stronger'. His plans for a stronger Egypt included establishing a minimum standard income or a minimum wage, restoring security within 100 days of taking office, re-equipping the Egyptian military from sources not funded by the United States, and appointing a young vice president, aged below 45. He also promised citizens' engagement through a 'participatory democracy' (Ayad 2013). In order to deliver his campaign messages, the candidate used some appeals and abandoned others such as:

Negativity and Attacks The campaign adopted a positive ethical approach which is why they did not attack or pursue negative campaigning tactics especially at the start of the campaign. However, according to El-Shahawy,[46] when Shafiq announced that he would run for the presidency, the campaign started attacking him by highlighting his negative points. In a press conference, the candidate was asked by a journalist about reports that Shafiq might run for president and Aboul Fotouh replied that it would be a disaster, adding that Shafiq was not fit to even run a district.

Amr Moussa was considered to be Aboul Fotouh's main opponent. As El-Shahawy explained, the campaign used to address issues like his age and the need for change, claiming that Egypt did not undergo a revolution just to have someone from the Mubarak regime again. However, the candidate was attacked by Islamists for not being Islamic enough while also being attacked by liberals for being an extremist.

Emotions The candidate appeared to be very emotional as El-Shahawy recalled—he cried two or three times during televised appearances. During the violent events that took place at the time of the campaign, such as clashes between police and protestors, the campaign used to send doctors to help with first aid, and sometimes Aboul Fotouh himself used to go. Two members of the campaign died in the various political clashes that took place and these were emotional times for the campaign that led to some sympathy.

Religious Both the candidate and the campaign were trying to distance him from his former affiliation with the Muslim Brotherhood. He was against the use of religion for the sake of appearances. He used to talk about what he described as a civilised and moderate Islam. Moreover, according to El-Shahawy, the campaign used to suffer from Islamist groups endorsing its candidate publicly, and this led to the loss of support among voters opposed to the Islamists.

Logic and Numbers were also used by the campaign, especially when talking about his electoral programme and plans for making 'Egypt stronger'.

3.4.3   The Campaign

Aboul Fotouh's campaign was formed after several brainstorming sessions, discussing whether the candidate would run for the presidency or support another candidate if he found a suitable one. Aboul Fotouh's decision to run for the presidency was taken after several stages, which was reflected in his statements: he initially said he 'might think' about running, then that he 'was thinking' of running, and the final stage when he confirmed that he 'would' indeed run.

According to El-Shahawy, during these stages the candidate tested the support he had by asking his supporters to collect 3000 signatures for him supporting his bid for the presidency, then asking for another 5000 and so on in order to gauge how much popular support he had. During the early period when he had not taken the formal decision to run, he used to have meetings with his supporters in places like his villa's basement or, later on, in a sporting club where he had supporters from the governorates. When they started formulating the campaign, it began with only four people, namely, the campaign manager, operations manager, spokesperson, and governorates co-ordinator. As El-Shahawy explained, these four people represented the campaign nucleus, and when the number of people working on the campaign increased and the campaign became bigger, the teams started realising what was missing bit by bit, such as the need for a dedicated media professional to deal with the media.

Unlike other campaigns, Aboul Fotouh's campaign did not start with structures or goals. They started with certain principles that they were keen to implement. El-Shahawy listed these principles as follows: 'to assign tasks only to professionals, to be ethical and conduct an ethical campaign, to be positive and conduct positive campaigning, and de-centralisation'. These principles also lengthened the process of new staff joining the campaign, as they wanted to make sure that anyone who would join them 'would share their same values'.

3.4.3.1   Campaign's Structures

3.4.3.1.1   Campaign's Staff

The campaign staff varied from one phase to another in its duration, which was more than a year. As El-Shahawy explained, 'it was flexible enough to change and to add the tasks needed over the campaigning period'. The campaign started with only four people, who were the campaign manager, operations manager, spokesperson, and governorates co-ordinator. After a period of time, the organisational structure evolved to include a range of operational committees that operated centrally, as follows:

a. **Strategic thinking committee:** responsible for converting 'the general theme of the election campaign into practicable do-able strategies'. This included setting the criteria for choosing the presidential team who would work with the candidate later on when he was elected. This comprised several specialisations including agriculture, energy, education, economics, and the like.
b. **Political communication committee:** responsible for following up and monitoring political developments and communicating with political forces and monitoring and following up other candidates' news. They would also help the candidate in setting his political agenda.
c. **Popular works committee:** this team was responsible for the campaign in the governorates. It was accountable for mobilising voters through various campaign events.

d. **Volunteer committee:** this was a simple committee responsible for counting new volunteers and registering their details on the database, besides providing them with the necessary training to understand more about the campaign and the candidate, how to use campaign materials, and what was expected from them.

e. **Marketing committee:** this committee was responsible for setting up the marketing strategy for the campaign, outsourcing companies to implement it, and organising events for the campaign and other related tasks.

f. **Media committee:** the media committee was responsible for both traditional and social media.

g. **Finance committee:** responsible for fundraising. Its role was limited at the start of the campaign as there was no law then to organise donations and fundraising. It probably only really started working after the law was passed. In the beginning, it used to bring in nonmonetary and in-kind contributions, rather than cash, for the campaign, and it used to train those working in the campaign on how to bring in contributions for events, such as projectors, lights, and campaign office space even if it was just a balcony in a flat.

h. **Egyptians abroad committee:** this consisted of volunteers living abroad who campaigned for the candidate in their respective countries. They were managed by the co-ordinator of the Egyptians abroad committee. The committee managed the candidate's visits abroad where he met Egyptians living in several other countries.

i. **The candidate committee:** this was his personal secretary and assistants. They were responsible for his appointments, clothes, flight tickets, and other such details.

These committees were working under the campaign's general manager, while the role of the operations manager was to follow its daily work and co-ordinate between the committees. At this stage, the role of the spokesperson was also replaced by the role of the media committee, which became responsible for media communications, candidate news, and candidate appearances in various media outlets. The candidate's meetings with foreign officials, academics, and journalists were organised with the candidate himself, his secretary, and the campaign's general manager.

In parallel with those committees was an advisory board that consisted of several advisors to the campaign. They were all public figures, experts, and academics from various backgrounds including Marxists, liberals,

Islamists, and others. This advisory board was responsible for the candidate's programme under the supervision of the campaign's general manager and for co-ordinating between the political communications committee and the candidate. With the increased number of volunteers, which exceeded 40,000 to 50,000 as El-Shahawy stated, and with the increase of the campaign's branches in several governorates, the campaign encouraged the idea of having several independent popular campaigns[47] that worked independently of the central campaign.

3.4.3.1.2 Management Style

As El-Shahawy explained, the campaign's structure was a matrix one, in which two or more duties may run through the same department or individual in both the central campaign and its branches in the governorates. The head office was responsible for the main duties such as PR, media, strategies, and political communications. The governorates' committees were mainly responsible for mobilisation, getting supporters, and conveying the message and ideas of campaign, but there was overlapping between some of the tasks.

Decentralisation was one of the core values and features of this campaign. As El-Shahawy explained, various teams were responsible for taking their decisions without referring back to the head office every time. This did not include strategic decisions like the political agenda and coalitions, as these were managed through the central campaign. For this reason, the campaign developed the internal slogan: 'you are the campaign'. Thus, according to El-Shahawy, when a team member called asking for money, they would reply 'you are the campaign', meaning that they should try to find the resources themselves. El-Shahawy further added that decentralisation worked well for the campaign as it allowed the central campaign to focus more on accomplishing high-level objectives away from local day-to-day work.

3.4.3.1.3 Campaign's Premises

During the early stages of the campaign, meetings with the candidate were held at his residence and other places such as sporting clubs. Later on, the campaign rented a place from one of the candidate's supporters for a symbolic rent, besides opening around 60 branches in the governorates according to El-Shahawy. These branches were either donated by volunteers and supporters or rented by the campaign.

3.4.3.1.4   Degree of Externalisation

The campaign resorted to outsourcing and hiring people from outside the campaign rather than the advisory board who acted as volunteers. This included a technical company that helped them establish a call centre with a number for the general public to call and ask about the campaign or the candidate, companies to organise big campaign events, and a marketing company for determining the campaign themes and designs. They also resorted to experts in the fields of marketing research, measurement of public opinion, and public speaking skills: the majority of whom were experts who were also friends and supporters of the candidate.

3.4.3.1.5   Internal Communication

The campaign staff used several methods to communicate with each other on a daily basis, including weekly face-to-face meetings at the start of the campaign, then daily meetings, and eventually 'sleeping in campaign headquarters near election times' as El-Shahawy explained. There were also mailing lists and phone calls, especially when dealing with the governorates.

3.4.3.1.6   Feedback

El-Shahawy described feedback in the campaign as 'one of the most painful things'. According to him, in Egypt, there were no bodies capable of conducting public opinion polls professionally except the government and the Muslim Brotherhood. Another option was the business sector, which was not used to conducting political public opinion polls. Thus, for the campaign 'there were no reliable sources to refer to'. They tried to develop a method of measuring public opinion by resorting to those who conduct it in the business sector, in order to develop a small public opinion polling centre as part of the campaign, but they did not succeed. Therefore, to get feedback they depended on the marketing team that mainly collected feedback from the call centres, the youth on Facebook, and events in the media: all of which 'proved to be unrepresentative and inaccurate' as El-Shahawy concluded.

3.4.3.1.7   Opposition Research

The campaign did not have a special committee for opposition research, and this responsibility fell to the political communications committee, along with the help of other committees such as the popular works committee, media committee, and marketing committee. According to

El-Shahawy, this was handled in a periodical manner with the campaign general manager.

3.4.3.1.8   Campaign's Duration

The campaign lasted for almost a year. It was divided into three stages as explained before: the 'might think to run' stage, the 'thinking to run' stage, and the actual running for president. During all of these three stages, the campaign was working for the candidate, although in different capacities. As with Moussa's campaign, El-Shahawy also believed that the long duration of the campaign was not in their favour, especially with rapid changes happening on the political arena that affected the campaign's work in general.

3.4.3.1.9   Campaign's Budget

According to El-Shahawy, the absence of rules regulating campaign finance at the time the campaign started (almost a year before the elections) did not help the campaign to plan ahead for their budget, nor allow it to collect donations from the start. Like other campaigns, Aboul Fotouh's campaign depended on volunteers buying the items they needed. The contributions were given in kind rather than in cash. All the in-kind contributions were not included in the campaign's financial report submitted to the Presidential High Elections Committee. At the beginning of the campaign, the candidate's family helped him a lot in funding his campaign. His brother had a printing house, and he would print there for free.

3.4.3.2   Campaign's Strategies

3.4.3.2.1   Voters' Targeting

The campaign divided voters into segments. According to El-Shahawy, the campaign was concentrating on:

> the undecided voters, the 'sofa party', and the mainstream who would not read the election programme and who just wanted to trust that the new president would not be an extension of the old regime, and those who wanted Egypt to be stronger in general in various fields.

However, because there was no real accurate data, they had to depend on their own estimations. As El-Shahawy explained, the campaign used all previous election and referendum results from after the revolution to get an estimate of the segments that could vote for their candidate. This led the campaign to concentrate on 19 governorates in Egypt, which El-Shahawy described as '19 falcons', to focus their campaigning work on. El-Shahawy explained how they surmised that if they concentrated on these 19 governorates, they would get more votes overall as they were not totally polarised.

The campaign also divided political forces on the street according to their presence and their numbers. At the start of the campaign, it concentrated on the Islamist vote as Aboul Fotouh was the only Islamist candidate at that time; other Islamist candidates joined the presidential race later on.

However, one of the main challenges that made it difficult for them to reach the voters—as stated by El-Shahawy—was the gap that appeared and later widened between Islamists and secular non-Islamists that occurred after the 19 March constitution, which led to a high degree of polarisation in society. This was one of the reasons that made the campaign concentrate on the mainstream, non-ideological, undecided voters. From the campaign's point of view, there was no point in spending time on people who have already decided who to vote for. In the targeted governorates, the campaign would mainly concentrate on, but not limit itself to, doctors, revolutionary youth, academics, and universities.

3.4.3.2.2 Narrowcasting Activities

As El-Shahawy explained, they did not carry out narrowcasting but rather targeted the middle-class, youth, and conservative voters throughout the campaign's messages and wide range of activities. These activities were mainly direct face-to-face activities, including candidate visits to various governorates, mainly the 19 falcons, other governorates, and candidate visits abroad and to universities. They also arranged face-to-face visits to senior families that the campaign saw as 'not polarised'. There were also special visits for specific groups like the disabled, demanding for and promising their rights, women's groups, trade unions, and chambers of commerce. Through the marketing department, the campaign sent out SMS campaigns as well, but this was on a small scale.

3.4.3.2.3 Free Media

The candidate used to appear extensively in all media outlets and talk show programmes, except those that El-Shahawy described as 'having a polarised presenter or a presenter with an agenda'. The main criterion for appearing on a specific programme was 'a desired target audience'. This is why the candidate appeared on an entertainment talk show for women where he talked about the women in his life, such as his mother and his wife, besides of course appearing on other political talk shows.

The campaign would not take payments for Aboul Fotouh's appearances but rather organised a deal where these channels would broadcast his campaign advertisements in exchange. They also used to ask the television programme the candidate would appear on to place a full-page or half-page advertisement in a newspaper before the programme was broadcasted.

The campaign did not like to be asked by presenters about their candidate's relationship with the Muslim Brotherhood. According to El-Shahawy, they used to threaten to leave the programme if asked these types of questions, as it was believed by El-Shahawy and the campaign that:

> it used to put the candidate into a corner, and made him lose votes from among those who did not want the country to be run by Islamists or people affiliated with the Muslim Brotherhood. It would also consume the time of the programme and would not allow the candidate to set out his opinion or programme messages regarding the rest of the issues.

The campaign used to prepare content and train the candidate in its use so that he would be able to concentrate on the main ideas and messages that he would like to send to his targeted voters during such televised appearances. The campaign would also make sure to receive the questions from the channel before the candidate's appearance. In the first stages of campaigning, they would take the themes of the questions. Towards the end, they used to organise the questions and programme details with the channel, as they saw it as a joint event between the channel and the campaign.

The campaign was also keen on international media. Foreign journalists and foreign officials visiting Egypt used to contact the campaign to meet the candidate. These meetings were organised through the candidate himself, the candidate's secretary, and the campaign general manager.

3.4.3.2.4   Paid Media

This was mainly during the marketing events, such as the campaign launching event in the Al-Azhar Park, where he was accompanied by his advisory board. Besides billboards on the streets, it also included the campaign's advertisements on television and online. Billboards and posters had the campaign's main colour which was orange. El-Shahawy explained that they chose this colour as it was good in personal communication, and it does not have the disadvantages of a strong colour like the red of Morsi's campaign. These printed advertisements had the candidate's photo and name followed by the words 'President of Egypt' and the campaign slogan. For TV, the campaign had official advertisements such as the one where the candidate appears introducing himself to the voters and setting his promises. There were also some advertisements made by volunteers and supporters outside the campaign, including animated songs. The campaign used them later on its social media accounts and website as they were created professionally. The campaign did not pay for broadcasting TV advertisements; they only paid for the production costs if the advertisement was not produced by volunteers. Newspaper advertisements were mainly done by the television channel the candidate would also appear on.

3.4.3.2.5 Debates
As explained before, the debate was supposed to be between several candidates, but all withdrew, leaving only Moussa and Aboul Fotouh to take part. According to El-Shahawy,

> Aboul Fotouh saw that the debate would be something new for Egyptians, and assumed that he would be able to get votes from it as it would be a chance to express his ideas.

El-Shahawy described the debate as a 'miserable night'. The campaign had some concerns and was not happy with the questions or the format the questions were asked in. For them, the debate started with questions about Aboul Fotouh's Islamist history, something the campaign did not want. For them, their candidate was forced to discuss issues he did not want to talk about. They were also unhappy with the format and the amount of time allocated to each candidate. From the campaign's standpoint, as El-Shahawy revealed, 'the debate merely led to character assassinations'. He further added that, 'it also gave advantages to those who did not participate, such as Hamdeen Sabahi'. According to El-Shahawy, the debate might have been successful in only two cases:

> since Aboul Fotouh and Moussa were the top two candidates in all public opinion polls, they should have been left to debate after all others had debated. Either that or that all the candidate should enter the debate at the same time

3.4.3.2.6 Internet and Social Media

The internet and social media team was part of the media team. The campaign had its own official website, and there was another personal official website for the candidate. The campaign had an official Facebook page and their official Facebook page for the campaign in each governorate. There was also an official Twitter account along with the candidate's accounts on Facebook, Twitter, and staff accounts. All of these were used to campaign for and support the candidate. As explained by El-Shahawy and Abu El-Gheit,[48] the campaign saw social media as an important outlet, especially in influencing the youth. The campaign had statistics saying that there were six million active Facebook accounts in Egypt at that time. Thus, for the campaign, those who were active could influence or help in spreading the candidate's message to others.

For the campaign, this type of media was important as it helped in dealing with the youth. However, the positive approach the campaign was adopting did not help them face the attacks coming from other campaigns, and they were only defensive in response. They also did not have the money for arranging an online response. As El-Shahawy explained, 'if they had had additional funds, they would have spent them on other departments in the campaign'. Further, the campaign did not imagine—as El-Shahawy explained—'that rival campaigns would spend large amounts of money to lie and spread rumours and conduct character assassinations'.

Nevertheless, due to the attacks they received towards the end of the campaign, they were able to develop defensive tools to reply to these allegations. For example, if a fake video appeared of the candidate, they would send it to a director or a picture editor who would give them a report proving why it was a fake and they would then publish these details.

The campaign remains convinced to this day that Shafiq's campaign was helped by Egypt's intelligence services in creating electronic committees and that whatever Aboul Fotouh's campaign did at that time, they would not have been able to counter the attack coming from both the Muslim Brotherhood and the state.

3.4.3.2.7 Campaign's Activities

The campaign used a diverse set of activities, such as direct face-to-face activities, including general candidate visits and narrowcasting activities to various governorates, mainly the 19 falcons, other governorates, and candidate visits abroad and to universities. They also arranged face-to-face visits to senior families that were not polarised. The campaign also established a call centre for the public to call and get information about the candidate or the campaign. The campaign also developed the idea of a double-decker open bus that would move between cities and campaign for the candidate. There were also special visits for specific groups like the disabled, demanding for and promising their rights, women's groups, trade unions, and chambers of commerce, besides the use of various media outlets as well. Through the marketing department, they advertised through billboards and posters. There were also some organised events like human chains, distributing brochures, and shows with projectors showing parts of his speeches in the streets and marketing events like the campaign's official launch in Al-Azhar Park.

3.4.3.2.8 Degree of Personalisation

As El-Shahawy explained, the campaign was keen on passing on news about the candidate's ideas and the main issues regarding his election promises from the beginning. This was done by the candidate himself when he appeared on media outlets. News about the campaign's activities was mentioned or passed to the media by the campaign staff. Campaign staff also appeared in the media to talk about themselves and their structure.

The campaign used to pass on news about the candidate and his activities. They found this easy due to their connections with journalists and those working in the media on the one hand, and on the other hand, public opinion polls published at that time put their candidate in second place, and thus the media was keen on following up his news.

The candidate also spoke about personal issues such as his family and their middle-class life and how they sacrificed for him, as well as the women who influenced him like his mother, and how his wife took care of the children when he was in prison. However, when his son was injured during one of the protests, the candidate refused to use it or to tell the media. One of the journalists once asked him why his house was in the name of his wife and not his, and he answered, even though these types of questions about wives and mothers are not generally acceptable in Egypt.

3.4.3.3 *Did the Campaign Matter?*

Despite efforts to conduct a professional campaign, Aboul Fotouh's campaign had shortcomings on the structural side, especially when comparing it to Morsi's and Shafiq's campaign. This shortage was clear in their work in the governorates. As El-Shahawy explained, they did not contact the senior families who were approached by Shafiq. On the one hand, they did not have access to them, and on the other they knew that they would not support Aboul Fotouh anyway. Instead, the campaign used to approach the youth, like pharmacists or youth lawyers, as they were the educated people in their villages. They also did not have an accurate way of getting feedback. These structural factors affected their ability to mobilise voters. According to Abu El-Gheit, who was responsible for the campaign in Asyut in Upper Egypt:

> the campaign was mistaken in not recruiting someone in each place they visited (no matter how small the place) to continue campaigning for the candidate, after the campaign left.

This shows the importance of having efficient experienced field co-ordinators on the ground, feedback, and vote-inducing activities, as will be explained in the next chapter. Moreover, the shortcomings were not only structural, as the candidate positioning made the campaign lose some of their targeted voters. For example, the candidate appearing to be a consensual politician who can get the support of various groups, no matter their background, led to several problems, as in some cases where the candidate's stance was seen to be insubstantial. For instance, for some Islamist groups he was not Islamic enough, as he did not say that he would implement strict Sharia law, and because of his famous visit to the Nobel Prize-winning novelist Naguib Mahfouz in the past. On the other hand, some liberals and non-Islamists accused him of being an extremist due to his previous affiliation with the Muslim Brotherhood and the Al-Gama'a Al-Islamiyya. He was sometimes described as a murderer due to his old opinions when he joined the Al-Gama'a Al-Islamiyya. The picture of him as an Islamist was highlighted once again after the Salafists decided on their own that they would vote for Aboul Fotouh and not for any other candidate.

El-Shahawy elaborated more regarding the Salafist issue, by describing an incident that might have caused them to lose votes, where some Salafists volunteered without contacting the campaign and made a song in support of the candidate. The song was made in the 'nasheed' style popular among Salafists, which does not use musical instruments. It differed from the campaign's songs which included music and women. This alternative type of unorganised and unofficial campaigning for the candidate, especially by Salafists, made Christians and other liberals afraid to support Aboul

Fotouh. And, according to the campaign, in the end they did not even receive the votes of the Salafists. For them Aboul Fotouh was not Islamic enough, and the Salafist leaders did not have control over their popular bases. But did their campaign matter? El-Shahawy believed that campaigns were important but that 'they were not the decisive factor'. As he explained:

the result of the election was a clear reflection of the political situation at the time and of how the election was engineered and managed, as well as the degree of polarisation the society suffered from, with its division into Islamist and secular blocs. The delay of the elections and the late announcement of the dates, in addition to candidates entering at the last minute, changed the calculations of other candidates and led to the final results.

However, he believed it had an important role because it resulted in Aboul Fotouh becoming 'known to the public'. He was not well-known beforehand to the ordinary public, especially in the governorates as both Abu El-Gheit and El-Shahawy explained. However, since the campaign made him well-known, the candidate was able to establish a student movement and political party called 'Strong Egypt'. For the campaign staff, 'the campaign was important as it created a third way separate from the National Democratic Party and the Muslim Brotherhood' as stated by El-Shahawy.

For them, the campaign cannot be compared with other campaigns abroad as there will be a significant gap, mainly because of what El-Shahawy called 'the way that democracy is practiced in Egypt, and how the election process was engineered, along with the high degree of polarisation in the society'. The campaign started before the PEC was formed and before any dates were known. Thus, according to El-Shahawy, it cannot be compared with a country where the dates are known beforehand and the laws are already set, especially those laws that manage donations. For Aboul Fotouh's campaign, it was very difficult to work without dates or laws.

El-Shahawy summarised the campaign's perspective by saying:

operational excellency was not the reason for the final result and Morsi's victory, but rather the engineering of the election itself by SCAF and the division of the people into Islamists and non-Islamists, as well as the increased polarisation that proved to be the decisive factors in the final result.

3.5   Hamdeen Sabahi

3.5.1   Sabahi: Short Biography

Hamdeen Sabahi is a Nasserist socialist politician and former Member of Parliament. He was born in 1954 in the Delta governorate of Kafr El-Sheikh. He was raised in a peasant family in the coastal city of Balteem, being the youngest of 11 children. Sabahi spent his childhood among other peasants and fishermen, and he worked as a fisherman in his younger years (Ibrahim 2012).

Sabahi was elected head of the Cairo University Student Union in 1975 and served as deputy chair of the General Federation of Students from 1975 to 1977. He also established the political Nasserist Thought Club to mobilise students on campus to defend the principles of Gamal Abdel Nasser's 1952 revolution (BBC news 16/5/2014).

In 1977, following the January popular uprising against President Sadat over the high prices of food, Sabahi publicly confronted the president in a televised meeting in which he spoke on behalf of the Cairo University Student Union. As a result, Sabahi was prevented from working as a journalist in the state media sector for several years (Ibrahim 2012).

Sabahi was a member of the Arab Democratic Nasserist Party, but his membership was suspended in 1994 due to internal conflicts between the party's youth, which included Sabahi, and the party's old guard of personalities who had been close to the late president Nasser. In 1996 Sabahi founded the Al-Karama party and was elected to the People's Assembly in 2000 and 2005 (Al-Arabyia 15/5/2012).

During the Mubarak era, he was arrested again in 1997 on charges of inciting agricultural workers to protest, due to some new legislation that strengthened the hand of landowners against poor tenant farmers. In 2003, as a sitting MP, his parliamentary immunity was lifted, and he was subsequently jailed for his involvement in organising demonstrations against the US-led war on Iraq that year. During the Mubarak era, Sabahi was one of the co-founders of the Kefaya ('Enough') movement, which emerged in 2004 and which opposed the inheritance scenario. In 2010, he was one of the co-founders of the National Assembly for Change (NAC), which called for constitutional reform and social justice. These two movements paved the road towards the 25 January Revolution. Sabahi participated in the 25 January Revolution and was slightly injured during anti-regime demonstrations in his home governorate of Kafr El-Sheikh (Ibrahim 2012).

3.5.2   Early Campaign: A Candidate from Among Us

As explained by Hossam Moeness—Sabahi's campaign manager[49]—a number of staff working in the campaign, including the campaign manager, already knew and had worked with Sabahi when they were students through the political Nasserist Thought Club, and later on after they finished university through Al-Karama party. Some of them already had experience or knowledge of elections in the governorates, as they had followed the parliamentary elections which Sabahi entered in his constituency, which was in one of the governorates.

At the beginning of 2010, there were calls from activists and opposition personalities for constitutional amendments to change article 76 in order to allow the option of multi-candidate presidential elections. There was an idea to collect signatures from the public to nominate public figures to run for election in protest to article 76. At that time, people working on Sabahi's presidential election campaign were collecting signatures from the public to nominate public figures such as Sabahi and Mohamed El Baradei to run for office. However, at that time their campaign was a political campaign rather than an election campaign. Their aim was to give Egyptians the option to witness and participate in real multi-candidate presidential elections, regardless of the candidate. As Moeness explained:

> We would collect signatures from the public and register them at the relevant registry office. Although we were working with Hamdeen Sabahi at that time, we were collecting signatures to nominate other candidates besides him, as we wanted to prove that there are other people in Egypt who can run for president other than just Mubarak and his son.

Their efforts were developed later into other formats, such as establishing the National Association for Change (NAC), which was formed by Mohammed El Baradei, the former head of the UN's atomic watchdog. These efforts continued until the 25 January Revolution. After the revolution, both Sabahi and the staff that used to work with him were aware that there would be an election. They wanted to continue what they had started before the revolution and nominated Sabahi to run for the presidency. Sabahi announced by the end of March 2011 that he would officially run for president and started forming his election campaign.

The slogan of his campaign was 'one from among us'. As Moeness explained, the slogan was suggested during the 2010 campaign by one of the youths who was supporting Sabahi but changed his mind in the 2012 elections. The campaign continued with the slogan, which they saw as a clear reflection of Sabahi's character.

The campaign also resorted to a mixture of appeals to mobilise and influence their targeted voters, such as:

Logic and Numbers These were used mainly in the campaign's electoral programme. However, as Moeness explained, their programme was too ambitious, as they were not aware of the real situation nor did they have the relevant dates or schedule for the election. They did not have access to the data available to the state. Nonetheless, according to Moeness, 'this was an advantage as well, as it made them think outside of the box'. Regarding the campaign, they believed that the voters in Egypt would not vote for a candidate for his programme but rather that experts in the various fields from among the elites would read the part they specialised in and may then campaign for the candidate through their own circles if they were convinced by the candidate's policies and plans.

Emotions As Moeness explained, Sabahi used emotional appeals 'unintentionally'. For example, he cried on-air during a television programme. For the campaign, this gave him credibility as he appeared to be sincere. The candidate was also keen on following Egyptian customs and traditions. For example, when Shafiq's wife died, Sabahi insisted on keeping with tradition and attending the customary Egyptian condolences service, despite disagreement from his campaign.

Religion Moeness explained that there was no pre-planned intention to use religion: 'he did not play on religion, but merely employed it in the manner that is the norm among Egyptians'. Sabahi quoted verses from the Qur'an, and if he was visiting a governorate during the time of Friday prayers, he would go with the local people and pray. However, he would not feign increased piety and pray each prayer at the mosque, preferring to do so when he got back home.

Negativity and Attacks As Moeness explained, the official campaign did not plan to conduct attacks or employ negativity. 'However, some unplanned attacks did use to happen from time to time.' In the beginning, this involved youths and volunteers on social media arguing over which candidate represented the revolution. The official campaign had to intervene to stop supporters of the revolution from damaging each other's candidates. Regarding the Muslim Brotherhood, there were general attacks from the campaign stating that they neither wanted the Muslim Brotherhood's candidate nor any candidate even close to that ideology. For Moussa, they used to attack his politics, not his character.

According to a member of the campaign, the main attacks which the campaign was unable to control were those against Shafiq. During Shafiq's first public conference, some of those working on Sabahi's campaign started throwing objects at him as a way to protest against him running for election. At that time, no one knew that they were from Sabahi's campaign, although the campaign came to know later. However, the campaign did use this later in front of the media to demonstrate that Egyptians were against Shafiq running for president.

Sabahi was attacked by other campaigns, including allegations that he was splitting the revolutionary bloc as he was running against other revolutionary candidates; but his campaign responded likewise regarding the other revolutionary candidates. There were other attacks and rumours regarding how he financed his campaign, given that he was not rich. As Moeness explained, 'because his profile was only raised during the last month, there was no time to attack him significantly'. He was mostly affected by these attacks after the campaign ended.

3.5.3 *The Campaign*

3.5.3.1 *Campaign's Structures*

3.5.3.1.1 **Campaign's Staff**

As Moeness explained, Sabahi's campaign was 'an extension of his previous political campaign', as staff members working in his campaign were working with him before the revolution asking for change, although they were not working solely for him at that time.

When Sabahi announced his intention to run for the presidency, his campaign was mainly formed from those who used to work with him on the political campaigns of signature collecting, those who worked with him on his parliamentary election campaigns, as well as youth from the Al-Karama party and some activists from the Revolution. He did not go to a company or other bodies to help him except for technical issues.

The campaign started with these committees:

a. **Media committee:** this was responsible for traditional media and social media.

b. **Governorates committee:** responsible for finding people who could join the campaigns in the governorates and campaign for the candidate there and mobilise them to vote on Election Day. Due to the candidate's family's large presence in one of the constituencies, they would also help him in the field. The governorates team used to mobilise people to go and vote in the election, even if they would not vote for Sabahi. The governorates team used to concentrate on the youth and students in big families, as they believed that modern-day family leaders could no longer force youths to vote for someone specific.

c. **Popular works committee:** responsible for planning and organising various campaign events such as conferences, open buses, door-to-door campaigning, and organising the candidate's visits to the governorates.

d. **Fundraising committee:** responsible for fundraising and securing funding for the campaign. At the beginning its role was limited due to the absence of laws regulating the issue of fundraising. Thus it used to depend on volunteers for their campaign to get the things it needed, mostly in the form of in-kind contributions. After the law was issued, the role of this committee became more active as it opened a bank account for donations and ran a campaign encouraging Egyptians to donate one Egyptian pound through SMS messages that were linked to the campaign's bank account. Alternatively, they could donate directly through the same account.

At a later stage, the campaign added two other committees:

e. **Egyptians abroad committee:** this committee mainly depended on volunteers. The campaign depended on the governorates committee to reach Egyptians abroad. There were many Egyptians from specific areas, for example, governorates such as Dakahlia, and especially in Kafr El-Sheikh, from which people went to work in Italy. Thus the governorate committee in Dakahlia used to connect them with Egyptians in Italy, and so on. This committee also helped Sabahi to travel abroad and meet Egyptians in other countries.

f. **Programme committee:** this committee referred to experts who had the same political stance and who volunteered and wrote the programme.

There was also a campaign co-ordinator who acted as the campaign manager and three assistant co-ordinators. Each of the three assistant co-ordinators was responsible for some of the committees above, as well as reporting to the campaign's main co-ordinator and manager. The candidate's son and daughter worked with the campaign as volunteers. His son, for example, was a cinema director and would help them create videos for the campaign. The situation was similar in Balteem, Kafr El-Sheikh, as his family was there helping the campaign and volunteering for him.

Despite the agreed roles, campaign staff would sometimes leave their roles to join political events taking place in the country which would delay campaign pre-planned events and activities. As Moeness explained:

> Due to the political developments taking place, the campaign found itself more like a political movement, participating in events and voicing opinions, rather than an election campaign. If the campaign planned something like brochure distribution, or any other such campaigning event, and then a political event took place or clashes erupted, they would leave the pre-arranged campaign event and head to the events taking place to participate.

3.5.3.1.2 Management Style

According to Moeness, the campaign used to differentiate between two levels, namely, the political sphere and the campaign or electoral sphere.

In the political sphere, there was differentiation between the candidate's political stance and the political stance of those working on the campaign. If they did not agree, everyone could participate as they wished. For example, the candidate could make a speech or voice an opinion, and the campaign would say something else. Moeness explained that this was part of the 'revolutionary spirit'. Everyone was different and it was not necessary to have the same political opinion or position, especially given that the majority of those working on the campaign came from the revolutionary youth and it was not easy to convince them of a specific stance, particularly regarding the army or SCAF. As Moeness explained:

> Many of the youths were not raised politically or had experience in a political movement to be able to know the importance of rules and organisation, and they used to revolt against anything. The campaign was aware of this and tried to absorb them.

Regarding the campaigning or electoral decisions, this too was divided into two parts. Decisions that dealt with the candidate himself, such as his visits or media appearances, would be discussed with him first, and if they did not agree, the final word lay with the candidate. For campaign decisions that did not involve the presence of the candidate himself, such as day-to-day activities and operations, the campaign used to manage these without referring to or informing the candidate. Thus, tasks related to the candidate were managed vertically, whereas tasks related to the campaign were managed horizontally.

3.5.3.1.3   Campaign Premises
The campaign's central office was in Lebanon Square in Mohandessin, Cairo. The campaign supporters used to pay its rent. For the governorates, the campaign used the Al-Karama party local offices, although the candidate was running as an independent. Some other small parties used to give them their branches in the governorates to campaign in such as the Nasserist party. In areas where the campaign had supporters, they used to rent places. Mostly, people would give them places in the governorates without the campaign asking. In Alexandria, for example, they had four places in addition to the local Al-Karama party branch.

On the issue of receiving places from volunteers, Moeness explained that some people used to donate flats or offices without the campaign even asking, to the extent that someone decided to close his work premises, which was a tyre workshop, and gave it to the campaign to use. However, the campaign explained that it did not use to manage all these places. In the beginning, they tried to do so, but after a while and towards the end of the campaign, the degree of volunteer activities and places became unmanageable.

Moeness gave an example of two incidents that showed the degree of unmanageable aid from volunteers, and that also reflected the lack of cohesion with the campaign. The first incident involved news, later known to the campaign, that some campaign staff were going to protest in front of the High Election Committee (HEC). As Moeness explained, the campaign was not aware of this at the time and was not able to determine whether they were really from the campaign or from among the candidate's supporters or just some people who were pretending to be from the campaign and who wanted to create problems between the candidate and the HEC. The campaign had to publish a statement denying involvement, and Sabahi had to speak publicly telling them not to go if they were really his supporters. The second incident was towards the end of the elections. During this time, the central campaign premises was full of volunteers whom they did not know. The campaign officials had a meeting with the candidate, and they said no one was allowed to go into the area they were meeting in. After finishing, as the campaign manager was leaving, he found that the volunteers were acting as if they were security and not even allowing those in the meeting to leave, some of whom they had never met. In this case, the volunteers were acting from excessive enthusiasm.

However, the campaign explained that volunteers were an essential part of their work, as they did not have access to some areas and yet they found the campaign's posters there, placed by volunteers without the knowledge of the central campaign. Even during election days, the campaign did not have enough people to act as its representatives in the polling stations. However, during those days, the campaign found many people who went to vote and did not find a representative from the campaign there and who then asked the campaign if they could act as representatives. The campaign took a risk and allowed them to represent the campaign officially. Moeness explained that this was a risky decision as they did not know these people. If someone untrustworthy went there, they might not give them the correct count or even fight with the judge or they might be working for an opponent's campaign. Nonetheless, their decision to allow them to be representatives was right at this stage, except where some of those representatives were very tired at the end of the day and went home to sleep after the counting ended without giving the final counting numbers to the central campaign until the next morning, thus leaving room for rumours that they were infiltrated by the Muslim Brotherhood.

3.5.3.1.4 Degree of Externalisation

The campaign hired only two companies: the first was an accounting company for the accounting and financial reports, especially those that would be submitted to the EHC. The second company was a social media company to help them with technical issues. All other specialists needed in other departments, such as advertising or programme writing, were volunteers from the campaign who were professionals in their fields.

Moeness explained that they were working more as a political movement, rather than an election campaign. They therefore resorted only to people who had 'the same political thoughts and ideas, and not professionals with different political opinions'.

3.5.3.1.5   Internal Campaign Communication

The campaign mainly depended on face-to-face meetings. There were daily face-to-face meetings between those working on the central campaign, and the governorates' co-ordinators use to come to Cairo every month to meet the central campaign as well. The second means of communication was daily mobile phone communications. As Moeness explained, emails were only used within the central campaign; in the governorates, this was not applicable as older people managing the work there did not have smartphones, or did not know how to use them, or had problems with internet connectivity.

For the campaign, it was not keen on using technological or expensive methods that would harden the communication process inside the campaign. It was keen to maximise the use of available affordable resources that their staff would be able to use without causing extra technological or financial burdens.

3.5.3.1.6   Feedback

There was no specific department for feedback. As explained by Moeness, the campaign received feedback mainly by sending people to public coffee shops to sit when Sabahi was on television and open the channel there without saying that they were from the campaign. They would then listen to people talking and commenting and get feedback this way. This was done in the both the governorates and in Cairo.

The campaign used to get feedback from social media as well, but they did not take the public opinion polls carried out in Egypt at that time seriously. As Moeness clarified, they believed these polls 'would not be professional, and they had no guarantee that the sample would not be biased and would be representative'.

Although the campaign did not have the infrastructure or resources for conducting scientific opinion polls, they were innovative in the way they gathered feedback. They did not depend on media reports or public polls conducted at that time, as other campaigns did. On the contrary, they innovated their own ways in to achieve their goal.

3.5.3.1.7   Opposition Research

As Moeness explained, the campaign did not have a specific department or committee for opposition research, but it used to get this information from other committees, such as:

a. Governorates committee: that used to write reports for the central campaign about opposing campaigns in the governorates.

b. Media committee: that used to follow up on opponents' news in both traditional media and on social media.

Moeness explained that they did not need any background research or any extra research on their opponents, as they already knew them from their previous work in politics. Thus, the opposing stances and opinions were clear from the start.

3.5.3.1.8 Campaign's Duration

The campaign duration can be divided into three stages. The first stage dates back to 2010 when youth activists were collecting signatures for some candidates, among them Sabahi, to run for the presidency. However, this campaign was not only for Sabahi, but it paved the way towards gaining him supporters and getting him known. This stage continued until the 25 January Revolution.

The second stage was after Mubarak's resignation, when they decided to activate their political movement and convert it into an election campaign. The third stage was when the election date became known and formal nominations were declared by the PEC.

Thus, the duration of the second and third stages of the campaign was more than a year. During this period, Sabahi's campaign was working as both a political movement and an election campaign, as Moeness explained.

Moeness commented that this long period caused them a lot of hassle as there were no regulations to follow, and they also did not know the election dates, leaving them unable to decide upon many things, such as how long to extend the rent contracts for their premises or if one of them wanted to take a career break from his job, when he could do it, and so on. On the other hand—as Moeness explained—the long period helped them to develop a relationship between the team members working on the campaign, as most of them had not worked closely with each other before. It also helped in making the candidate well-known to the public.

3.5.3.1.9 Campaign's Budget

In the beginning, the campaign did not have any money and did not manage to acquire cash. They used to depend on volunteers in providing the campaign with necessities such as paying rent, providing equipment, or providing the campaign with branches or office space. As Moeness explained, 'during this stage, there was no actual budget: whenever the campaign needed money, they started thinking about how they could get it'.

Towards the end of the campaign, when the law allowed them to collect money, they started a fundraising campaign urging supporters to donate one pound through SMS or through the campaign's bank account. For Moeness, the SMS campaign demonstrated that 'those who donated small amounts of money contributed two thirds of the money collected'. It was an indication of the type of people supporting them. They were not businessmen or millionaires but either students or lower-income people.

Moeness explained that they were not affected by the maximum spending limit, as they did not have enough money and thus did not reach it. However, they were affected by the limit of donations per person. The campaign saw this as impractical because if a donor wanted to donate more that the allowed amount, they could give it to a member of the family to donate on their behalf. The campaign also explained that there was no real means of providing accountability for those who exceeded the limit. The campaign was also affected by the short timespan for collecting and spending the money for campaigning.

3.5.3.2 Campaign's Strategies

3.5.3.2.1 Voter's Targeting

There was an assumption among the public that since the candidate was a socialist and a Nasserist, he would target the poor and lower classes, including peasants and workers. However, Moeness explained that 'due to changes in the society over the past years, those who agreed with his speeches and ideas were often from the middle and upper classes as well'.

This is why the campaign concentrated on the cities that witnessed the revolution and mainly on middle and educated classes and youths living therein. The campaign was also keen on sending reassuring messages to different segments in society, such as businessmen, clarifying the candidate's stances on issues like development and capitalism.

However, Moeness pointed out that the main problem in reaching the target audience was that candidates were not allowed to access the voter database during the presidential elections. The campaign explained that this was not the case with the parliamentary elections, where a candidate could access the database for his constituency. As Moeness explained:

In the same year, there were parliamentary elections and candidates in each constituency were allowed to access the databases for their constituency. A group like the Muslim Brotherhood, which had candidates in every constituency, therefore had access to voter databases for almost the entire country, which was a privilege Sabahi's campaign did not have.

3.5.3.2.2 Narrowcasting Activities

In addition to general campaigning activities, the campaign in each governorate used to invent its own unique narrowcasting events to their targeted voters. These were mainly initiatives from each governorate to be organised individually. Moeness gave an example of narrowcasting events in the canal area, as the campaign organised a day for fishermen, where they heard their problems and passed the information to the central campaign to work on.

3.5.3.2.3 Free Media

For the campaign, television was an important outlet to convey their own and their candidate's messages. According to Moeness, 'there was freedom of expression at that time and people still used to watch television'. This is why Sabahi appeared on all channels, including Islamic and Christian ones, and he appeared in various formats, one of which was with his family.

With the local media, the campaign had two issues as Moeness said. The first was that the candidate himself was a journalist and had personal relations with most of the other journalists. Thus, he used to appear with some of them as he was unable to refuse due to these personal relations: 'if he had said no, they might get upset.' The second issue was that 'media used to put Sabahi in a separate category from the frontrunners', and thus they had to accept the timing that was given to the candidate. They were also unable to control when they could appear during the first stages of the campaign. Later on, they were able to control this, as all channels wanted Sabahi to appear with them.

With the international media, the campaign had the same problem, namely, that 'the international media also did not consider him a frontrunner'. They were not paying attention to the candidate, and he did not have access to them; and when the international media started noticing the candidate towards the end of the elections, the candidate and the campaign were busy with other priorities like reaching voters and mobilising them. According to Moeness, despite the importance of free media outlets to the campaign, the campaign did not have much luck with the free media, both local and international, especially at the start of their campaign.

3.5.3.2.4   Paid Media

The campaign did two official advertisements, which involved a short documentary about the candidate and endorsements from public figures including Khaled Said's mother, whose death sparked the 25 of January Revolution.[50] There were other advertisements and songs done by Sabahi's supporters without the involvement of the campaign. The campaign also had posters, brochures, and billboards advertising for Sarahi. It had the campaign's slogan 'a candidate from among us' along with a verse from Quran which meant 'there is no victory except from God', an action that was explained by some as a way to influence traditional Muslims (Shoman and Saleh 2013). The colours of his posters were white and black, which gave an impression of his clarity and decisiveness and tendency to implement clear solutions (Ibid. 2013).

According to Moeness, the campaign did not actually pay for the production or for the broadcast of the advertisement in case of TV and radio. Director and prominent filmmaker Khaled Youssef—who supported Sabahi—provided the advertisement for free. The campaign also agreed with some channels to broadcast them for free. They also ran one advertisement on the radio which was narrated by famous people who had volunteered in the campaign. For printed advertisements, when fundraising was allowed by the new law, the campaign started putting up billboards and posters.

3.5.3.2.5   Debates

Unlike other campaigns, Sabahi wanted to participate in a presidential debate with the frontrunners. However—as Moeness explained—the media did not pay attention to him and only offered him a chance to appear with low-profile candidates 'who did not represent significant political trends or political thoughts in society'. According to Moeness, the candidate saw debates as a 'right of society and a chance for Egyptians to know the real differences between the candidates'.

As explained, the only debate that took place was between Moussa and Aboul Fotouh. According to Moeness, Sabahi's campaign saw it as technically good from the format side of things, but content-wise, the candidates were fighting rather than debating. Accordingly, the campaign saw that what happened between the other two candidates in the debate was in Sabahi's favour, as undecided voters went to him and not to the other candidates, due to perceived faults revealed during the debate.

3.5.3.2.6 Internet and Social Media

Internet and social media were part of the overall media team. They were an extension of the media team but with a different audience, mainly the youth. For social media, the team used to formulate the general strategies and left it to a company to help them in implementing these strategies, as well as helping them in organising live events on social media.

For the website, the campaign created this with the help of volunteers. It was used as a source of information for the general voters, and it was also used to upload the campaign's materials for those working in the governorates to print and use.

According to Moeness, the campaign did not have any 'electronic committees' such as Morsi's and Shafiq's campaign. Their social media team was mainly concerned with redistributing content from the candidate's and the campaign's activities, besides launching some live events for social media audiences.

3.5.3.2.7 Campaign's Activities

The campaign organised a variety of events, such as a touring bus, conferences, visits to governorates, human chains, and meeting people in coffee shops. In addition to normal campaigning events, each governorate used to invent its own unique events; some of which were narrowcasting events, others were general events. The campaign also used social media, traditional media, and advertisements to reach its target voters.

3.5.3.2.8 Degree of Personalisation

The campaign was keen on passing news about the candidate himself and his opinions. During the candidate's appearances in the media, he used to add a personal touch. He once appeared with his family on a television programme, and on another programme he recited some poetry he wrote when he was in prison.

According to Moeness, 'the act of reciting poetry that he wrote gave him credibility as he did not appear fake'. It also made some youths, who loved poetry, support him. The candidate was fine with introducing his family, who were already known, such as his daughter, who was a presenter, and his son, who was a cinema director, until attacks and comments criticised his family's appearances for reminding people of Mubarak and his ever-present son.

The campaign was also keen on passing news about the campaign itself such as events that it organised, its statements and stances, and any endorsement they took from public figures.

3.5.3.3 Did the Campaign Matter?

Sabahi's campaign was different from the other studied campaigns in terms of the way it was managed. As explained, its candidate's positions and those of his staff could be completely different, unlike other campaigns which were keen on abiding by their candidates' positions and stances. The campaign was only different as it managed to invent innovative ways to reach its goals despite a lack of resources. The main success of the campaign was that Sabahi became the third winner and the election dark horse, which was one of the main election's surprises. But did the campaign help in this success, or was the rank Sabahi achieved a result of other factors? This question was asked to Moeness, Sabahi's campaign manager.

Moeness replied that 'the campaign was very important but not the decisive factor'. According to Moeness, the campaign staff were the ones working with the people, not the candidate. Some voters may support a candidate or participate because those working on the campaign were nice to them. Others may hate a candidate because someone in the campaign treated them badly. Thus, the campaign played a massive role in reaching out and communicating with voters. The campaign was also important because even if the candidate did not win, he could organise his supporters into a political party or for any other political activity.

However, as Moeness explained:

> Even the best campaign cannot guarantee victory, as the political equation in Egypt at that time involved overlapping factors that played a role in determining the results of the election.

Among these factors—as Moeness elaborated—were 'what the regional and western powers wanted'. The campaign believed that Morsi came to power because the regional powers did not want Shafiq and because they wanted to control the country: 'This was why, for example, the electoral forgery case was not concluded.' Another important factor for the campaign was the issue of the law and its tailoring, such as 'the immunity given to the PEC's decisions'. There was no separate committee to consider appeals against PEC decisions. A third factor was the manipulation of people's awareness through the media or through what Moeness described as 'planting people in villages and companies to influence voters', in addition to the involvement of SCAF in determining all the political details. For Sabahi's campaign, all of these factors combined 'proved to be more important in determining the final result than the campaign itself'.

3.6   CONCLUSION

This chapter offers a detailed overall understanding of how each campaign was planned and implemented by giving a detailed account of the campaigns' structures and strategies. In addition to this, the chapter gave a practitioner account of how the campaigns were managed and whether the campaign staff see campaigns as an important factor in influencing election results. The next chapter will build upon the data presented here and offer an analytical comparison in terms of the professionalism of the five studied campaigns and the impact on election results.

NOTES

1. This was proven later—after Morsi's winning—incorrect. See Chap. 5.
2. Interview with Yehia Hamed, Morsi's campaign spokesperson and former investment minister during Morsi's term in presidency.
3. According to Hamid, the Brotherhood had already tried to convince three independent candidates from outside the Brotherhood to run for the presidency, but they refused (Hamed 2016).
4. PEC refused and excluded ten candidates who did not meet the criteria. Among them, four famous characters: Khairat Al-Shater, Omar Soliman, Hazem Salah Abu Ismail, and Ayman Nour.
5. Morsi submitted his nominations papers on 8 April 2012 in the morning. The PEC closed the door for submitting nominations papers on 8 April 2012 at 14:00 PM. For more information see Al-Masry Al-Youm newspaper edition on 9 April 2012.
6. Interview with Yehia Hamed, Morsi's campaign spokesperson and former investment minister during Morsi's term in presidency.
7. Interview conducted with Abdel-Galil El-Sharnouby in October 2016. El-Sharnouby held several official positions in the Muslim Brotherhood such as head of media unit which was responsible for all the governorates, deputy head of the Brotherhood's media unit, member of the weekly newsletter committee, ex-editor-in-chief of Ikhwan online website.

8. For more information about the Brotherhood's internal structure, methods of recruiting members, how to become a Brotherhood, and different ranks and authorities inside the organisation, see Trager 2011.

9. The extent of total obedience of Muslim Brotherhood members led non-Muslim Brotherhood members to describe Brotherhood members as 'sheep' ('khirfan' in Arabic) obeying their shepherd. For more info about obedience in the Brotherhood, see Masoud (2014: 155–169) and Trager (2011).

10. The Muslim Brotherhood denies having an office in London. However, I managed to visit the office which is based in Cricklewood Road in North West London in May/June 2013 while covering a TV package for BBC Arabic TV. The office was exposed later by other British media (see: Both 2014; Loveluck 2014; Wynne-Jones 2014).

11. Chapter 5 proves that this claim is not true.

12. The guidance office is the highest body in the Brotherhood. It consists of approximately 15 members, headed by the Supreme Guide. For more information, see Trager 2011.

13. For more details about Muslim Brotherhood internal organisational structure, see Trager 2011, 2016.

14. Electronic committees are equivalent to astroturfing. For more details, see social media section in Chap. 4.

15. In 2012, one GDP was equal to approximately ten LE.

16. These allegations were widespread and were also mentioned to me by other campaigns who believed it was true.

17. Email from Abby Berg-Frank Wolf's office—on 27 October 2016.

18. Personal interview on 28 February 2017.

19. The term and practice will be explained in detail in the next chapter.

20. For more info, see Al-Watan newspaper special file on the topic on 31 March 2013.

21. For details about Morsi's governing, see Chap. 5.

22. Speculations that Mubarak's own son Gamal Mubarak would inherit his father Mubarak and be the president of Egypt after him.

23. These names were overshadowed by the inheritance scenario and the name of Mubarak's own son Gamal Mubarak.

24. Interview with Mahmoud Ibrahim, Internet and Social Media Manager in Shafiq's campaign.

25. Interview with Mahmoud Ibrahim.

26. Interview with Ahmed Shafiq on CBC TV, broadcasted on 1 May 2012.

27. See social media section in this section and social media analysis in Chap. 4.

28. Protests in front of Shafiq's headquarter ended with setting it on fire.

29. Quotations in this section are from Mahmoud Ibrahim, unless otherwise stated.

30. Added in one title due to similarity in Shafiq's campaign.
31. Morsi's campaign was the shortest campaign.
32. I was not able to verify his name or relation to the candidate, as the campaign refused to reveal his identity upon his request.
33. Allegations were based on UAE hostile tensed relations with the Muslim Brotherhood and Shafiq's staying there after losing the election. However, I was not able to verify these allegations.
34. For more info about Sufism in Egypt, see Daily News Egypt on 21 October 2012 and Harvard Religious Literacy project 2016.
35. Interview with Yara Khalaf, campaign's media team.
36. Interview with Moataz Kotb, the campaign's IT and social media manager.
37. Ordinary Egyptian uses Quranic verses and poetry in their ordinary talks as a way of showing emphasis, eloquent, or rhetoric.
38. Interview with Ahmed Kamel, Moussa's campaign.
39. These were the parliamentary elections that were conducted around six months before the presidential elections. Hamzawy was elected as an MP in Heliopolis in Cairo.
40. Campaigns by volunteers and candidates' supporters without the official involvement of the candidate and their team.
41. For more info about Pope Shenouda III, see BBC News 17 March 2012.
42. For role of the Coptic Church in Egyptian politics, see Fahmi 2014.
43. For more info about Ultras and role in politics, see Dorsey 2012; Elgohari 2013.
44. Some of these activities were meant to be narrowcasting activities for their targeted groups but at the same time can be considered as general campaign activities as it was enhanced by media coverage to a wider audience.
45. Interview with Lamia Kamel in May 2012.
46. Interview with Mohamed El-Shahawy, Aboul Fotouh's campaign manager.
47. A group of volunteers who support and admire the candidate can run a campaign to support him on their own. They don't have to necessarily know him in person.
48. Responsible for the campaign in Asyut governorate.
49. Interview with Hossam Moeness, Sabahi's campaign manager.
50. Said was beaten and tortured while in police custody in 2010. This lead to the creation of a Facebook page called 'we are all Khaled Said' through which the revolution was organised. The page which had hundreds of thousands of followers urged Egyptians to participate in anti-government demonstrations on 25 January 2011—Egypt's National Police Day. Eighteen days later, Mubarak was forced to resign.

REFERENCES

90 Minutes, Morsi TV interview, 2012. [television programme, video, online]. Al-Mehwar TV. YouTube. Available from: https://www.youtube.com/watch?v=kD5cSN1ThPA [Accessed 1 February 2017].

Abdelghany, I., 2012. The truth about 50 million dollars U.S. gave to Morsi's campaign. *Masress* [online], 5 August 2012. Available from: http://www.masress.com/october/129708 [Accessed 3 September 2016].

Ahram Online, 23/6/2013. UPDATE: Morsi prison escape referred to Egypt prosecutors. *Ahram Online* [online], 23 June 2013. Available from: http://english.ahram.org.eg/NewsContent/1/64/74704/Egypt/Politics-/BREAKING-Morsi-prison-escape-referred-to-Egypt-pro.aspx [Accessed 3 September 2016].

Al-Jazeera, 2011. Muslim Brotherhood dismisses Aboul Fotouh. *Al Jazeera* [online], 19 June 2011. Available from: http://www.aljazeera.net/news/arabic/2011/6/19/%D8%AC%D9%85%D8%A7%D8%B9%D8%A9-%D8%A7%D9%84%D8%A5%D8%AE%D9%88%D8%A7%D9%86-%D8%AA%D9%81%D8%B5%D9%84-%D8%A3%D8%A8%D9%88-%D8%A7%D9%84%D9%81%D8%AA%D9%88%D8%AD [Accessed 19 September 2016].

Al-Arabiya, 15/5/2012. Revolutionary Youth Coalition supports Sabbahi for president. *Al Arabiya English* [online]. Available from: http://english.alarabiya.net/articles/2012/05/15/214193.html [Accessed 19 September 2016].

Al-Hagag, Y., 2014. Court reviewing sources of Morsi's campaign funding. *Al-Dostor* [online], 17 February 2014. Available from: http://www.dostor.org/156380 [Accessed 1 February 2017].

An Appointment with the President, Morsi interview, May 2012. [television programme, video, online]. Al-Nahar TV. YouTube. Available from: https://www.youtube.com/watch?v=pgORX8lD_Fs [Accessed 3 September 2016].

Ashour, M., 2013. Al-Jalad: Arab figure participated in Morsi's election campaign. *Al Watan* [online], 12 March 2013. Available from: http://www.akhbarak.net/articles/11719316-الموقع-من-المصدر-الجلاد-شخصية-عربية-تشارك [Accessed 3 September 2016].

Awad, M., 2012. Ex-military man says can lead Egypt transition. *Reuters* [online], 16 February 2012. Available from: http://uk.reuters.com/article/uk-egypt-presidency-shafiq-idUKTRE81F0LE20120216 [Accessed 19 September 2016].

Ayad, H., 2013. Independent candidates' elections programmes. *In*: Rabeea, A., ed. *Presidential election 2012*. Cairo: Al Ahram Centre for Political and Strategic Studies, 151–169.

BBC Arabic, 22/1/2012. Egypt: Ahmed Shafiq campaign confiscated videotapes after BBC recorded with him. *BBC Arabic* [online], 22 January 2012. Available from: http://www.bbc.com/arabic/middleeast/2012/01/120122_egypt_shafiq.shtml [Accessed 19 September 2016].

BBC News, 16/5/2014. Hamdeen Sabahi: Egypt presidential candidate. *BBC News* [online], 16 May 2014. Available from: http://www.bbc.co.uk/news/world-middle-east-27441418 [Accessed 19 September 2016].

BBC News, 17/3/2012. Obituary: Pope Shenouda III. *BBC News* [online], 17 March 2012. Available from: http://www.bbc.co.uk/news/world-middle-east-17416731 [Accessed 19 September 2016].

Black, I., 2012. Mohamed Morsi: Brotherhood's backroom operator in the limelight. *The Guardian* [online], 25 May 2012. Available from: https://www.theguardian.com/world/2012/may/25/mohammed-morsi-muslim-brotherhood [Accessed 3 September 2016].

Both, R., 2014. The Muslim Brotherhood's new nerve center: Cricklewood? *The Guardian* [online], 1 April 2014. Available from: https://www.theguardian.com/world/2014/apr/01/muslim-brotherhood-cricklewood-london [Accessed 1 February 2017].

CNN Arabic, 1/5/2012. Splits in the Muslim Brotherhood after announcing that Shater would run for presidency. *CNN Arabic* [online], 1 May 2012. Available from: http://archive.arabic.cnn.com/2012/egypt.elections/4/1/egypt.shater/ [Accessed 1 February 2017].

Daily News Egypt, 21/10/2012. Sufi Islam in Egypt. *Daily News Egypt* [online], 21 October 2012. Available from: http://www.dailynewsegypt.com/2012/10/21/sufi-islam-in-egypt/ [Accessed 19 September 2016].

Dorsey, J., 2012. Egyptian ultras emerge as powerful political force. *Huffington Post* [online], 11 December 2012. Available from: http://www.huffingtonpost.com/james-dorsey/egypt-ultras_b_1870016.html [Accessed 19 September 2016].

Eissa, I., 2013. *Eissa: Mohamed Morsi did work as a consultant for NASA* [video, online]. Cairo: Al Qahira w-Alnas. YouTube. Available from: https://www.youtube.com/watch?v=AabgQbzRywo [Accessed 3 September 2016].

El-Gundi, Z., 2012. Abdel-Moneim Abul-Fotouh. *Ahram Online* [online], 2 April 2012. Available from: http://english.ahram.org.eg/NewsContent/36/124/36854/Presidential-elections-/Meet-the-candidates/AbdelMoneim-AbulFotouh.aspx [Accessed 19 September 2016].

El-Sherif, A., 2012. Will the Muslim Brotherhood's gamble on al-Shater pay off? *Carnegie Endowment for International Peace* [online], 13 April 2012. Available from: http://carnegieendowment.org/sada/?fa=47836 [Accessed 1 February 2017].

Elgohari, M., 2013. Egypt's ultras: no more politics. *Jadaliyya* [online], 30 June 2013. Available from: http://www.jadaliyya.com/pages/index/12475/egypt's-ultras_no-more-politics [Accessed 19 September 2016].

Fahmi, G., 2014. The Coptic church and politics in Egypt. *Carnegie Middle East Center* [online], 18 December 2014. Available from: http://carnegie-mec.org/2014/12/18/coptic-church-and-politics-in-egypt-pub-57563 [Accessed 19 September 2016].

Fathi, Y., 2012. Ahmed Shafiq. *Ahram Online* [online], 2 April 2012. Available from:http://english.ahram.org.eg/NewsContent/36/124/36798/Presidential-elections-/Meet-the-candidates/Ahmed-Shafiq.aspx [Accessed 19 September 2016].

Habib, M., 2013. *The Muslim Brotherhood between rising, presidency and erosion of legitimacy.* Cairo: The International Group for Publishing and Distribution.

Harvard Religious Literacy Project (RLP), 2016. Sufism in Egypt. *Harvard Divinity School* [online]. Available from: http://rlp.hds.harvard.edu/faq/sufism-egypt [Accessed 19 September 2016].

Ibrahim, E., 2012. Hamdeen Sabbahi. *Ahram Online* [online], 2 April 2012. Available from: \http://english.ahram.org.eg/News/36856.aspx [Accessed 19 September 2016].

IkhwanWeb, 7/5/2012. Dr. Mohamed Morsi – a brief biography. *IkhwanWeb* [online], 7 May 2012. Available from: http://ikhwanweb.com/article.php?id=29964 [Accessed 3 September 2016].

Knell, Y., 10/3/2012a. Egypt candidate: veteran diplomat, Amr Moussa. *BBC News* [online], 10 March 2012. Available from: http://www.bbc.co.uk/news/world-middle-east-17234124 [Accessed 19 September 2016].

Knell, Y., 13/4/2012b. Egypt candidate: moderate Islamist, Abdul Moneim Aboul Fotouh. *BBC News* [online], 13 April 2012. Available from: http://www.bbc.co.uk/news/world-middle-east-17356253 [Accessed 19 September 2016].

Knell, Y., 23/4/2012c. Egypt candidate: Ahmad Shafiq, former prime minister. *BBC News* [online], 23 April 2012. Available from: http://www.bbc.co.uk/news/world-middle-east-17788595 [Accessed 19 September 2016].

Loveluck, L., 2014. Egypt's Muslim Brotherhood launches fightback from Cricklewood flat. *Telegraph* [online], 12 January 2014. Available from: \ http://www.telegraph.co.uk/news/worldnews/africaandindianocean/egypt/10567230/Egypts-Muslim-Brotherhood-launches-fightback-from-Cricklewood-flat.html [Accessed 1 February 2017].

Masoud, T., 2014. *Counting Islam: religion, class, and elections in Egypt.* Cambridge University Press.

PEC website: 2012 presidential elections. [online] Egypt. Available from: http://pres2012.elections.eg [Last Accessed 1 Feb 2014].

Shoman, M. and Saleh, A., 2013. Campaigns' strategies & tactics in 2012 presidential elections. *In:* Rabeea, A. H., ed. *Presidential election 2012.* Cairo: Al Ahram Centre for Political and Strategic Studies, 205–239.

Trager, E., 2011. Unbreakable Muslim Brotherhood: grim prospects for a liberal Egypt. *Foreign Affairs* [online], 90 (5), 114–126. Available from: https://www.foreignaffairs.com/articles/north-africa/2011-09-01/unbreakable-muslim-brotherhood [Accessed 1 January 2017].

Trager, E., 2016. *Arab Fall, how the Muslim Brotherhood won and lost Egypt in 891 days.* Washington, DC: Georgetown University Press.

Wynne-Jones, J., 2014. Egypt's Muslim Brotherhood open London office... above a disused kebab shop in Cricklewood. *Daily Mail* [online], 13 January 2014. Available from: http://www.dailymail.co.uk/news/article-2538755/Egypts-Muslim-Brotherhood-open-London-office-disused-kebab-shop-Cricklewood.html [Accessed 1 February 2017].

Youssef, B., 2013. *Bassem Youssef and the Supreme Guide's prompts to Morsi: retribution, mate* [video, online]. Cairo, Egypt: Al-Bernaeg. Available from: https://www.youtube.com/watch?v=zhGJmztZYcc [Accessed 3 September 2016].

Zane, K., 2013. Obama's secret $8 billion bribe to the Muslim Brotherhood, *Western Journalism* [online]. Available from: http://www.westernjournalism.com/obamas-secret-8-billion-bribe-to-the-muslim-brotherhood/ [Accessed 3 September 2016].

CHAPTER 4

Analysing the Campaigns in Light of Their Professionalisation

This chapter aims to analyse the five studied election campaigns by comparing and analysing their structure (hardware) and strategies (software) based on the professionalisation index which was applied separately to each campaign in the previous chapter. By analysing the campaigns' professionalism, the chapter explores which campaigns were more professional and tries to answer the question: did professionalisation play a role in determining the election results. In other words, was there a direct relationship between campaigns' professionalism and the election results? The chapter argues that professionalisation played a significant role in the first round of elections which left both Morsi and Shafiq as the top two front runners, giving them the chance to compete again in the second round of elections. However, professionalisation did not play the same role in determining the result of the second round of elections, as there were other determinant factors such as voters resorting to punitive voting.

4.1   Campaign Structure

A good campaign structure is vital to any election campaign as it represents the 'organisational preconditions' for campaigning, which acts like the campaign hardware (Tenscher et al. 2012). This good structure (hardware) facilitates the 'communication flows' between the candidate, various political actors, media, and voters (Esser and Strömbäck 2012).

© The Author(s) 2018   157
D. Elsheikh, *Campaign Professionalism during Egypt's 2012
Presidential Election*, Political Campaigning and Communication,
https://doi.org/10.1007/978-3-319-75954-8_4

A well-designed infrastructure and the employment of necessary qualified staff also help the campaign to fulfil its daily tasks which are usually
many in number and require more than one person to carry out. These
tasks vary from traditional campaigning activities to administration within
the campaign. The variety of tasks and relatively large number of people
working in the campaign require a solid internal infrastructure similar to
that of companies. This infrastructure should be flexible enough to deal
with the candidate and his advisors on the one hand and volunteers and
activists in the field on the other (Maarek 2011).

However, like any company, good infrastructure alone does not necessarily guarantee success, as this is affected by other things such as the staff
chosen, relationships between staff, poor or good communication behaviour within the teams, decisions taken, energy, and the enthusiasm of those
working in the campaign (Maarek 2011). This is why the role of a campaign manager is of great importance as he is the one to ensure a smoother
workflow and working relations in the campaign. However, there are
other obstacles that may affect the campaign structure on which both the
campaign manager and the candidate may not have the upper hand.

Philippe J. Maarek highlights what he describes as 'psychosociological
handicaps' (Maarek 2011: 180) that differentiate a campaign from a company and can also differentiate one campaign from another. Among these
handicaps is the lack of 'past history', which played a significant role in the
2012 Egyptian presidential elections. This lack of past history and previous experience can delay or prevent the campaign from taking decisions
that would have otherwise been based on previous experience, knowledge,
or previous work habits. The lack of experience could cause a campaign to
make naïve decisions or take a longer time to finalise a decision regarding
a trivial issue. The 'past history' also plays a role in knowing how the candidate can obtain funding from contacting previous donors, or those the
candidate or campaign are aware of whose previous history and experience
informs them that they could donate. In the 2012 Egyptian elections, the
first top three candidates in the first round of elections already had a long
history of electoral campaigning in Egypt through parliamentary elections
and through other forms of political activism in the Egyptian political and
public spheres.

For instance, Mohamed Morsi had the Muslim Brotherhood group
behind him, making use of all its 'past history' and previous electoral data.
The same applies to Ahmed Shafiq; although officially he did not have a
political party behind him, he recruited those who had a 'past history' in

performing that role in elections within the dissolved National Democratic Party (NDP). The same applies to a greater extent to Hamdeen Sabahi, who has previous experience in parliamentary elections or in other forms of political mobilisation and campaigning such as the campaign to collect signatures to change Article 76 of the constitution. The luxury of 'past history' was not one enjoyed by the other two campaigns: Aboul Fotouh and Moussa. This is why, for example, Moussa's campaign did not know earlier on about those 'brokers of elections and billboards' who acquired permission from councils for strategic places to put up posters and then sold them to others at higher prices, making a business out of it. Likewise, Aboul Fotouh's campaign complained of not having access to adequate previous electoral data to build upon, saying that, 'past experience could provide us with more historical data about voters' trends, managing electoral debates, and fund raising techniques' (Al-Shahawy 2016).[1]

The next section will analyse the campaigns' structure depending on the professionalisation index which reflects the main indicators according to which the structure can be considered 'professional'. The more the structure has from these indicators, the more professional it is. These indicators are summarised by Tenscher (2013: 245–246) as follows: (a) 'a growing structural, financial and personal capability for cost-intensive campaigning which includes the centralisation of campaigns organisation', (b) 'Professionalisation of campaigns activities and actors, which includes the process of consulting, externalisation and commercialisation of campaigns tasks', and (c) 'the change from "selling" to "marketing" the political product, which includes the use of marketing techniques, opposition research, opinion polls ...etc.' These indicators are reflected in the following nine criteria that will be discussed in detail in the following section: campaign staff, management style, campaign premises, degree of externalisation, internal campaign communication, feedback, opposition research, campaign duration, and campaign budget.

The first step towards building the campaign structure, which would then determine the campaign's strategies, was choosing the campaign staff as the harmony of the campaign team would depend on it (Maarek 2011: 181).

4.1.1   Campaign Staff

Campaign staff refers to 'the institutionalized permanent and temporary staff members involved in the planning, organisation and implementation of the election campaign at the national level' (Tenscher et al. 2012: 161).

This is a wide definition that involves a variety of positions and roles within the campaign which all play a vital role. Due to budget and time constraints, it is not expected that a campaign will fill all positions with professionals who have previous experience in campaign work. However, there are two key positions that require professionals to ensure a campaign's internal efficiency, which reflects later on the campaign strategy. These two roles are the position of the campaign manager and the position of the field co-ordinator (Maarek 2011). This part discusses both roles as an indication of how staff were chosen in the campaigns and the level of their professionalisation.

4.1.1.1 Campaign Manager

The campaign manager is always chosen by the candidate himself as the candidate needs someone they can trust on a personal level and who can stand in for him in some of his duties or make decisions on his behalf. The campaign manager is vital to the campaign as an organisation as he then hires other members of the campaign and manages them, besides co-ordinating and supervising with outside agencies and organisations exterior to the campaign. Maarek concludes that dismissing the campaign manager during the course of the campaign has a negative effect on the campaign, even if the campaign manager did not do his job as planned, as previous experience from various campaigns shows that this was a 'bad omen' for the campaign (Maarek 2011: 183). This emphasises the importance of choosing a professional campaign manager in order to maintain the stability and efficiency of the overall campaign. In Egypt's 2012 campaigns, all campaigns had a manager, although the role and efficiency varied from one campaign to another.

In Morsi's campaign, the campaign was already formed before the Muslim Brotherhood's decision to nominate Morsi instead of Khairat Al-Shater. Thus, the candidate did not play a role in choosing the campaign manager or most of the campaign staff that were already chosen by the Muslim Brotherhood and who were already members of the Muslim Brotherhood. Moreover, the Muslim Brotherhood and the Freedom and Justice Party were already campaigning for the candidate.

Essam Hadad, a member of the Muslim Brotherhood's Guidance Bureau, was chosen as the campaign's manager. After Morsi was elected as president, Hadad was appointed as the president's advisor for foreign affairs and international cooperation, which again shows the amount of trust he had in him.

In Shafiq's campaign, the candidate himself chose a trusted person, General Ibrahim Manaa, as his campaign manager. General Ibrahim Manaa was an ex-army officer, who was known in Egyptian local media as Shafiq's secret keeper. Even though he was the official campaign manager who dealt with the public and managed campaign staff, the actual campaign manager who was working secretly was, as explained before, the journalist Abdallah Kamal, who acted as the campaign's mastermind. However, he was only known to a small circle within the campaign.

Amr Moussa also had a favoured trustee. He chose his previous office manager, the veteran diplomat Hesham Youssef, as his campaign manager. Sabahi chose Hossam Moeness, who has the same political inclinations and who managed his political signature campaign previously. Hossam came from a banking background. For Aboul Fotouh, although there was no previous experience between him and his campaign manager, he chose Mohamed El-Shahawy, from the marketing sector, as he was among the first people to contact Aboul Fotouh after the revolution asking him to nominate himself for the presidency. He was also from the same political school of thought as both were dismissed from the Muslim Brotherhood.

From the above, it is clear that trust, political stances, and previous knowledge were the main criteria for candidates to choose their campaign managers, and not necessarily previous experience on electoral campaigns. This shows that personal trust preceded professionalism in all the five campaigns when choosing a campaign manager. This gives an indication that other positions also might have been filled by loyal staff rather than professional staff. This was clear in the way some campaigns appointed their field co-ordinator.

4.1.1.2 Field Co-ordinator

The second key position was the field co-ordinator. Unlike the campaign manager, the field co-ordinator may not have direct access to the candidate; instead he has to work directly with the central campaign. The field co-ordinator is mainly responsible for organising the ground campaign as in deciding which neighbourhoods to visit, which houses, and sending volunteers out knocking on doors.

Maarek (2011: 183) explains that the position of the field co-coordinator intersects three categories of players from contradictory backgrounds. These categories are (a) activists and party members, (b) sympathisers and volunteers who are not necessarily professional, and (c) the central campaign, which may convey unclear messages, especially if it has a poor structure.

Staff in these categories may be working according to different methods and may have some tensions between them due to their professionalism or closeness to the candidate. The role of the field co-ordinator is equivalent to the governorates committee or governorates co-ordinators in the Egyptian campaigns. This role was significant in the first round of the elections as it aimed at mobilising and securing voters in various governorates[2] to vote for their candidate. It was a determinant factor in securing enough votes for both Morsi and Shafiq to pass the first round and compete in the second round of elections.

For Shafiq's campaign, one of its main strategies was what was known within the campaign as 'five thousand is equal to five million', where the campaign resorted to those from the former NDP who had past experience in dealing with governorates, especially the villages. Each of these had the responsibility of mobilising a thousand voters to vote for Shafiq, meaning that in total the five thousand representatives could secure five million votes, and this helped Shafiq enter the second round of elections. In Shafiq's campaign, the role of the field co-ordinator was to provide the campaign with trusted representatives, contact them on a daily basis, and develop methods to monitor their performance. The field co-ordinator was also responsible, along with his team (the five thousand representatives), in organising the candidate's visits to the governorates—including villages and cities—and meeting with senior families there. The field co-ordinator also had NDP data from previous elections, which mainly helped the governorates teams and the campaign in general in developing strategies to secure votes.

Although Morsi's campaign did not have a title called 'field co-ordinator' or 'governorates committee' within the campaign's structure, these roles were part of the events and on-the-ground committees which were responsible for organising the campaign's and candidate's events in the various governorates. The role was also embedded in the way the Muslim Brotherhood as a group, or the Freedom and Justice Party, used to campaign for the candidate, where each member—that is, each Brother—of the Muslim Brotherhood group and party used to campaign and mobilise voters, especially in the governorates, to vote for their candidate. In other words, and although there were no accurate figures for members of the Muslim Brotherhood, if there were five thousand active members that would campaign and mobilise a thousand voters to vote for their candidate, taking into consideration the Muslim Brotherhood members themselves, the campaign would easily secure the five million votes (exactly

5,764,952 votes) Morsi gained in the first round that secured him a place in the second round. This could resemble Shafiq's main strategy in securing votes, which was summarised in 'five thousand equal five millions'. The field co-ordinator position was also present in Moussa's and Aboul Fotouh's campaigns, although they were not as effective as they had planned. This can be explained by the fact that neither of the two campaigns employed professionals who had worked as a field co-ordinator before, thus not having a database of voters to mobilise, nor did they have links to the key figures that can mobilise voters, especially in governorates, unlike Shafiq's and Morsi's campaigns who had this privilege.

For Moussa's campaign, the field co-ordinator's job was equivalent to the governorates co-ordinator and field manager. The campaign describes this role as the 'executive arm' (Khalaf 2016).[3] However, due to the lack of previous experience, the role was not as effective as previously thought. The campaign realised that it did not meet the effective people in the governorates: those who can mobilise voters in the governorates or those who can go and vote on election days. As the campaign explained, those who endorsed the candidate in villages, 'would come to campaign rallies in large numbers, sometimes more than 22,000 of them, to attend an event for the candidate, but they would not vote, attending the events largely out of curiosity' (Khalaf 2016). The ineptitude of the field co-ordinator's role was also clear with some examples the campaign gave while interviewing them, such as not being fully aware of the election brokers' game, not contacting representatives in various governorates early enough, and more importantly not having a strong method of monitoring the families or representatives they had agreed to work with. This explains the state of shock they were in after the results appeared, as it was against their expectations and calculations.

For Aboul Fotouh's campaign, the field co-ordinator's post was equivalent to the popular works committee, which was the team responsible for working in the governorates and mobilising voters therein. The committee's role was also weak in comparison to Shafiq's and Morsi's campaigns. Aboul Fotouh's campaign did not contact senior influential families in villages, and as explained in an interview with Mohamed Abu El Gheit, who was responsible for the campaign in Asyut in Upper Egypt (Personal interview, May 2016), 'The campaign was mistaken in not recruiting someone in each place they visited (no matter how small the place) to continue campaigning for the candidate, after the campaign left.' Again, the campaign did not have a solid mechanism to monitor the performance of their representatives in the governorates, nor did it have access to influential people therein who could mobilise voters or a fixed group of campaigners who could continue to campaign for the candidate in each place he visits. According to Abu El Gheit, they would visit some small places and convince voters there of their candidate, but another candidate would go to the same village and convince the same people of another candidate.

For Hamdeen Sabahi's campaign, the field co-ordinator post was equivalent to the work of the governorates committee, which used to campaign for the candidate in governorates and mobilise voters there to vote and campaign for the candidate as well. In Sabahi's campaign, the governorates committee took a different approach which concentrated on reaching and mobilising young voters. The campaign believed that after the revolution, and due to changes in society where the youth in families became more educated than their family seniors, they would no longer go and vote as was dictated to them, even if they appeared to be obeying (Moeness 2016).[4]

The campaign had advantages over Moussa's and Aboul Fotouh's campaigns, namely, their past experience working on the ground, whether in the parliamentary elections in the governorates, and had the privilege of having Sabahi's big family living in one of the governorates and already campaigning for him. It appears that the campaign's bet on the youths in the governorates rather than senior families was a sound decision as it positively affected the results of the first round of elections, allowing Sabahi to beat other candidates, mainly Moussa and Aboul Fotouh. The bond Sabahi's campaign was able to make with youth in the governorates became evident during a visit to one of the villages immediately after the results of the first round of elections until the end of the second round of elections. During this period, visits to one of the villages involved a meeting with a group of youths (who were not affiliated to the campaign) and some of them less than 18 years old, thus they could not vote. Nonetheless, they explained how they supported Sabahi by standing in front of polling stations urging those who had the right to vote to go and vote for Sabahi. This observation confirms what Sabahi's campaign manager said (Moeness 2016), which is that they found people they did not know contacting the campaign and asking to be the campaign's representatives in polling stations where the campaign had no representatives. These examples show unplanned support from the youth in governorates which stresses the importance of the role of the governorates committee (i.e. field co-ordinator).

From the above, it appears that only Morsi's and Shafiq's campaigns had professionals in the field co-ordinator position. After them comes Sabahi's campaign who already had some experience in mobilising voters in governorates. At the bottom of the list comes Moussa's and Aboul Fotouh's campaign. The reason for this could be understandable, as the only two forces who had this experience were the NDP and the Muslim Brotherhood. The Muslim Brotherhood had its own candidate to work for and the NDP people were approached by Shafiq. Although there were other NDP people who used to work in elections, they were not approached by any of Moussa's, Aboul Fotouh's, or Sabahi's campaigns who wanted to keep their image and avoid resorting to staff of the NDP. At the same time, there was no guarantee for them that ex-NDP staff would be happy to work for them even if they were well paid. This explains why the rest of campaigns did not approach professionals who already had experience of field co-ordinator work.

4.1.1.3 Other Positions

Other positions in the campaign, including the campaign treasurer and cabinet, were present in all campaigns as explained in the previous chapter. Their roles were roughly the same, and their performance was determined by other factors such as the candidate himself, the candidates' personal relations, and laws organising the campaigning process, as explained in previous chapters. The only clear difference in role would be for the media department in Moussa's campaign which was given to a media and PR company. The same can also be said of Aboul Fotouh's campaign which gave the media a priority. This priority given by both campaigns to the media helped a lot—along with other factors—in framing their two candidates as the front runners. However, this did not have any effect on voting as was demonstrated by the election result where Morsi and Shafiq emerged as the two front runners.

The similarity in the rest of roles in the five campaigns made the field co-ordinator role (whatever its name was in each campaign) the most influential position, the position which played a significant role in determining the results of the election as it was the one securing the votes from the villages in the governorates. The professionalism of the field co-ordinator posts, mainly in Morsi's and Shafiq's campaigns, suggests that their role might have impacted the election results and helped Morsi and Shafiq to be the top candidates in the first round of elections, allowing them to compete again in the second round of elections. Unlike the rest of candidates, both Morsi's and Shafiq's campaigns resorted in general to professional staff who had previous experience mainly in parliamentary elections, which made them precede other campaigns in terms of professionalised staff with past experience in elections.

4.1.2   Management Style

The management style reflects 'the degree of centralisation of the campaign management in the hands of the leaders at the national level' (Tenscher et al. 2012; Tenscher 2013). It is argued that 'a more top-down internal structure and hierarchical culture' would make it easier for implementing the changes required for professionalisation (Gibson and Rommele 2001: 37; Norris 2000). Those responsible for decision making can urge the rest of the staff to adhere to their will and decisions in implementing professional techniques and strategies.

The importance of having a coherent internal structure—usually presented in an organisational chart—lies in its ability to improve operational efficiency by defining the roles and responsibilities of team members (Sullivan 2010) and in determining the workflow, decision making, and final responsibility. It also makes it easier to add new positions when needed (Ingram 2011). A good internal structure should ensure the adaptation of communications to guarantee efficient flows of information between various teams (Hill 2011).

The most common management styles are vertical and horizontal task divisions. In the vertical structure style—known as 'tall' companies—there is a manager at the top making decisions, delegating jobs and authority to lower-level managers (Huebsch 2010). As you move down the chain, at each level authority and responsibility decreases (Joseph 2017). According to this structure, information flow is either downwards or upward (Ostroff 1999). Its main advantage is that it is better in assigning tasks and generally easier to manage (Huebsch 2010). The vertical tasks' management, however, has major disadvantages such as the slow process of making decisions due to its bureaucratic shape (Ostroff 1999).

Alternatively, the horizontal flat management style is usually preferred, especially in new or small businesses due to its efficiency in the short term. Horizontal structures usually have fewer management levels, with each level responsible for a particular field (Griffin 2010). It usually ensures better employee morale and synergy as they are involved in decision making (Bass 2011). Decisions are taken within teams according to their specialisations or targets, and tasks are often completed more quickly and effectively. However, the main disadvantages tend to be that different teams tend to make decisions without paying attention to the probability of conflicting with other teams' goals … that is, without taking into consideration other aspects of the campaign. Further, specialised teams sometimes overestimate their roles in relation to other teams which may lead to serious mistakes. It could also lead to increased costs as each team may try to increase its budget at the cost of others, viewing its role as more important than other roles. This is why the horizontal management style is usually advisable only if the campaign has a strong campaign manager and a strong field co-ordinator (Maarek 2011), although it is most appealing due to its fast process of decision making (Ostroff 1999).

Despite the importance and necessity of deciding a management style, it would appear that the five studied campaigns did not pay much attention to which management style they needed to adopt. It looks like none of the campaigns decided beforehand which management style to follow. They only became developed through practice and within situations as they occurred and required decisions.

The campaign structure itself was not finalised until towards the end of the campaigning period. At the beginning of most of the campaigns, only the candidate with the campaign manager and a few members were involved in planning and decision making for the campaign. During the campaigning period, campaigns were adding teams and expanding their structures depending on the situation at the time. It would appear that most of the campaigns started with a vertical style, but the managerial tiers under the candidate or the campaign manager were not structured till towards the middle or the end of the campaign when all the teams were formed.

When asked about their organisational structure, most of the interviewees from the various campaigns could provide no clear answer. The question had to be simplified for most of them as to whether they had to get approval for decisions or whether they decided on their own and the relationship between different teams and with the campaign manager and candidate.

It appeared that most campaigns had two levels of internal management style. The first was a vertical management style between the campaign manager/candidate and heads of various departments/teams. The second was a horizontal management style, beneath the candidate, that is, between various departments/teams and inside each of the teams.

However, this horizontal style lacked co-ordination in some points as will be explained.

For Moussa's campaign, the main management style was horizontal as each team was working and taking decisions separately without the need to get approval from the candidate or campaign manager, except for strategic political decisions which had to have the input of the candidate himself and thus the importance of the second style of vertical management applied. The vertical management style was also applied between some of the teams in the governorates and their relative department in the head office. For example, the media team in the governorates would report vertically with the main media team in the head office.

However, this horizontal style led to some problems in Moussa's campaign, mainly with their marketing team. The marketing job was assigned to a professional marketing company very early on, earlier than the formation of all other teams inside the campaign. Neither the candidate nor the campaign manager interfered with their job. However, the output of their work was not up to standard and did not come into line with what other departments such as the PR and media departments were trying to do. For example, they printed the poster with a grey background, and Moussa was described by his opponents as a 'grey' person due to his job as a diplomat, and other teams in the campaign such as the PR and media teams had to work to counteract this.

For Aboul Fotouh's campaign, the campaign was a matrix where tasks between governorates and the central campaign used to intersect, with some overlapping between tasks. On the other hand, the main theme of the campaign was decentralisation, especially when it came to the relationship between the central campaign and the other branches in various governorates. For the campaign, decentralisation allowed the central campaign to focus more on accomplishing high-level objectives away from local day-to-day work.

For Sabahi's campaign, it differentiated between two levels: tasks related to the campaign itself, which were managed horizontally, and tasks and decisions related to the candidate were managed vertically, where they had to refer ideas to the candidate to be approved before being implemented. For example, a decision needed for campaign staff to go and campaign in a particular area—without the candidate present—would be taken horizontally, whereas a decision needed to involve the candidate in the activity—that is, going with the campaign staff to particular area—would be taken vertically.

Morsi's campaign did not develop a specific management style which was due to the 'tight timeframe', as explained by Yehia Hamed in a personal interview, although each team was specialised in its role and had certain tasks to manage horizontally. Each team within the campaign, or a member of the party, could go and fill any gap they found over the course of the campaign, which was probably done through the vertical style of management as someone would probably have had to decide who would go and fill which gap. The Muslim Brotherhood itself is a hierarchical organisation founded in 1928. It has an embedded centralised vertical management style, depending on a top-down chain of command and obedient members, which was clearly reflected in the way the campaign was working, taking into consideration that the campaign was formed almost at the last minute, which indicates that members of the campaign would still follow management in the way they were used to. This would suggest that at least major strategic decisions would be concentrated in the hand of its 'war room' (Scammell 1998) whether it was the campaign managers, or the Muslim Brotherhood Guidance Office, or the Freedom and Justice Party, or a 'war room' that included members from all the three bodies.

Shafiq's campaign did not differ a lot from Morsi's campaign. Although there was a horizontal management style at the management level beneath the candidate and campaign managers, the campaign had its own secret 'war room' that used to meet daily in various places and decide on the candidate and the campaign. There was a direct relationship between the war room and some team leaders to highlight what needed to be done. This was clear in the way Abdallah Kamal—secret campaign manager— would highlight items for the social media manager or meet and start commenting on candidates' performances on social media outlets, for example. There was also a direct relationship between the 'war room' and the governorates team (i.e. the field co-ordinator).

Despite general agreement within each campaign on the way they worked, the management style adopted was not strict as changes could happen, and the candidate or the campaign manager could intervene and change or oppose decisions taken by the campaign, such as the previously explained example of the debate: both Moussa's and Aboul Fotouh's campaigns refused the candidate's participation in the debate, but both candidates took the decision and participated. Apart from Morsi's and Shafiq's campaigns, it looks like the management style did not play an important role in the 2012 campaigns' structures. Disagreement or any conflicts that arose were dealt with collectively by discussion with the campaign manager and the candidate himself, if required. However, the involvement of Morsi's and Shafiq's 'war room' at various stages, with decisions taken in their campaigns, demonstrates the centralisation of power in the hands of this war room through a vertical, hierarchical top-down management style—despite the presence of the horizontal style as well—which suggests that they were able to push for the changes required for professionalisation without staff resisting, as at the end the candidates and their 'war rooms' had the upper hand.

The professionalisation index assesses the degree of centralisation of campaign organisation based on the degree of the centralisation of the campaign management in the hands of party leaders. The more centralised, the more professional it is. By applying the index, it appears that both the Morsi and Shafiq campaigns were the two most centralised campaigns, thus the more professionalised. On the contrary, Aboul Fotouh's campaign was the least professional as it was totally decentralised.

4.1.3   Campaign Premises

The campaigns' separate premises became an important feature of professionalised campaigns, which indicates the presence of a separate team to manage the campaign apart from the main parties' premises (Strömbäck 2009), usually known as the 'war room' (Scammell 1998) where the concentration of power (Lisi 2013) and decision making rests. This is why choosing campaign premises is a very important step towards building the campaign's infrastructure. They would have to accommodate individual staff members from varied backgrounds, with differing skills and roles, who had never worked together before (Maarek 2011). A lot of attention should be paid to the headquarters as it has to ensure the co-ordination of messages and management of the campaign (Strömbäck 2007: 54), and it has to have responsibility for the whole overall strategy of the campaign (Gibson and Römmele 2001: 33). Therefore, it has to be designed to ensure maximum internal communication from one side, and from the other side it has to be open to the outside word to avoid rumours (Maarek 2011), false speculations, or general gossip by the media or the public. This is why the premises—mainly the headquarters—should be located in a central location for easy access and a relatively short distance from TV channels and other political parties, along with being easy to access for volunteers and the public as well.

The campaign premises give credibility to the campaign and give proof to the public that the campaign cares about them. For example, if the campaign opened a branch in a village or governorate, it would give an indication to those living there that the campaign cares about them, in comparison to a campaign that did not open places there. It also gives a privilege to the campaign as it allows it to know its actual presence in this area; are voters aware of their presence and of their candidate, do they visit the premise, and how they interact with the campaigns' activities in the area? The local premises also help the campaign to know the problems facing the people living in this place and what issues will make them support the candidate. All this information could be communicated back to the central campaign and help in amending or designing a more targeted message to these voters.

A well-designed headquarters helps in creating the image of the candidate. Does it look like a presidential office or is it a chaotic place that doesn't reflect the image of a president?

The premises make the campaign more accessible to the public as well. It could encourage citizen participation or engagement with the campaign. People may be reluctant to visit and engage in a campaign, even if they support the candidate, if, for example, they had to travel or pay extra for transportation to get to the campaign premises.

For the headquarters of the central campaigns, all five campaigns managed to have a central office near the city centre, which is almost equidistant from the locations of Egyptian TV, media TV centres, local newspapers, parliament, and Tahrir Square. The locations of the premises were well served by public transportation as well. The main difference perhaps was in internal design. Moussa's campaign was very keen on making the premises appear as a presidential office. As explained before, they were keen to have separate and well-equipped offices for journalists, and a photo booth for any photos that would be taken for the campaign. This is in contrast to other campaigns who were not interested in these details.

For campaign branches in other governorates, it varied from one campaign to another. Opening campaign branches was an easy task for Morsi's campaign as it had all the offices of the Freedom and Justice Party, alongside any other offices the Muslim Brotherhood owned that were opened to campaign for the candidate. The rest of the campaigns had to start from scratch and choose strategic places in the governorates and rent them or take the places that volunteers or supporters gave them. Sabahi's campaign was helped by some parties such as the Nasserist Party with some of its offices in the governorates. Other than this, it was mainly volunteers giving them places that could be a whole flat, shop, balcony, or a room in a flat.

Thus in terms of the campaign premises, there was no difference between campaigns with regard to the presence of a main central headquarters. The differences only appeared in the relative importance of the headquarters. Shafiq campaign, for example, had its main headquarters which was thought to be their war room, but they left it for volunteers and media and they used to have their meetings in other places, especially towards the end of the campaign. The same would apply for Morsi's campaign as the concentration of power and decision making was not limited only to the campaign headquarters, as there were additional 'war rooms' in the Freedom and Justice Party, known as the political arm of the Muslim Brotherhood group, and in the Muslim Brotherhood guidance office as well. Another difference would be the internal design of the headquarters which Moussa's campaign was keen on, unlike other campaigns.

In terms of the campaigns' premises in the governorates, it appears that Morsi's campaign excelled other campaigns in this aspect. This is due to the organisational back up it had from both the party and the Muslim Brotherhood group. Other campaigns tried to overcome Morsi's advantage by accepting places offered by volunteers, which showed public support and engagement, but at the same time showed the lack of resources they had.

4.1.4   Degree of Externalisation

The degree of externalisation refers to the 'number of temporary dedicated agencies and political consultants and experts occupied with election campaign jobs' (Tenscher et al. 2012: 17). In the age of professionalisation, election campaigns became more dependent on professional experts and consultants (Strömbäck 2008), making 'no room for amateurs' (Johnson 2001). Whether they are paid or not, they add credibility to the campaign and add to the morale of the staff as it gives the impression that everything is under control (Maarek 2011). The reliance on professional experts led the campaign to enter the postmodern phase (Norris 2000). Many campaigns not only hire external professionals but also increase the professionalisation of its own staff (Esser and Strömbäck 2012).

The need for professional consultancies was one of the main themes of the 2012 Egyptian presidential campaigns. It only differed over whether these professional consultancies were already part of the campaign staff or part of the volunteers working in it, or whether the campaign had to resort to additional consultancies from outside the campaign, and whether they had previous experience in campaigning. For Morsi's campaign, the party and the campaign already had their consultancies and professionals in almost every field. The campaign also had an affiliated public opinion polling centre and an affiliated media company. It also had its own experts who helped in writing the election programme. Thus, the need for full-time additional external experts was limited.

For Shafiq's campaign, which did not have an official party behind it, it resorted to experts and professionals on two levels. The first level was hiring them as a part of the campaign staff. The second was resorting to experts who were not members of the campaign. On the campaign staff level, the campaign resorted to field co-ordinators from the dissolved NDP to become part of the campaign and help them with the governorates. It resorted to professional journalists, a professional social media team, and a professional media company who were all part of the campaign. From outside the campaign's full-time staff, the campaign resorted to around 20 experts to help in writing the candidate's vision.

For Aboul Fotouh's campaign, the campaign resorted to experts from outside the campaign mainly to help with technical issues in establishing the call centre, an event and marketing company, public opinion polls, and public speaking skills. Other specialisations were provided from within the campaign's staff such as the advisory board which helped in writing the programme, the media, and the marketing committee which all involved professionals.

For Amr Moussa's campaign, the majority of the expertise needed was hired as part of the campaign as well as the media and PR company which was responsible for the media committee in the campaign, or the advertisement team which was another company, or the IT team which mainly specialised in technical and IT issues. This, along with the advisory board, acted as the candidate cabinet and helped in writing the programmes. The campaign resorted to external experts mainly in getting some research undertaken and analysing data, besides resorting to volunteers, mainly friends in the media or diplomats, to help them reach the voters abroad.

For Sabahi's campaign, the campaign managed to have all the necessary experts as volunteers in the campaign, to the extent that they did not have to pay for advertisements, for example, as explained in previous chapter.

They only resorted to a social media company to help them with technical issues and an accounting company to help them with the financial issues.

From the above, the two campaigns that proved keenest to hire external full-time professionals were Shafiq's and Moussa's campaigns. They were keen on having full-time experts as part of their campaign staff. Each was responsible for their team or task. This action proved to be important as the campaign was guaranteed full loyalty by those they employed. Freelance or part-time consultancies can work with various campaigns at the same time, which was shown to have happened in this election. During the author's interviews with campaign staff for the sake of this study, it became evident that some experts, mainly academics and researchers, worked for more than one campaign at the same time, for example, in providing them with research or data. The campaigns were not aware of this during the time of elections. This is why hiring experts as part of the official campaign staff might have been a better option in the Egyptian case, as even if the expert tried to work in another campaign at the same time, both campaigns would know about it which would ruin his reputation.

For Morsi's campaign, although the campaign sourced all its experts and professionals from the party and the Muslim Brotherhood, it may well be that the campaign was self-contained enough and did not need outsiders to be involved. It also prevented outsiders knowing its secrets, which could perhaps be published later in the media. Trust and confidentiality were among the main themes controlling the way Morsi's campaign worked. This was made clear to the author in the reluctance in answering some of the questions asked during the interviews, which other campaigns replied to openly. Although all campaigns resorted to professional experts—whether they acted as volunteers or they had full-time jobs or part-time jobs—the main difference was those professionals' past experience in the campaign and election field. In terms of this political experience, both Morsi's and Shafiq's campaigns were ahead of the rest of the campaigns, which had professionals, but, on the whole, it was the first time for them working in a nationwide election campaign. Based on this, the degree of externalisation of Morsi's and Shafiq's campaigns was better than the rest of the campaigns.

4.1.5   Internal Campaign Communication Structures

Effective communication inside a campaign is vital to ensure the campaign's targets are met and decisions are well understood and implemented. Effective communication ensures synergy and good relations between the campaign's teams. However, the term 'internal communication structures' does not refer to the reliance on traditional means of communication that prevailed in almost all the five studied campaigns. According to Tenscher (2013: 254), the term refers to 'the existence and the use of "new" communication media for internal campaign communication and the mobilisation of party members'.

Although all the campaigns were keen on maintaining effective communication, or in other words avoiding miscommunication between staff internally, this was done mainly through traditional means of communication such as daily face-to-face meetings in all central campaigns, along with mobile phone calls throughout the day. The use of emails was limited to sharing big files, data, or brochures.

In each of the governorates, there were also daily meetings or phone calls between staff. The communication between the central campaigns and governorates differed from one campaign to another.

Shafiq's campaign established daily communication waves between the central campaign and the governorates. Morsi's campaign did not have a fixed system for communication between the central campaign and the branches in the governorates. It used to depend upon the situation. Moussa's campaign had daily phone calls between their field co-ordinator and the governorates and emails from the central media team and equivalent media teams in governorates.

Aboul Fotouh's campaign used phone calls as well and emails to send brochures and campaign materials for governorate offices to print. For Sabahi's campaign, the main methods of communication with the governorates were daily phone calls and bringing in those working in the governorates each month for a face-to-face meeting at the central campaign.

Thus, internal communication was almost the same within the different campaigns, as they all depended on traditional mediums as the main means of communication. The only differences would be for Moussa's campaign, which managed to use a bigger variety of methods than other campaigns, such as walkie-talkies, or WhatsApp, or three different sim cards with the three different telecommunication companies. A second difference would be for Shafiq and the communication waves with the governorates. This would make Moussa's campaign the most professionalised campaign in terms of the internal communication structure implemented. After it comes Shafiq's campaign due to establishing the daily 'communication wave'. There was not a noticeable difference between Aboul Fotouh's and Morsi's campaigns in this regard. Although Sabahi's campaign did not use techniques that were consistent with the professionalisation index, it employed other ways and techniques to maximise its chances. The campaign did not use 'new' communication mediums. On the contrary, it used to bring in the staff in governorates for a monthly face-to-face meeting at the central campaign headquarters. This was very understandable as it was suitable for its targeted audience. However, due to the resource gap, Sabahi's campaign was not able to challenge his rivals. In other words, in the case of Sabahi, following the Tenscher index by using new communication means might have led to miscommunication inside the campaign. This highlights another aspect of professionalism which is trying to perform better depending on the resources available. This might not be the most professional, but in a way, it is still professional especially if they are unable to achieve the same as those with more resources.

4.1.6   Feedback

Feedback is essential for any campaign and any message it delivers. Feedback allows the campaign to alter or change its message, tactics, or strategies. It also allows the campaign to know about its actual presence on the street, that is, what the public—mainly voters—thinks about the candidate, whether they support him or not and whether they are likely to vote for the candidate. Feedback can be assessed by several means such as from public opinion polls and focus groups that allows the campaign to learn about 'voters' sentiments' and feedback from media monitoring that allows the campaign to learn about the 'journalists' sentiments' (Esser and Strömbäck 2012: 299).

In the case of Egypt, due to a lack of data and lack of efficient accurate public opinion polls,[5] there was a lack of accurate data which the campaigns could have built upon. This was mainly the case for Moussa's and Aboul Fotouh's campaigns. Other campaigns tried to find a way of getting feedback from other sources.

Morsi's campaign did not have the same problem that faced other campaigns in getting feedback as the Muslim Brotherhood already had its own affiliated centre that conducted public opinion polls, which was, according to Yehia Hamed, an accurate way of getting the feedback the campaign needed.

For Shafiq's campaign, it depended mainly on its five thousand representatives in the governorates to get them the required feedback. There are no details on how those representatives used to get the feedback, but it was mainly through their observations, not properly conducted public opinion polls. It also depended on its social media team who used a 'Tweet deck' programme in following everything said about Shafiq on Twitter. The main problem facing Moussa's and Aboul Fotouh's campaigns was that they were depending heavily on the data available in the media and on public opinion polls that were proven not to be accurate. Aboul Fotouh's campaign tried to develop a way to get its own feedback by resorting to the business sector but the project failed.

For Sabahi's campaign, they did not depend on public opinion polls. Their past experience in the political field made them aware that polls would not necessarily be accurate. According to Hossam Moeness, there was no guarantee that they would not be biased, or that the sample would be representative, or that those working on it would be too lazy to get a representative sample. Instead Sabahi's campaign used to depend on observation by participation, where the campaign staff would go into a coffee shop and open a discussion with those sitting there about the presidential candidates without saying that they were from Sabahi's campaign or go to coffee shops and open places when Sabahi was on the television and listen to what the public was saying. Again, while Sabahi's campaign did not stick to the index on how to get its feedback, it was more innovative than other campaigns such as Moussa's and Aboul Fotouh's. The latter depended on media and public opinion polls, but Sabahi was better in finding new ways—not covered by the index—amid a shortage of resources, in order to maximise his chances.

In the professionalisation index applied as a framework to this study, Tenscher (2013: 254) assesses feedback mainly through two methods which are '(a) commissioned or independently conducted opinion polls and (b) focus group analysis'. By applying these two methods to the five studied campaigns, it became clear that only Morsi's campaign had a professional way of measuring feedback as it had its own affiliated centre to measure feedback scientifically. Other campaigns had their own methods which did not include commissioning opinion polls or conducting focus group analysis.

4.1.7 Opposition Research

Opposition research is considered to be fulfilled if the campaign has a dedicated unit to conduct regular and frequent research into the opposing campaigns, both before and during the election campaign. The result of this research should be distributed and integrated later to the rest of the campaign by giving it back to relevant departments which will help in amending their strategies (Gibson and Rommele 2009; Tenscher et al. 2012)

In the 2012 Egyptian campaigns, each campaign developed its own internal way of conducting research on their opponents' candidates. In the interviewing process, all campaigns—except Morsi's campaign—highlighted that they did not need to conduct background research or research on the candidates' previous positions. This was because, for all of the candidates and their campaigns, these positions were already clear in the minds of the campaign's staff and the candidate. The campaigns were more interested in monitoring other campaigns and what other campaigns and candidates were doing during the campaigning period.

Again, Morsi's campaign surpassed other campaigns in this regard as well as they had a unit dedicated to monitoring other campaigns.

For Shafiq's campaign, they did not have a separate unit for opposition research. They depended on their five thousand representatives in the governorates, their secret campaign manager himself, what was written on social media, along with what was given to them by other departments.

For Moussa, Aboul Fotouh, and Sabahi, they did not have a separate unit to monitor other campaigns. They mainly depended on media reports conducted by their media units, along with other information that would come by now and then from the teams in the governorates or other departments in the campaign.

However, it looks like there were weaknesses in the opposition research in Shafiq, Moussa, Aboul Fotouh, and Sabahi's campaigns, as none of them were able to discover and exploit the contradictions in Morsi's speech during the time of elections, such as the 'Qassas' (retribution) and NASA examples elaborated on in previous chapters.

In terms of the professionalisation index, the degree of opposition research should assess if the campaign developed an independent structure to monitor its political opponents (Tensher et al. 2012; Tescher 2013a, b). By applying the index, it appears that only Morsi's campaign was professionalised in terms of having a separate body to monitor its political opponents, that is, Morsi's campaign exceeded other campaigns in terms of the opposition research.

4.1.8   Campaign Duration

The presidential election law determined the campaigning period to be from only three weeks before the actual date of the election, until two days before the election's first round. In the second round, it would start a day after announcing the result of the first round and end a day before voting starts for the second round. This was implemented by the High Elections Committee ruling Number 10, deciding the dates for the first round to be from 30 April to 21 May. The second round would be from the second day of announcing the results until midday on 15 June.

Many political forces saw the three-week period as insufficient. This led the People's Assembly (the lower parliamentary house) to amend the law on 7 May, making the campaigning period start from the first day of opening the door for nominations till the date of the elections, even cancelling the period of silence prior to voting. This was dismissed by the Supreme Constitutional Court, which insisting on starting the actual campaigning period after nominations were accepted formally, and further insisted on the period of silence as it was a right for voters to have time to think over their preferred candidates and to compare them without being subject to influence or pressure from the candidates (Rabeea 2013).

For all the campaigns, except Morsi and Shafiq, the campaign duration lasted for more than a year, as they had announced their decisions earlier than both Morsi and Shafiq, whose announcements of their decisions to run came at the last minute.

According to the professionalisation index, the longer the overall duration of the campaign is, the more professionalised it is. The overall campaign duration includes preparation, planning, and implementation of the campaign until the Election Day (Tenscher et al. 2012; Tenscher 2013). This would mean that Moussa's, Aboul Fotouh's and Sabahi's campaigns were more professionalised in terms of the relatively long period of campaigning they enjoyed.

However, this long campaigning period highlighted contradicting views from the campaign staff interviewed. The dilemma for both Moussa and Aboul Fotouh was that the longer campaign time gave an opportunity for opponents, media, and even the public to have enough time to research the candidates' weak points and attack them. This is unlike short campaigning periods, as no one has enough time to research and attack the candidates. On the other hand, the short period of campaigning would not allow the candidate to be well-known enough to the public.

The long period of campaigning led the candidates' campaigns to be impacted by the political polarisation that took place during the campaign year, such as the rule of law versus the rule of the Revolution, constitution first or election firsts, the Law on the Exercise of Political Rights, and other issues explained in previous chapters, which led to an increase in the polarisation of society and affected the candidates as well. Any stance the candidate took, even if this stance was not to have a stance, would be used against them, or gaining supporters for one side would mean a loss of supporters for the other side. Thus the long campaign created greater challenges for the campaigns.

The debate around the duration of campaigning highlights concerns about whether it is applicable in the Egyptian case—mainly in the 2012 presidential elections campaign—to say that the longer duration the campaign, the more professional it is, as it appeared that the shorter duration was better for both Morsi and Shafiq. On the contrary, the longer duration was detrimental to both Moussa and Aboul Fotouh. Yet it is too early to generalise, as the duration is not the only factor that indicates whether the campaign is professional or not or if the model applies fully; other factors highlighted in the professionalisation index should be taken into consideration as well.

4.1.9   Campaign Budget

The election law regulated the amount of spending and donations for each campaign. The spending limit was ten million Egyptian pounds (approximately around one million GDP[6]) for each candidate in the first round and two million Egyptian pounds (around 200 thousands GDP) in the second round. There were also some restrictions, such as that every candidate should open a bank account for cash donations in one of the banks agreed upon by the committee. Donations were to only be from Egyptians, and donations could not exceed 200 thousand Egyptian pounds (around 20 thousands GDP) from one individual. Despite these regulations, there was no actual way of monitoring or punishing those who exceeded these limits.

There was also no accurate way in this research to verify the budget or money spent by each candidate. Media reports estimated that 100 million Egyptian pounds were spent during the elections. Other estimations suggested that some candidates spent more than four times the amount before the start of the official campaigning period, such as Hazem Salah Abu Ismail, who was dismissed from the presidential race as his mother was proven to be American and who had printed 10 million posters at a printing house. This estimation is based on the fact that the cost of one poster was four Egyptian pounds at that time. Thus, the total cost of the printed posters was 40 million, in addition to his other forms of campaigning which meant even more spending (Ezzabawy 2013).

For the five studied campaigns, especially those campaigns that started early, such as Aboul Fotouh, Moussa, and Sabahi, the delay in issuing rules for budget and spending regulations till towards the start of the campaign period led to a state of confusion and uncertainty and issues with regard to planning. The campaigns were not able to start fundraising or to plan ahead with regard to spending. To overcome this situation, all campaigns resorted to in-kind contributions rather than cash, especially at the beginning. Cash was used on advertisements and other forms of campaigning, which the High Elections Committee could easily know about and verify from other governmental sources and reports.

The issue of the budgets witnessed many rumours and uncertainties, with media reports suggesting that Shafiq was taking money from the United Arab Emirates, since it is against the Muslim Brotherhood. Other reports were about Morsi taking money from both Qatar and the United States as explained in previous chapters.

Rumours also faced some of the candidates who refused to publish their financial disclosure reports to the public, although they were submitted to the HEC. For example, both Moussa and Shafiq refused to publish them to the public, saying that issues like their salaries and financial situations should remain confidential. This led to a large amount of rumours against them.

Despite all this, the financial documents submitted to the HEC did not exceed the limit. However, at the same time, during the interviews with campaign staff, members from all campaigns stated that if the in-kind contributions had been calculated into the budget, this would mean that the total amount spent on campaigning would have exceeded the maximum limit permitted by the HEC. Thus, only the bills paid by the campaign itself, and not its supporters, were documented in the financial reports, and not the actual costs.

The professionalisation index evaluates the professionalisation of the election budget based on the election campaign expenditures of each candidate's campaign per eligible voter (Tenscher et al. 2012, Tenscher 2013). By applying the limit set by the election law on the number of eligible voters which was 50,996,746[7] voters would mean that the campaign expenditures are 20 piasters (around 2 pence) per eligible voter, which is very low. However, it is very difficult to assess or know the actual expenditure of each campaign due to the complexity and sensitivity of the issue. Officially, all campaigns adhered to the official limits, as reported in the figures they submitted to the HEC. Only Sabahi's campaign says that it did not reach the ten million maximum limits decided by the law—without calculating the in-kind contributions. All campaigns expressed—informally—that if they calculated the in-kind contributions, they would have exceeded the maximum limit. This research was not able to verify the actual budget for each campaign.

4.1.10   Which Structure Was More Professionalised?

From the above overview, it appears that the structure of Morsi's campaign was the most professionalised structure. This was due to their past history in campaigning in Egypt, the expertise of its staff, mainly their expertise in the governorates (field co-ordinator position), their centralised management style, the widespread nature of their premises due to the use of their already available party premises and finally the presence of separate units for feedback and opposition research. The second most professionalised structure was implemented by Shafiq's campaign. This was also due to their past history of campaigning in Egypt, the expertise of its staff mainly their expertise in the governorates (field co-ordinator position), their centralised management style, their externalisation in terms of hiring external professionals, and their ways of getting feedback and opposition research, although not having separate units set up for these functions.

The result that Morsi's structure was the most professionalised is almost the same result that Tenscher et al. (2012: 155) reached while studying the professionalisation of election campaigns in four EU countries. Tenscher et al. (2012: 155) concluded that the campaign structures of big parties were more professionalised. This result can explain why Morsi's campaign structure was more professional than other campaigns, as it already had the required funds, resources, and people who are available to big established parties in most developed democracies, which was not the case with other campaigns. Moreover, Tenscher (2013: 249) concludes that smaller political parties will try their best to compensate for the structural disadvantages they have by being more innovative in strategic development. But was this applicable in the Egyptian case? The next section will try to answer this question by analysing the strategies (software) of the five studied campaigns according to the professionalisation index.

4.2   CAMPAIGN STRATEGIES

Determining an effective strategy is essential for any campaign (Lees-Marshment 2001; Burton and Shea 2015; Sides et al. 2012). A good strategy should help determine what the campaign will look like: What is the main theme of the campaign? What methods and tactics will the campaign utilise in order to achieve its goals? And how will the campaigns make full use of the limited resources they have while maximising the return? The strategy should also guide the campaign staff on what to do at each stage of the campaign, especially when situations change. A good campaign strategy should also be coherent, meaning that any decision taken should be correlated with the campaign's other decisions (Maarek 2011). It should also be suitable to and understandable by the candidate and their staff who put it into practice (Burton and Shea 2015)

This section will analyse campaigns' strategies based on the professionalisation index which reflects the main indicators according to which the campaign's strategy can be considered 'professional'. The more the strategy demonstrates the presence of these indicators, the more professional it is. These indicators are summarised by Tenscher (2013: 246) as follows: (a) efforts to influence the media's agenda and shaping public opinion, (b) focusing on free media channels, mainly TV including talk shows, (c) the use of paid media such as paid advertisement, (d) segmentation of voters into target groups to be contacted by narrowcasting and micro-targeting, and (e) focusing on the candidate through personalisation. In studying the five Egyptian campaigns, these indicators are reflected in the following eight criteria, which will be discussed in details in the following section: targeting, narrowcasting activities, free media, paid media, debates, internet and social media, campaign activities, and the degree of personalisation.

A first step in determining a good strategy is to know who your target audience is. This would help in determining the campaigns' tactics and means of communication in reaching and influencing this targeted audience or type of voter, as follows:

4.2.1   Targeting

Voter targeting reflects the number of segmented targeted groups that the campaign identifies in order to contact and mobilise (Tescher 2013a, b: 255). The idea behind the segmentation of voters, as Burton and Shea (2015: 106) explain, is to divide the voters according to other common characteristics rather than the traditional ones such as age, sex, or demographical locations, thus concentrating campaign efforts by GOTV activities (Gerber and Green 2008) on them, more than the rest of voters, in order to maximise the votes that the campaign requires to win the election.

In general, both the candidates and the campaigns are faced by two major challenges. The first is to admit that they will not appeal to every voter and that all voters will not be flexible enough to give the campaign a chance to convince them of their candidate. This is especially the case if the voters have already pre-decided who they will vote for due, for example, to party loyalty. Thus there is a need to divide voters into segments. The second challenge is to be able to locate and find those voters who may vote for the candidate or at least could be influenced by the campaign's activities and who may become convinced and vote for the candidate. From this comes the need for the segmentation of voters, whose main goal was to comprehend each voter's needs in order to communicate with them successfully (Cwalina et al. 2011: 81).

A campaign can divide voters according to four ways. Cwalina et al. (2011) differentiate between two levels of voter segmentation: primary and secondary. Primary segmentation divides voters according to two main criteria which are party identification and voter strength, which assesses the voters' level of attachment to a party. The second level of segmentation divides voters according to geographic, demographic, behavioural, and psychographic segments.

A third way of segmenting voters is to divide them into decided and undecided voters, who can be divided into campaigning-period deciders or last-minute deciders (Chaffe and Rimal 1996). However, with the difficulty of reaching voters and thus dividing them, a fourth way of segmentation could be via primary and secondary targets. Primary targets could be to identify people to act as 'opinion relays' and convince them of the candidate so that they can convince other voters in turn. Secondary targets include targeting the voters through one of the criteria mentioned above (Maarek 2011).

In order to be able to divide voters into segments, there is a need for information about the voters. In most countries, there are many sources that gather information about voters, such as voter databases, general census records, results of previous elections, and lists of union members or other associations (Maarek 2011).

The level of available data, however, differs from one country to another. In some countries, such as Egypt, personal data on a nationwide level is not published or given to candidates, as it is considered a matter of national security or for the sake of protecting individual privacy. The main problem that faced all the campaigns, except Morsi and Shafiq's, was that the voter databases were not available to their campaigns. According to Hossam Moeness, Sabahi's campaign manager, the voter databases were only allowed for candidates in the parliamentary elections, as each candidate can ask for the voter database for his or her constituency. However, this was not allowed in the presidential elections, so as not to give out personal data about all the voters in the country to one person or candidate (Moeness 2016). Nonetheless, although all the candidates should not have access (theoretically) to voter databases, Morsi's campaign had the database of each separate constituency, as they had candidates in the parliamentary elections that took place that same year. The same applied to Shafiq's campaign, as it had the voter databases from previous elections prior to the revolution from their field co-ordinator (Moeness 2016).

Amid this absence of data, and the unequal access thereto, each campaign tried its best to identify and divide their targeted voters through a mixture of the four ways mentioned above. The most commonly targeted audience among all of them was what is known as the 'sofa party', despite small differences in the groupings that come under the definition of 'sofa party', which were explained in previous chapters. This indicates the undecided voters that are not affiliated to a specific party, in this case one that was not affiliated to Islamists, the old regime, or the revolutionaries.

For Morsi's campaign, in the first round of elections, the campaign's main targeted voters were the Islamists. In the second round, the campaign extended its targeted voters to include revolutionaries and the 'sofa party'.

Regarding Shafiq's campaign, the targeted voters did not differ from the first to second round of elections. The campaign mainly concentrated on targeting conservative voters in society, those who were against the Muslim Brotherhood and the 'sofa party', which the campaign divided into the subcategories mentioned in previous chapters.

Moussa's campaign mainly targeted the 'sofa party' and divided it into subcategories. They did not target other segments, although they sent them some campaign messages. This proved to be the wrong choice, as they did not try to secure a solid base in the same way as other candidates, especially given that the sofa party is a very loose term that involves too many people with different backgrounds whose main common interest is that they are not interested in politics or do not take actions.

Aboul Fotouh's campaign used the parliamentary election results to decide upon 19 governorates, thus targeting voters according to geographical and behavioural categories. In the beginning, this segmentation included the Islamist voters, revolutionary voters, and the 'sofa party'. However, after the Muslim Brotherhood's announcement to nominate Al-Shater and then Morsi, the campaign only concentrated on revolutionary voters and the 'sofa party' in the 19 governorates it chose.

Sabahi's campaign targeted youths in the cities that witnessed the revolution, using the geographical and demographical criteria available.

A common comment made by all campaigns, except Morsi and Shafiq's, was that the undecided voters, or the 'sofa party', were not necessarily active or paid much attention to politics, nor were they ready to take political decisions. This was clear in what Khalaf (2016) told the author: that targeted voters were attending events largely 'out of curiosity' but would not actually go out and vote. This was confirmed by Aboul Gheit (2016),[8] who mentioned that when they went to a village and convinced voters to vote for them, after a couple of weeks another candidate would go and the same voters would tell the second candidate the same thing: that they would vote for him instead.

Perhaps this may be explained by the timing of exposure to the candidate's message and the time the voters would take to make their final decision (Chaffee and Choe 1980). This means that the candidate should have visited those undecided voters or presented his message to them at a time nearer to the election when they would be most likely make their decisions or by returning to reinforce their message, as well as employing 'get out the vote' tactics. The power of GOTV is not about reminding voters of election dates by pre-recorded messages and leaflets but by personalising the importance of their vote, going back to voters who initially showed interest, or by just being around as many non-voters will vote if they think that they are being watched since the decision to vote is shaped to a great extent by one's social environment (Gerber and Green 2008).

From the above, it appears that the most professionalised campaigns in terms of targeting their voters were Morsi's and Shafiq's campaigns. This was mainly due to the fact that they had voter registration lists from previous elections, in addition to a base of loyal supporters. Add to this a professional field co-ordinator who knows how to reach these targeted segments, and all these factors helped them to identify and segment their voters and more importantly to be able to reach them. This was not the case with other campaigns that chose a vague, widely targeted group which other campaigns were competing for as well, besides not being able to reach them effectively.

4.2.2   Narrowcasting Activities

Narrowcasting became an essential feature of postmodern campaigns. In pre-modern campaigns, campaign managers were described as 'mobilisers', as 'broadcasters' in modern campaigns, then as 'narrowcasters' in postmodern campaigns (Esser and Strömbäck 2012). Unlike broadcasting, which means delivering messages to the masses, narrowcasting means delivering information or messages to a narrow group within the public. Essentially, in an election campaign, narrowcasting means delivering a campaign message to a segment of targeted voters, and not all the voters. A campaign may need to send specific messages to a certain segment of voters who have different interests and fears. The reason a campaign may resort to narrowcasting could be to gain the support of a certain segment of voters by making them some promises or that the candidate would appeal most specifically to one target group. The campaign may also resort to narrowcasting to send messages to some segments among the voters who are not the campaign's targeted voters, just to reassure them or perhaps even to frighten them. Narrowcasting can be done through various means of communication, such as face-to-face communication or through mass media outlets, such as specialist mass media outlets that target specific audiences or specialised programmes in general outlets. In Egypt, for example, there are television channels and programmes that target women, youths, Muslims, or Christians.

Aboul Fotouh's campaign did not carry out narrowcasting but rather targeted the middle class, youth, and conservative voters throughout the campaign's messages. Both Sabahi and Moussa carried out narrowcasting towards certain groups, either by face-to-face meetings whose content was published in media outlets and included no targeted promises or in special television programmes or on channels that target certain audiences. Most of the promises given to them were from the candidates' programmes. Sabahi held some closed meetings with workers whose factories were closed because of the revolution, or farmers, or university students. Moussa's campaign did the same with groups such as those working in the communication sectors, union members, or disabled people. However, the content of such meetings was all published in the media after the event.

For both Morsi and Shafiq's campaigns, they did the same but there was also some face-to-face narrowcasting that was not published in the media and that involved secret promises or secret reassurances to certain groups. As explained in the previous chapter, Shafiq's campaign, for example, gave some indirect promises to certain groups. For Morsi, the campaign did not speak about secret promises, but it is believed that Islamist groups were promised special posts in the event of Morsi winning. This is due to his choosing more than half of the committee that was responsible for drafting the Egyptian Constitution in 2012 from among Islamist groups (Al-Arabiya 29/11/2012), besides appointing many members of the Freedom and Justice Party in governmental posts after being elected.

The professionalisation index assesses the degree of narrowcasting according to the number of activities aimed at the target group through various direct communications (Tenscher et al. 2012). By applying the index, it appears that all campaigns—except Aboul Fotouh—resorted to narrowcasting. However, messages that were narrowcasted in both Moussa's and Sabahi's campaigns were usually reinforced by being broadcast later to wider voters, either by the campaign itself or by the media. This was unlike Morsi's and Shafiq's campaigns where narrowcasting was not transformed to broadcasting later, apparently so as not to lose votes from one section of the electorate while securing the votes of another due to the controversies of their narrowcasted messages. In terms of which campaign was more professionalised in resorting to narrowcasting activities, it was difficult to assess objectively because of the unavailability of all the messages that were narrowcasted and its importance. This was due to either the memory or the reluctance of the interviewees when asked about more details.

4.2.3 Free Media

Media play an important role in the campaign period, as they act as a vehicle for both the candidates and the campaigns to deliver their messages to the voters. Voters are unlikely to receive the information they need directly from the candidate, but from mass media (Gibson and Rommele 2001). Candidate participation in the media stabilises the agenda-setting media effects, as important or controversial news from the candidates or campaigns will always find its way into the media in most cases. In the 2012 Egyptian elections, campaign relations with the media were affected by three main factors: access to the media, media bias towards candidates, and the degree of a campaign's dependency on the media as a reflection of the final results.

4.2.3.1   Access to the Media

Towards the start of the official campaigning period, the main theme for election coverage was in the form of dedicated programmes designed to interview various candidates. Some of these programmes had a panel of experts to ask and discuss issues that they specialised in with the candidates. For example, an economics expert would ask the candidate about his economic policies, and so on. Other programmes had an audience within them. These types of programmes depended on interviewing each of the candidates in a separate episode. This meant that candidates had equal access to these programmes, and the channels themselves did not want to appear biased. The problem of media access, however, was before the start of the official campaigning period, as most candidates started campaigning a year before the official starting date.

Both Moussa and Aboul Fotouh did not have a problem accessing the media. This was mainly due to their contact with those working in the media and at a later stage because of opinion polls that showed both Moussa and Aboul Fotouh as the top candidates. Hiring professionals to lead the campaigns' relations with the media was a successful decision as well. They managed to frame their candidates as front runners and create a mainstream belief—with the help of the polls—that their candidates were the two front runners, as explained in previous chapters. Moreover, there was a common belief among many journalists and intellectuals that Moussa's campaign was the most professionalised campaign. This was due to the professional way that his media department was dealing with them, being keen to frame his campaign in a professional way.

In contrast, Sabahi had a problem accessing the media. Although he was a journalist and had personal relationships with many journalists and presenters working in the field, he was seen by them as having no chance. Thus, he was not able to get the same attention from the media. Moreover, he sometimes had to appear in the media either at times he did not want or in an outlet he did not want, as he could not refuse due to his personal relations with those working in these outlets and risk upsetting them.

For Shafiq's campaign, his history with the media was not good, but he still had access to them. The media was interested in following up his stories, as for them he was a controversial character. On the other hand, there was a belief among the campaign's higher echelons that the media would not be the decisive factor in the result of the election and that what is said in the media does not necessarily reflect reality. For Morsi's campaign, he did not have a problem accessing the media early on due to joining the presidential race late.

4.2.3.2 Media Bias

Campaign messages can be subject to three types of media intervention: heavy intervention, medium intervention, or no intervention at all (Paletz 2002). In the 2012 elections, there was heavy journalistic intervention that exceeded the normal news coverage. The media played an important role in creating a common public perception that Moussa and Aboul Fotouh were the two front runners. The implication was that if there was going to be a second round of elections between two candidates, they would be Moussa and Aboul Fotouh. This explains why there was a state of shock when the actual results appeared showing that the second round would be between the two most polarising candidates: Shafiq and Morsi.

There is no clear evidence to suggest a reason for this bias. However, it might have been due to several combined factors, such as active media departments in both Moussa's and Aboul Fotouh's campaigns, personal relationships between both candidates or their campaigns' media departments with media personnel, the media depending heavily on opinion polls available at that time showing both candidates as the front runners, or the media trying to perform a gatekeeper role and support the two most moderate candidates: Moussa's with his reconciliatory speech and Aboul Fotouh with his consensual speech. This was in stark contrast to Shafiq and Morsi's polarising speeches.

4.2.3.3 Dependency on the Media as a Reflection of Voter Behaviour and Future Decisions

Both Aboul Fotouh's and Moussa's campaigns relied heavily on the media as an instrument to change voter behaviour and as a real reflection of their preferences and future voting patterns: the belief in a strong media effect and that media was a representation of what the public thought was an essential part of their campaign logic. This could be due to their lack of experience in elections and campaigning, the active media departments in both campaigns in contrast to their field co-ordinators, and finally, the lack of resources that made them depend on media as the primary method of communication and a main source of feedback as well. Academic studies on the role and effect of mass media during the 2012 Egyptian Presidential Elections are limited. They also depended on a limited sized sample, thus their findings cannot be generalised.[9] Phillips (2013) concluded that mass media have a significant effect on voters' final decisions during the elections, arguing that the sample's respondents who followed mass media during the elections were highly affected by them in shaping their voting decisions, unlike those who did not follow it and who disagree that it had a role. However, El-Khoreiby (2013) concluded that mass media had a limited effect on influencing a voter's decision to elect a specific candidate in the 2012 elections. Despite this, they were able to change some voters' attitudes towards candidates, as voters did not like the candidates' media performances. However, those who changed their electoral decision did not admit resorting to the media in taking information about the new candidate they voted for, and it did not affect their new decision either (El-Khoreiby 2013: 196–197). The difference in the findings between the two studies could be because of the limited samples they used. It could also be interpreted that respondents in favour of a media effect could have used media for reinforcement only, getting the required information and not necessarily changing their vote to correspond to media reports. However, for the sake of this study, the election's result supports the argument of this study that media did not have an effect on the election outcome as was expected by the campaigns of Moussa or Aboul Fotouh. They were not the two front runners despite media predictions.

The professionalisation index assesses the relevance of free media though the subjective opinion of the campaign manager regarding the importance of their candidate's presence on various free media outlets (Tenscher et al. 2012). The question was asked to campaign managers at the time of campaigns. Both Moussa's and Aboul Fotouh's campaigns invested heavily in gaining media coverage. Their investing in the media represented a clear theme of their campaign tactics and logic. Sabahi's campaign tried but he did not have the same access at the beginning of the campaigning period. Both Morsi's and Shafiq's campaigns did not see the media to be significant, especially when compared to their investment in the governorates. Thus in terms of professionalisation and the use of free media, Moussa's campaign was the most professional campaign in this regard. It hired a professional media and PR company to assure its media presence through several tactics as discussed in the previous chapter. The second most professionalised campaign was Aboul Fotouh's who hired a professional journalist to assure a media presence.

4.2.4   Paid Media

Paid media allows the campaigns to communicate their messages while guaranteeing that there will not be any sort of journalistic intervention (Esser and Strömbäck 2012). Paid media—usually known as advertisements—can be made through mass media channels such as TV, radio, the internet, newspapers, or in the form of campaign literature such as flyers, leaflets, brochures, billboard, posters, and similar means (Cwalina et al. 2011). Some studies argue that television advertising is the main method by which political campaigns communicate with their targeted voters (Wisconsin Advertising Project 2017). Despite the importance of advertising, there is no academic consensus on its influence on the final voting decision according to Cwalina et al. (2000) who compared the effects of candidates' advertisements in three countries. Their research differentiated between three types of influences of advertisements: (a) advertisements can reinforce already existing voting preferences, (b) advertisements can weaken or change already existing voting preferences, and (c) advertisements neither weaken nor reinforce existing voting preferences. This is mainly due to other factors such as the candidates themselves, or their advisors, or differences in the countries (Cwalina et al. 2011).

In Egypt, at this point, there is no scientific research to measure the influence of the 2012 campaigns' advertisements on voters' behaviour. During the campaigning period, the most used advertising methods were TV advertisements, billboards, and posters. All the five campaigns were keen on advertisements as a way for reaching the voters. Advertisements were mainly used to give more information about the candidate, or to reinforce the candidate's position and messages, or just to simplify the candidates' promises to the general public, or to make the slogan and name easy to remember. However, it did not seem that those working on the campaigns had a sincere belief that advertising can affect the voters' final decision. For them, it was one of the factors but not the main factor. As explained by most of the interviewees, advertising would play a role in voters' final decisions in areas where people do not access the internet, such as the governorates or in areas with high percentages of illiteracy. In other areas, such as the capital or among more educated classes, it was understood that advertising was bought by the campaign so could say what it wants to say without intervention, even if there was exaggeration. Conversely, the campaigns were keen on advertising as it gives impression of having money and resources. It also showed respect to the voters in terms of doing its homework and duty to reach them and not taking them for granted. It shows that they can deliver professional content and that they care about the voters and are taking campaigning as a serious matter. Further, they are differentiating their campaign from other campaigns that do not have any money or any resources at all which indicates that they don't have a base or supporters in the street or even people around the campaign who are willing to sponsor it. It also sets the subject or issue agenda for the public sphere.

Regarding the high cost of TV advertisements, most campaigns managed to broadcast their advertisements for free on television channels in return for the candidate appearing on the same channels. Some campaigns, like Aboul Fotouh's, made a deal to even publish a page or half-page advertisement in newspapers before the candidate appeared on their channel. Other campaigns, such as Sabahi's, already had professionals within their campaigns who produced their advertisements for free, following which the campaign later managed to also broadcast for free in return for the candidate's appearance on the channel.

These advertisements came in short documentary format showing the candidates' past and future plans and the type of endorsements the candidates received from the public, for example, Sabahi's endorsement by Khaled Said's mother (the icon of the revolution) or Shafiq's endorsement by the mothers and wives of policemen killed or wounded during the revolution. Shafiq also had another advertisement that compared him to Lula da Silva, the former president of Brazil. Morsi's supporters took this advertisement and put it on YouTube as if it was for Morsi. Morsi broadcast another advertisement of him receiving endorsements from ordinary citizens representing different groups and ages, each saying their reason for endorsing him. This included a Christian cleric although he did not appear giving his reason for endorsing Morsi, he appeared only in the background of general photos among others who appeared to support him.

Despite the importance of advertisements for Moussa's campaign, they were not successful due to problems with the marketing team, as discussed previously. Most of these advertisements had longer versions to be played on the internet and in the conferences. However, the campaign did not make other advertisements to replace those they did not like, apparently due to time and money constraints.

Thus, the use of paid media was almost the same for all the studied candidates, and its importance to the campaign managers was almost the same: each campaign used advertisements to reflect its candidate's positioning and send a message through the advertisement that addressed a target audience. The only difference, perhaps, in the paid media was the series of vague teaser billboards that was made by Shafiq's campaign, making them more noticeable than opponents' advertisements. Thus, according to the professionalisation index which assesses a campaign manager's subjective assessment of the use of paid media, it appears that the degree of professionalisation of the paid media was almost the same in all campaigns.

4.2.5   *Debates*

Although debates are essential parts of campaigning in western democracy, this was not the case with the Egyptian elections. In established democracies, debates are believed to give voters a chance to compare candidates' stances simultaneously. They also allow voters to see a candidate's on-the-spot reactions, unlike other formats where candidates would have already prepared answers for questions. Hence, debates attract more audiences than other formats, meaning a greater chance to deliver the campaign's message and a greater chance to alert or influence voter behaviour (Benoit 1999). Debates are believed to help candidates have equal access to the mass media (Coleman 2000). The influence of debates does not end after their broadcasting but extends as media analyses who the winner is, which may also affect voter attitudes (Maarek 2011).

Despite this importance, most candidates in the 2012 Egyptian election did not agree to participate in debates. As discussed in previous chapters, the debate was supposed to be conducted between the majority of candidates, who refused to appear as they did not see that it could help them to win. Only Moussa and Aboul Fotouh agreed to participate as they saw it as a chance for a form of campaigning in Egypt unseen before. On the other hand, Sabahi wanted to participate with top candidates but was not allowed by the media, which did not see him as a front runner (Moeness 2016).

The issue of debates highlighted how the three candidates, namely, Moussa, Aboul Fotouh, and Sabahi, wanted to engage in a practice that they saw as essential to democracy and encourage democratic behaviours and practices. This was unlike Morsi and Shafiq who would only conduct activities that they believed would help them gain more votes. At the same time, however, the conduct of the debate showed a lack of effective planning from both sides and perhaps a lack of understanding of the Egyptian voters (i.e. would the Egyptian voter be happy seeing future presidents attacking and fighting each other or would the Egyptian voter still see the president as a pharaoh or a strong man who cannot be attacked publicly?)

Despite some useful information highlighted in the content of the debate, which further highlighted the candidates' opinions and stances, some other factors influenced voter reception of the information. Voters only select information they find useful for them (Cwalina et al. 2011). This is why they selected the candidates' performances as represented in their fighting and attacking each other, and not the actual information or arguments both candidates were trying to convey to them in the debate.

For Moussa, it appeared that one of his main aims was to prove Aboul Fotouh's Islamist affiliations, which was something Aboul Fotouh was trying to hide. At the same time, Aboul Fotouh's aim was to highlight Moussa's relation to the old regime, something Moussa was denying. The result was an increased degree of attack by both sides, something Egyptians are not used to. This is why Sabahi's campaign believed that he would not have faced the same fate in the debate. For them, Sabahi's history is 'clean, and full of political and ethical struggles' (Moeness 2016). Thus, according to the campaign, 'he would not have faced the same fate' (Moeness 2016). However, this cannot be proved on a practical level, as Sabahi did not participate in the debate; and if he had participated, other candidates might have raised other concerns such as his work or his future plans for the country, if their plan was to attack him.

Ironically, it appeared that the sole beneficiary of this debate was Sabahi, as polls conducted after the debate showed a boost in his popularity, unlike Moussa's and Aboul Fotouh's who lost support. This result concurs with El-Khoreiby's (2013) conclusion that some voters changed their support for their chosen candidates because of the way they performed on TV and that they did not depend on media in making their second voting choice … in this case, choosing Sabahi.

Aside from the content of the debate, it would also appear that both Moussa's and Aboul Fotouh's campaigns did not pay attention to the debate's technical side, such as the way the candidate would stand, the décor, the director shots, and other such details. They did not seek the help of an independent director. Instead, they took their instructions from the channel's director. Many details were missing, one of which was toilet breaks, for example. Neither of the campaigns, nor the channel itself, considered that the two candidates' advanced years would necessitate a toilet break, meaning that they stood for more than six or seven hours without going to the toilet until this was highlighted during the advertisement breaks. Their campaigns used the advertisement breaks mainly to prepare for the other rounds of the debate.

Although the original professionalisation index (Tenscher et al. 2012) did not put debates as a separate indicator, they played an important role in determining the results of the 2012 elections, as it made both candidates who participated lose support from the electorate which is believed to have affected the result. Participation also showed the candidates were willing to adopt new techniques and methods which they believed were part of the professional campaign they were trying to conduct. Moreover, it shows their efforts in influencing the media's agenda and shaping public debate and highlights their use of the free media channels on which the debate was broadcast. All these reasons lead to adding debates as a separate criterion while studying the 2012 Egyptian campaigns. In terms of the professionalisation of the use of debates, Aboul Fotouh's and Moussa's campaigns were the most professionalised, but as explained, it did not help them to get more votes. On the contrary, participation in the debate made them lose support. This finding suggests the importance of previous experience in elections, as candidates and campaigns with previous experience in elections understood that they would not get more votes from debates.

4.2.6   *Internet and Social Media*

All campaigns resorted to the internet and social media as a way of campaigning. Their use of digital technology was a clear reflection of their adopted strategies, whether the campaigns would stick to their brand image as a priority or would do anything in order to win.

Some studies assessed the role of social media in framing the 2012 elections (Khamis and Mahmoud 2013) and the candidates' usage of social media (Elsebahy 2013) by conducting a content analysis of their Facebook and Twitter pages. Khamis and Mahmoud (2013) argued that online campaigning played an important role in building the candidates' positive image and diminishing the image of opponents. Elsebahy (2013) stressed the crucial role it played in the elections by acting as a promotional tool, attacking tool, sarcastic tool, and rumour-spreading tool as well as helping voters to interact with the campaigns freely.

However, the importance of the use of social media and the internet did not lay in its role as a gateway to information or in interacting between voters and campaigns, which all campaigns did. Its importance was in the use of what is known in Egypt as 'electronic committees', which was the real and crucial difference between the campaigns and which was not discussed by the academic studies analysing candidates' use of social media or the social media role in the elections so far.

The term 'electronic committees' is equivalent to what is known as astroturfing. Astroturfing is the attempt to hide the real sender of the message to make it appear as if it was sent by the public to create artificial support. Its aim is to 'create an impression of widespread grassroots support for a policy, individual, or product, where little such support exists' (Bienkov 2012). The same can be the case for using negative comments to give a misleading impression of strong opposition, seeding rumours or false accusations. This can be done via the creation of a large number of fake online identities in order to mislead the public or change its opinion by showing that there is a large degree of support for, or rejection of, a certain policy or candidate. In an election campaign, astroturfing can be used to show public support for a certain candidate and public rejection of another candidate. It can further be used to destroy a candidate's image by attacking him and making it appear as if these attacks are coming from the general public. Technology also helped in easing the work of 'astroturfers', due to the availability of various software that can help in creating fake identities to make it to look like an authentic and real profile, and it can also generate different IP addresses for them (Monbiot 2011), making it very difficult to uncover.

The only two campaigns that decided to resort to astroturfing were Morsi and Shafiq's campaigns. The other campaigns, such as Moussa's and Aboul Fotouh's, did not use it, both due to the brand they were trying to maintain and also due to not having the financial resources or manpower.

Regarding Shafiq's campaign, there was a strong belief among the other campaigns that Shafiq's social media team was managed by the intelligence services: a belief that was clearly objected to by the campaign's social media manager, Mahmoud Ibrahim, who felt bad that his efforts were not credited to him, saying: 'It is not fair to find that all of our efforts and professional work are credited to other services in the state which did not help us at all' (Ibrahim 2016).[10]

As explained by Mahmoud Ibrahim, Shafiq's campaign did not have the budget to resort to computer programmes to help them in their astroturfing campaigns. Instead, they depended on his campaign's social media team, which consisted of 24 staff, each of them managing 20 fake accounts, making a total of 480 fake accounts. As explained in previous chapters, these accounts were used to fulfil four main objectives: (1) to attack other campaigns, (2) to stop rumours being spread about their candidate, (3) to consume the time of opponents' campaign staff and delay them from performing their other tasks, and (4) to support those who support Shafiq online from being attacked by opponents.

For Morsi's campaign, the official campaign and current officials in the Muslim Brotherhood deny resorting to any astroturfing or creating social media fake accounts to do the astroturfing through, as mentioned by Yehia Hamed (2016),[11] 'Why would we resort to fake accounts. We already have our members who are active on social media.' Other ex-Muslim Brotherhood members confirmed that the Muslim Brotherhood had resorted to astroturfing in all previous elections, including parliamentary elections and during other incidents when public opinion needed changing or influencing, or to put pressure on the government, or impact generally held beliefs.

This is why it makes logical sense that it was used as well during the presidential election which was even more important to them. However, astroturfing by the Muslim Brotherhood was not limited to the use of social media. According to Abdel Galil El-Sharnoby (2016),[12] astroturfing in the Brotherhood was done through: (1) face-to-face communication, as every member of the Muslim Brotherhood is a member of its media machine, thus every member promoted what they were requested to through face-to-face communication or through their own personal social media accounts; (2) creating fake accounts on social media; (3) hacking a famous person's account and using it to broadcast what they want as if it is the person's own opinion; and (4) establishing social media pages to attack the Muslim Brotherhood. The reason for this was to control the type of attack on the Brotherhood and to give credibility to its members, who are not known as such to the public, who are writing and attacking the Muslim Brotherhood so as to use them later on to pass on certain opinions; (5) penetrating the opposition by making Brotherhood members that are unknown to the public join the opposition group, pretending they are not Brotherhood members, and thus affect the decision process there; and, (6) penetrating well-established media organisations by the same methods through planting Brotherhood members therein who can provide help when needed.

According to El-Sharnoby, the Muslim Brotherhood had its own IT department which not only bought software to help them achieve their goals but also produced software internally, regardless of the cost. These types of software used to help them in the process of securing the process of communication through the internet. For example, it helped them to secure emails from governmental monitoring or hacking of other political forces. It also helped them to publish stories from abroad to be seen in Egypt, even when the government banned the website in Egypt. The active IT department would suggest it had a role in Morsi's campaign, mainly in astroturfing. However, it was difficult to confirm in this study as current available Muslim Brotherhood members or campaign staff denied the whole idea of astroturfing.

From the above discussion, it is clear that astroturfing played an important role in the 2012 presidential elections, mainly for Morsi's campaign, then Shafiq's campaign. It is also clear that, at that time, the other campaigns did not have a clear strategy to combat it, especially given that the 'electronic committees' were not a well-known term at that time. It was only explored after the election ended.

On the one hand, the other campaigns stuck to their 'ethics' as a brand for their campaigns. On the other hand, they did not have a clear vision to deal with it. A common complaint from the three other campaigns was how their time was consumed by social media, which was one of the main aims of Shafiq's astroturfing campaign. Being penetrated by the Muslim Brotherhood was one of the fears faced by Sabahi's campaign during polling days (although it did not actually occur): again, one of the aims of Morsi's astroturfing campaign.

With the absence of clear ways in Egypt to monitor or differentiate astroturfing from real communications during 2012, astroturfing messages were often picked up by traditional media and treated as real messages, utilising the political information cycle (Chadwick 2011), creating a state of scepticism and confusion among the electorate. It might also affect social media academic research, as research that was done on social media at the time did not pay attention to this phenomenon and did not have ways to identify it. Although astroturfing might have been helpful to both Morsi's and Shafiq's campaigns in general, it was harmful for the democratisation process in Egypt as it hindered the process of constructive debates, mainly on social media, and lowered trust in real authentic grass-roots movements which might have been useful for the democratisation process in Egypt. All this doubt and uncertainty was then transmitted to the public sphere as well by various means such as traditional media taking what is on social media as a real reflection of the society or through face-to-face communication.

Although the professionalisation index does not add the internet and social media as a separate criterion so as not to be biased towards new technologies such as CAMPROF (Tenscher and Mykkänen 2014), the internet and social media are added here as a separate criterion due to its role in identifying the campaigns' logic and strategies. Key is the potential of digital technologies for influencing the media's agenda and shaping the public sphere, particularly considering the role the internet and social media played in the eruption of the 25 January Egyptian Revolution (Elsheikh 2011). In terms of professionalisation of the internet and social media, it appears that both Morsi's and Shafiq's campaigns were more professionalised in terms of their usage of the internet and social media: because of their dependence on it they developed tactics to make the most use of it. Unlike the rest of the campaigns that did not focus on creating specific content for the internet, with the exception of some content specifically made for the internet, the majority of the campaigns' internet content was just either rebroadcasting messages broadcast on other outlets or a reaction to the attacks they were facing from Morsi's and Shafiq's campaigns.

4.2.7   Campaigns' Activities

Apart from the use of media, the five studied campaigns used a wide range of activities to reach their target voters. Their activities were almost the same in all campaigns. When a campaign pioneered and used unusual methods during the Egyptian elections, other campaigns used to repeat the method used. The most common practice used by all campaigns was face-to-face communication. This would include governorates visits, or knocking on doors, or canvassing, or the electoral conferences which were a famous form of campaigning activity. Perhaps the only difference would be the Muslim Brotherhood which depended on their female members for face-to-face campaigning with other women in areas the Muslim Brotherhood are not popular in or areas they do not have a base in (Shoman and Saleh 2013). This was unlike other campaigns which did not strategically make use of women in that way, perhaps deeming it unnecessary since women were already part of their campaign either as staff or volunteers.

With regard to the professionalisation of campaign activities, the professionalisation index assesses the degree of media-oriented pseudo-events in the campaign (Tenscher et al. 2012). Pseudo-events (Boorstin 1961) mainly refer to activities planned ahead and organised for the sake of getting media coverage, or in other words, staged events. In Egyptians' minds, the idea of pseudo-events is usually coined with a scene in a 1995 comic movie called *Toyour elzalam* or *Birds of Darkness*. In this scene, a corrupted lawyer who acts as a campaign manager takes the candidate to a poor area, where the candidate is approached by a citizen of those living in the area. The candidate felt very disgusted by this citizen commenting that he has scabies. But his campaign manager urged the candidate to kiss him, telling him to kiss him on his mouth as cameras were approaching. After the cameras took the photo, the candidate pushed the citizen away from him. This stereotype of the pseudo-events made campaigns very reluctant to admit if their events were pseudo ones.

Having said that, by applying the professionalisation index, it appears that all the five campaigns were competing to gain the media attention and coverage by creating these types of events. These included press conferences, events for the formal inauguration of the campaign or for the announcement of the campaigns' programmes. Some campaigns introduced new forms of activities that were repeated by all other campaigns. These forms of new activities included long support marches, double-decker buses, and human chain activities.

For example, Aboul Fotouh's campaign asked his supporters to walk to the place of his events, such as when his supporters went to his electoral conference in Cairo Youth Centre walking on foot around three kilometres through Cairo's streets (Shoman and Saleh 2013). The action caught media attention of course. There were also the double-decker buses used by various campaigns; although they were not able to verify who pioneered this as every campaign said that they were the first to use them, it was still new for Egyptian campaigns. Long human chains were another theme of the campaigns. It was first practised by Morsi's campaign, whose chain was described as the longest in the world (Shoman and Saleh 2013). This was repeated later by the other campaigns. Some campaigns were also concentrating on candidates' appearances with ordinary people such as Moussa sitting on the floor with ordinary citizens and eating with them using his hands instead of cutlery, to refute his image as a diplomat who has no relation to ordinary citizens.

The logic behind those activities was that wider media coverage would influence the voters' final decision. It would reinforce the decisions of the supporters who see their candidate undertaking activities covered by the media which reinforce his image and messages and, on the other hand, providing the public sphere with content to discuss and debate. They were hoping that it would also affect the sofa party, especially knowing that not all the voters would know that these activities were designed primarily to gain media coverage. Some citizens think that the media were interested in such events due to the importance of the candidate himself or because of the popularity of the candidate. The more the campaigns believe in the importance of media in influencing the voters, the more it would depend on such pseudo-events. Thus it appears that these events were not for the sole aim of media coverage, but media coverage was used as a means to reach the voters. In terms of the professionalisation of campaigns' pseudo-events, there was a high degree of competition between all the five campaigns, making them with almost the same degree, especially towards the end of the campaigning period.

4.2.8   Degree of Personalisation

Personalisation became a key concept in postmodern campaigns, reflecting changes that occurred to election coverage over time mainly due to the rise of TV and the decline of party affiliation (Van Aelst et al. 2012). Personalised stories attract media attention (Strömbäck 2008) and candidates themselves try to appeal to voters on the basis of respective similarities (Garzia 2011). However, the assumption that the coverage is converted in favour of personalisation (McAllister 2007) is not purely supported by other academics (Karvonen 2010; Kriesi 2012). This may be due to differences at the time of conducting the studies—or due to differences between the political and institutional structure in which the election took place, that is, presidential or parliamentary elections (Garzia 2011)—or the absence of a clear definition of what is meant by the term personalisation (Van Aelst et al. 2012). This is why Van Aelst et al. (2012) differentiates between two forms of personalisation. The first is known as 'individualisation' where the concentration of media coverage is on the individual candidate, rather than his institution/party. The second type is known as 'privatisation' where the concentration of media coverage is on the personal characteristics and the personal life of the individual candidate (Rahat and Sheafer 2007).

Despite distinguishing between 'individualisation' and 'privatisation', the case was a little different in Egypt as all the candidates except Morsi did not belong to any party. Thus the term 'individualisation' is not applicable in comparing between candidates. Personalisation in the case of the five studied campaigns would mean media coverage of the personal characteristics and the personal life of the candidate, that is, 'privatisation'. The importance of privatisation lies in the emotional aspect it involves which is believed to influence voters' behaviour and their reception to the candidates' messages (Abelson et al. 1982; Cwalina et al. 2011; Wattenberg 1987). This is why candidates often participate in three different types of media outlets which give them the chance to highlight their personal character: indirect political broadcasts, infotainment broadcasts, or pure entertainment programmes (Maarek 2011).

The perceived effect of the personalisation thesis on voting behaviour has changed over time. It was first argued that voting on the basis on personality is irrational (Converse 1964; Garzia 2011) as voters are deceived and manipulated by professionals and image makers working with the candidate. However, recent studies consider it as a rational voting strategy that depends on the degree of voters' sophistication and education (Glass 1985; Garzia 2011). Others argued that voting behaviour would depend on personality in the presence of some conditions at the time of the elections, such as the absence or presence of a dominant culture of opinion and the presence of a systematic crisis (Garzia 2011), which were both available in the 2012 Egyptian election: it happened after a revolution, amid trials of corruption and accusations against previous regime leaders and amid a high degree of polarisation. The importance of personalisation in influencing voters' decisions in Egypt 2012 elections was also proved by Farrag (2013) who found that the voters' evaluations of the candidates was based on the candidates' personal characteristics. El-Khoreiby (2013) also found that candidates' image, which was based on personal traits, is one of the main factors that motivated voters to vote for a specific candidate.

The professionalisation index assesses personalisation depending on the subjective assessment of campaign staff of the significance of issue-oriented campaigning, both candidate and issue-oriented campaign, or only candidate-oriented campaign. By applying the index both subjectively through the assessment of the interviewees and objectively through the assessment of the researcher, it would appear that all the campaigns were both candidate and issue oriented, although the degree varied as follows:

Candidates who were not well-known to the public had to focus at first on introducing themselves to the voters by concentrating on privatisation and highlighting their career and public work path and so on. Other candidates used personal stories to create a link and appear closer to the voters. In general, all campaigns were both candidate and issue oriented. However, Moussa and Aboul Fotouh had an extra feature: they were keen on highlighting stories about the campaign staff themselves. Their campaign staff would participate in media outlets to talk about the campaign and their roles therein. The aim was mainly to create a public perception that their candidates hired professionals to run their campaigns and would do the same when they reached the presidential office.

Personalisation appeared through participating in indirect political programmes or features about the candidates or participating in purely non-political entertainment programmes. Participating in indirect political programmes was common for all the studied candidates, such as participating in talk show programmes. Feature stories about the candidates were also common across all candidates. Moussa's campaign was distinct among the campaigns as it was keen on providing the media with topics, ideas, and contacts for the features. One of the reasons they were doing this was to give the media some substance to work with and, to an extent, control what they would write about him. The main difference was the candidate's or campaign's willingness to participate in purely entertainment-based programmes, which was only done by Sabahi and Aboul Fotouh.

The personalisation thesis has been studied extensively as highlighted above. However, so far, there are not enough studies to assess the impact of personalisation methods used by the five campaigns on the Egyptian voters in the 2012 elections. Having said that, it appeared that using a mixture of news passed to the media and adding a touch of personalisation did play an important role in making the candidate closer and more well-known to potential voters. Participation in such programmes gave substance for the media to work with, instead of leaving the floor for the media to dig alone for stories that the candidate might not be happy with. These could be talk show programmes, which all candidates participated in, or features about the candidates, which distinguished Moussa's campaign who were keen on giving ideas and contacts for features to media outlets.

In terms of the professionalisation of the use of personalisation in the campaigns, all the five campaigns were nearly similar as all of them were both candidate and issue oriented.

4.2.9   The Professionalisation of Campaign Strategies

By analysing and comparing the strategies adopted by each campaign, there is a clear indication that campaigns which did not have a party or a big organisation supporting them were trying to compensate the shortage they had in their structure by concentrating more on their strategies. This result agrees with Tenscher's conclusion that (2013: 249) the smaller political parties try their best to compensate for structural disadvantages by developing more innovative strategies. This was clear in the way both Moussa's and Aboul Fotouh's campaigns pioneered with regard to utilising free media and debates. They also came in the same category as other campaigns with regard to the professionalisation of their usage of pseudo-events and personalisation. However, the professionalised structure of both Morsi and Shafiq had influenced the degree of the professionalisation of some of their strategies making them more professional than the rest of the campaigns, such as in their targeting and use of the internet and social media. Therefore, overall theirs were the two most professionalised campaigns as they had more overall professionalised criteria in both the structures and the strategies than the rest of the campaigns. However, another important factor has influenced the degree of the professionalisation of all the campaigns' strategy which was the logic behind the strategy of Morsi and Shafiq from one side and the rest of the three campaigns from the other side. This difference in the logic influencing the campaign strategies will be discussed in the next section.

4.3   STRATEGY ANALYSIS

The goal of all five campaigns was to reinforce the decisions of their supporters and to gain the support of undecided voters in order to win the election. For both Morsi and Shafiq, they already had a solid base of supporters that the rest of campaigns could not compete with. Instead, they were competing with the rest of campaigns for the undecided voters as well.

The rest of the campaigns, including the three of Moussa, Aboul Fotouh, and Sabahi, did not have a solid base of supporters, and thus they were trying to create one by influencing the undecided voters, which was referred to here as the 'sofa party'. On the other hand, they were trying to influence the votes of those supporting the revolution.

The revolution's supporters could have acted as a solid base for candidates who were saying that they represented the revolution, but since there was more than one candidate making this claim, and since the revolution did not have a leader to direct the votes, votes of those supporting the revolution were split between the revolutionary candidates and cannot be considered as a solid base for any one of the candidates.

This difference influenced the strategy of the campaigns. For Morsi and Shafiq, both candidates had already established an image long ago and were building upon it by any means that they could to secure as many votes as possible, mainly from the 'sofa party'.

They were ready to do anything that could help them win and leave anything that would not fulfil that aim regardless of the brand they had already created long ago.

On the other hand, the other candidates were trying to create a consistent brand and were only prepared to make moves that would enhance this brand and abandoned anything that contradicted the brand, even if doing so would help them win.

This difference in secured voters, which led to a clear difference in adopted strategies, put both the Egyptian voters and campaigns to the test regarding which approach is more effective in the elections: sticking to the brand versus doing anything to win.

4.3.1   Sticking to the Brand

There is no academic consensus on whether branding should be applied to politics as a communication strategy or not. Those who oppose the idea of applying branding to politics, see that it can lead to undesirable effects such as narrowing the political agenda and political disengagement (Scammel 1999; Smith and French 2009). Meanwhile, those who support it see that it can lead to sociological, rational, psychological, and cultural benefits (Smith and French 2009). These benefits could lead to a more connected electorate, which is crucial to democracy.

This debate was reflected in the Egyptian campaigns, as campaigns which stuck to their brands did not win. Essentially, those who won in the first round of the election were not concentrating on the coherence of their brand. On the contrary, those who did not win were paying too much attention to their brand.

Coming from a business and commercial marketing background, both Moussa's and Aboul Fotouh's campaigns stuck to branding their image

(Moussa with his PR and media team, who worked in the business sector before, and Aboul Fotouh's campaign manager was also formerly from the business sector). The same applied to Sabahi's campaign, which built on the revolutionary spirit that prevailed in Egypt at the time of starting his campaign.

A brand is defined as: 'A name, term, sign, symbol, or design, or a combination of them which is intended to identify the goods or services of one seller or a group of sellers and to differentiate them from those of competitors' (Smith and French 2009: 211).

Theoretically, all the candidates satisfied this definition: they had a name that was repeated in all media outlets and was written everywhere, whether on street walls, on billboards, or advertisements, and each had a symbol that represented him, and in a country like Egypt symbols play an important role for illiterate voters who cannot read names but can recognise the symbol. Each candidate tried to present himself as different from the others, giving voters a reason why should they vote for him instead of his opponents.

According to psychology learning theory, voters remember a brand by linking individual pieces of information (Smith and French 2009). This confirms the importance of sustaining credibility through the coherence of a campaign's messages, behaviours, and attitudes and avoiding any conflicting messages, along with integrity and competence (Cwalina et al. 2011).

Several statements were made by the three campaigns that indicated that sticking to the brand they were trying to create was the main theme of their strategy, such as by sticking to positive campaigning, participating in activities they thought would enhance democracy, avoiding astroturfing, and more importantly preserving their moral integrity and competence as a core feature of their image (Cwalina et al. 2011).

As an example, Aboul Fotouh's campaign had what they called 'campaign values', which delayed the process of choosing campaign staff to make sure they had the same set of values, and they did not resort to astroturfing or attacking their opponents. They participated in the debate as they thought it would enhance democracy. For Moussa's campaign, this was clear as well in their positive campaigning approach, even when they had a chance to attack, such as Shafiq's daughter's photo that they had, along with participating in the debate and not playing upon 'polarisation behind closed doors' (Khalaf 2016). Sabahi's method did not differ very much, as his campaign tried to stop revolution supporters who were supporting different

'Revolutionary' candidates from attacking each other, and he wanted to participate in the debate.

The time they started their campaigns played a role in determining their strategy. As they were starting their campaigns at the time when Mubarak left power, morals at that time were high on the agenda. Candidates built upon this: each portraying himself as a supporter of the revolution who can rebuild the country, each with his own philosophy and programmes.

However, when the campaign duration grew, many political incidents happened that changed the positive morals prevailing after the revolution. These incidents included the debate around whether to have the constitution first or election first, SCAF's way of managing the transitional period, and the increase in the death toll due to clashes that took places in the streets in several forms, including but not limited to between protesters, or protesters and police. All these incidents led to a polarised society, a polarised public sphere, leading to a polarised electorate by the time of election. However, the candidates' brands did not evolve to match these developments. They were concentrating on the reconciliation approach for Moussa, the consensual approach for Aboul Fotouh, and the revolutionary approach of Sabahi, although not something over which he had a monopoly, as other candidates were using the same tactic. Amid polarising speeches from other candidates and a polarised society, these three candidates did not develop their brand enough to meet the challenges that evolved over the course of the campaign. This led to their disconnection from the electorate.

In other words, for Aboul Fotouh and Moussa, the differences between them were not clear enough for the polarised voters. As explained in previous chapters, the desire to satisfy all voters made them lose voters as well: making Aboul Fotouh not Islamist enough for some Islamist voters and too Islamist for liberal voters. It further made Moussa an old regime figure, but not enough so, for supporters of the old regime, and not revolutionary enough for the revolution's supporters, and so on.

They concentrated on their images more than on the real politics. They concentrated on media appearances and marketing their brand more than securing a number of votes from the governorates. Their insistence on a coherent brand led to them not playing enough politics and neglecting to do what other campaigns did, as if their brands were enough to mobilise the voters, especially the ordinary non-polarised voters to go and vote for them on the Election Day.

Although the branding may have had some positive effects for the campaigns or the candidates, it did not help them to win. Sticking to the brand alone perhaps made the candidates appear to be fanciful, unrealistic, or unaware of the Egyptian electoral tradition and unable to influence Egyptian voters and their voting behaviour.

4.3.2   Everything to Win

On the other hand, the other two candidates, Morsi and Shafiq, already had strong, polarising brands. Morsi represented the Muslim Brotherhood even while trying to appear in the second round as the revolution's candidate. Shafiq represented the old regime, even while trying not to appear as such and just as an employee of the state, whoever ruled it. The reality did not matter to the voters as these ideas were already carved into their minds as stereotypes: that Morsi represented the Muslim Brotherhood and Shafiq the old regime.

Instead of working on changing this stereotype or brand or rebuilding their image to appeal to all voters, they built upon what they already had in order to concentrate on having a secure number of votes that would get them past the first round of the election. They were not keen on changing their image; on the contrary, they reinforced it, mainly during the first round, and they were prepared to do anything in order to win votes. On the other hand, they were not ready to conduct campaigning activities that might cause them to drop votes, even if it would cause them to lose the undecided voters. Winning votes was priority number one for them.

Despite being culturally limited (Isotalus and Aarnio 2006; Isotalus 2011), the functional theory (Benoit 2001) would be best for explaining both Morsi's and Shafiq's campaign strategies. According to this theory, (a) voting is a matter of comparative judgement; (b) candidates must differentiate themselves from opponents through their campaign messages; (c) candidates have three options to increase (preferably), namely, acclaiming or self-praising, attacks to make opponents lose preferability, and defending to restore lost preferability; (d) these three functions, namely, acclaim, attack, and defence, can be fulfilled by concentrating on policy and character; and, (e) candidates don't need to persuade everyone to vote, but rather a secured majority to make him win (Benoit 2001, 2002, 2007 ; Isotalus 2011).

Because voting is a matter of comparative judgement, voters will only judge and vote for the candidates based on the differences between them.

Voters will have no reason to prefer a specific candidate if there are no differences at all between them (Isotalus 2011). For both Morsi and Shafiq, the differences between them were sharp and clear. Furthermore, the differences between them and the rest of the candidates were sharp and clear enough as well. This apparently gave them an edge over the other candidates, who looked nearly the same or, in other words, the differences were not clear enough or were not polarising enough to satisfy the already polarised electorate.

These differences were reflected in their messages through a polarised and clear discourse at the time of the campaign. This again highlighted the differences between them to ordinary voters and reinforced the decisions of the polarised supporters.

Both candidates made full use of the three functions mentioned above: they had a history that allowed them to praise themselves. For Morsi, it was his history of opposing the old regime and being previously imprisoned. For Shafiq, it was his history as a state figure and the ability to manage which highlighted his leadership abilities. This acclaiming function was not clear enough among the other candidates, who did not have a history of opposition like that of the Muslim Brotherhood, or a history of working in the state and implementing real physical projects such as the airport, or even a history of united support to make them appear to be the sole representative of the revolution.

Both candidates also relied upon attacking to minimise the support and appeal of the other candidates. This included direct attacks on other candidates or resorting to astroturfing, which the rest of candidates did not include in their strategies.

Morsi and Shafiq also used defensive strategies to defend against any general attacks against them and tried to make use of these attacks to guarantee their secured voters.

In their discourses, both candidates focused on their policies and characteristics. In their policies, they concentrated on their past deeds, future plans, and general goals for Egypt. For their characteristics, they concentrated on reinforcing the images they had, instead of creating new ones. Shafiq, for instance, concentrated on appearing to be the strong state candidate who can restore security and safety to Egypt's streets, something that was absent after the revolution.

Both candidates also concentrated on guaranteeing their secured votes and not losing any by trying to convince everyone to vote for them, which differed greatly from the strategies of other campaigns, especially Moussa and Aboul Fotouh, who tried to please everyone with their discourse. From the above: although the functional theory acts as a method of analysis and not a step-by-step guide for campaigns to follow, it appears that candidates who adopted it as a strategy in the first round of elections were likely to win, unlike other candidates who stuck only to their brand.

4.4   Campaigns' Professionalisation and Election Results

As elaborated, the two most professionalised campaigns were those of Morsi followed by Shafiq as they fulfilled more professional items in both indices, leading to a more overall professional campaign.

According to the party-centred theory (Gibson and Rommele 2001, 2009; Strömbäck 2008), there are several factors that would force a political party to resort to professionalism in their campaigning. These factors are internal such as seeking votes in order to win, ideology,[13] size, resources, internal centralisation, and leadership change; and external factors such as electoral shock by loss of incumbency.

In terms of the 2012 elections, some of these factors could explain why Morsi's campaign resorted to professionalism: it was seeking votes as its ultimate goal; as an organisation it had a high level of resources, with a high level of internal centralisation represented in its hierarchal structure both in the party and in the group; it had a conservative ideology; it had several changes in the both the group and the party, including party formation after the revolution and appointing a new leader. However, although it did not suffer from loss of incumbency, it suffered from some internal problems which led to the dismissal of some of its members.

Although theoretically the theory cannot be applied to Shafiq's campaign as he was not officially representing any party including the dismantled NDP, practically some of the factors are still applicable to his campaign such as it was seeking votes as its ultimate goal, the conservative ideology of the dismantled NDP which was still embedded with the campaign, the internal centralisation of the campaign, leadership change as the NDP was already dismantled, and the loss of incumbency after the revolution.

Despite the significant role that professionalism might have played in the first round of elections, leading to their winning in the first round, it was not the only decisive factor in determining their victory in the second round of elections. There were other factors that played a role in the election results along with the campaign's role, such as, but not limited to, (a) absence of electoral alliances in the first round of elections, (b) differences between big cities and villages in the governorates in terms of mobilising voters and voting behaviour, and (c) punitive voting prevailing in the second round of the election.

4.4.1   Absence of Electoral Alliances

In the 2012 presidential elections, the competition appeared to be between three forces: the Muslim Brotherhood, the old regime, and the revolution. Both Morsi, the Muslim Brotherhood candidate, and Shafiq, who theoretically represented the old regime, did not need to enter into a coalition with other candidates as they already had a solid base of voters, and they were sure of their capability of winning in comparison to other candidates who were also classified as Islamists or from the old regime. Those who were in great need of a coalition or alliance were the revolutionary candidates. There were some attempts to form a coalition between the main five revolutionary and reformist candidates in order to avoid the predicted fragmentation of votes (Al-akhbar 17/05/2012). These attempts were based on a united election programme and a united one candidate that represented all of them. In other words, only one of the five candidates would run for presidency and the rest would be vice presidents or would take senior roles when the chosen candidate that represented them all won. However, all these attempts failed due to various reasons such as disputes over who would take which role, that is, who would withdraw and who would run for presidency and similar issues. This led to the nomination of three candidates representing the revolutionary side who were Hamdeen Sabahi, Abdel Moneim Aboul Fotouh, and Khaled Ali and two other reformists' leftists' candidates who were Abu Al-Izz Al-Hariri and Hisham El-Bastawisi.

The result of the first rounds of elections reflected the necessity of a coalition due to the fragmentation of votes as each of them took the following numbers of votes (Tables 4.1 and 4.2):

The total number of votes gained by the five revolutionist and reformist candidates was more than ten million votes. This exceeded the number of votes collected by either Shafiq or Morsi. In other words, if the five candi-

Table 4.1 Revolutionary candidates' results

Candidates	Number of votes[a]
Sabahi	4,820,273
Aboul Fotouh	4,065,239
Khaled Ali	134,056
Abu Al-Izz Al-Hariri	40,090
Hisham El-Bastawisi	29,189

[a]Number of votes as appears on EHC website 2012

Table 4.2 Second round of elections' results

The two top candidates	Number of votes
Morsi	5,764,952
Shafiq	5,505,327

dates had entered into a coalition, the result of the election might have been finalised in the first round by the winning of the revolutionary/reformist camp in opposition to the old regime and the Muslim Brotherhood.

The same might have been applicable even if the three revolutionary candidates only had entered into a coalition or alliance, as the total of votes gained by Sabahi, Aboul Fotouh, and Khaled Ali exceeded nine million votes, again, exceeding the number of votes gained by either Shafiq or Morsi.

These assumptions are still theoretical as it is not necessarily the case that all supporters of a specific revolutionary candidate would vote for the candidate remaining. Nonetheless, this assumption still has some validity because if this coalition existed, revolutionary supporters would find themselves forced to choose between a Muslim Brotherhood candidate who they certainly did not want, an old regime candidate that they did not want, and only one revolution candidate who agreed with them even if he wasn't their ideal candidate. In such a case, they would find no choice rather than choosing between the three camps and voting for the candidate that best represented the revolutionary coalition. However, neither of these scenarios happened in real life.

4.4.2   *Voting Behaviour Differences Between Various Governorates*

This chapter stressed the importance of the field co-ordinator role, especially in the governorates. The chapter also highlighted some problems that faced campaigns like Moussa's and Aboul Fotouh's in various governorates in terms of which voters they should mobilise and how to mobilise them to go and vote on voting day. The argument was that getting the vote out from villages in the governorates would be different from major urban cities such as Cairo and Alexandria, for example. This indicates the need to mobilise voters with GOTV activities in the governorates and villages perhaps more than the capital and other urban educated cities. The chapter argued that both Morsi's and Shafiq's campaign were the only campaigns that resorted to professional field co-ordinators with past experience in mobilising voters in governorates in previous Egyptian elections.

Election results supported these arguments as they showed the nature of elections and competition which varied between various governorates. In his analysis of voting results in the 27 Egyptian governorates, Masoud (2014: 188–194) argued that villages identical in many social and economic factors voted differently depending on the candidates' 'embeddedness' in local communities. This result supports this chapter's argument on the importance of the field co-ordinator role who was the one responsible for creating this 'embeddedness' on behalf of the candidate in various governorates by contacting and mobilising ordinary voters, families, community leaders, officials, and influential people there.

The results of the first round of elections represent a good reflection of the governorates' electoral behaviour due to the availability of all candidates who represented different political trends and thoughts. This is unlike the second round, which was limited to two candidates only, where Egyptians resorted to punitive voting as will be explained in the next section.

The results[14] showed two main surprises. The first was that Morsi and Shafiq were the two top winners who would compete in the second round, and not Moussa and Aboul Fotouh, who were thought to be the front runners according to public opinion polls and media estimations at campaigning time. The second surprise was that Sabahi was in third place which was unexpected, even after the rise of his support after the debate between Moussa and Aboul Fotouh per public opinion polls conducted at that time.

By analysing the voting results of the first round, it appears that there was a clear difference in the governorates' voting behaviours as follows: Urban governorates voted for Sabahi. Delta and Northern governorates voted for Shafiq. Upper Egypt and border governorates voted for Morsi. The results also showed a clear drop in the Muslim Brotherhood's electoral support in comparison to the parliamentary elections which were held around six months[15] before the presidential elections.

Sabahi achieved the first rank in well-educated urban governorates such as Cairo, Alexandria, Port Said, and along the Red Sea with Kafr El-Sheikh, his home governorate. He also got the second place in votes in semi-urban governorates such as Giza, Garbeyia, Dakahlia, Ismailia, Suez, and Damietta. This means that Sabahi gained more than 70% of his overall total votes from these urban and semi-urban governorates.

Sabahi getting most his overall number of votes from urban and semi-urban governorates was another surprise. Due to the nature of his campaign's speech and his Nasserist background, it was assumed that Sabahi would get his votes from poor and uneducated areas (Masoud 2014); especially as his campaign slogan was 'one from among us', reflecting that he was one from the ordinary Egyptian citizens, not the well-educated upper middle-class citizens.

Masoud (2014: 188–194) also found a negative correlation between Sabahi's vote share and both the crowding rate and percentage of adults working in agriculture. This is another way to prove that Sabahi did not get his votes from farmers or poor areas which are overcrowded.

Shukr (2013: 299–301) explains this phenomenon by highlighting the fact that voters' behaviour in urban well-educated cities is different from rural ones as those living in major urban cities are supposed to be more educated and more immersed in politics taking place in the streets around them, which would affect their rational independent voting choice.

The result also showed that Sabahi won his own governorates, which proves the important role of the field co-ordinator. In Kafr El-Sheikh, all Sabahi's extended family played the role of his field co-ordinator. He was also embedded and well-known by voters there as he had represented them before in parliamentary elections. However, the results also showed that he was not able to mobilise enough voters in Kafr El-Sheikh to vote on Election Day as the voters' turnout there was only 42.9%.[16]

Being unable to mobilise more voters from his own governorates—taking into consideration all the help he had from his family and friends there—highlights the issue that he was not able to do the same with the rest of governorates, especially that he did not have the same people working for him on the ground. In other words, perhaps if his campaign was able to mobilise enough voters to go out and vote on Election Day from several governorates, including his own governorate, he might have been able to secure the number of votes he needed to outperform Shafiq in the first round: all that he needed was less than 700,000 votes, which was the difference in votes between him and Shafiq. This again proves the necessity of having a professional field co-ordinator with experience, something Sabahi's campaign lacked.

Quite the contrary to Sabahi's results, Morsi took the majority of votes in the border governorates and Upper Egypt including Giza. These areas—especially the villages—are characterised by high levels of illiteracy, a weak economic situation, lack of a multicultural environment, and loyalties to bigger families and tribalism (Shukr 2013: 299–301).

The number of registered voters in these governorates was approximately nine million, which represented 18% of the number of registered votes in all Egypt. Morsi gained around 2.2 million of the valid votes in these governorates, which represented 37% of the total votes he achieved in the first round of elections. This could be explained by the fact that the governorates' social, economic, and cultural situation plays a role in both influencing voter attitudes and in determining voting behaviour. It can also be explained by the active role the Muslim Brotherhood played in these areas. In other words, what Shukr explains as the role played by the alliance of poverty, ignorance, and tribalism in backing candidates who use religious slogans in their campaigns (Shukr 2013: 300). Again, the results showed that a field co-ordinator who understands the nature of his voters and their areas would be able to mobilise them using appeals they would understand and affect them.

Morsi's results also showed that the Muslim Brotherhood had lost more than half of its voting bloc in comparison to its results in the parliamentary elections (Al-Saadawy 2012). In the parliamentary elections, the Muslim Brotherhood took around 10.5 million votes. However, in the first round of elections Morsi only took around 5.7 million votes, outperforming Shafiq with a narrow victory of only 882,000 votes (Al-Saadawy 2012). This can be explained due to people's dissatisfaction with the performance of the parliament in various cases, one of which is the constitution assembly explained in Chap. 2.

Another loss for the Muslim Brotherhood in this election was the significant drop of votes it had in its traditional strongholds (Al-Saadawy 2012). Morsi came second or third in a number of governorates which were known for their support for the Muslim Brotherhood and were even described as Islamist friendly areas such as many governorates in Delta and Northern Cairo (Al-Saadawy 2012). Most of the Delta and Northern Cairo governorates—which were traditionally described as Islamist friendly areas—voted for Shafiq. In five[17] out of ten governorates, which have more than 29% of the electorate in Egypt, Shafiq got more than 34% of the valid votes, leading him to secure more than 2.5 million votes of his overall approximately 5.5 million votes he got in the first round from these governorates alone. In other words, Shafiq secured 45% of the overall votes he got in the first round from these five governorates only.

These surprising results could be explained by two main reasons. First is the way Shafiq's campaign was working as it was concentrating its mobilising and campaigning efforts more on the governorates with high numbers of registered voters. The second reason, as revealed by Shafiq's campaign, was that since these areas were known as being Muslim Brotherhood-friendly since Mubarak's era, the NDP started concentrating on having an electoral base in these areas through various means; one of which was training field co-ordinators to be able to mobilise people in these areas. Shafiq's campaign resorted to these trained field co-ordinators to help him in his campaign (Personal interview, Ibrahim 2016).

The above overview proves that voting behaviour varies between governorates. It also varies between urban and rural areas. This is why the role of an experienced field co-ordinator—who understands these differences—is significant in getting out the vote from them. The next section explains how Morsi and the Muslim Brotherhood managed to restore and gain more votes in the second round with the help of the punitive voting.

4.4.3   Punitive Voting

This chapter indicates that the professionalisation of the campaigns of Morsi, then Shafiq, was a main contributory factor that led to them winning the first round of elections. However, in the second round of elections, the situation was completely different. The competition and polarisation were fierce between them. It divided the electorate into two main binary camps: Islamic state versus secular state and pro change versus status quo. In other words, the possibility of the return of the old regime represented by Ahmed Shafiq, the last prime minister in Mubarak's era, versus the possibility of having a president from the Muslim Brotherhood.

The first round of elections showed the actual support and voting base for both Morsi (5.7 million votes) and Shafiq (5.5 million votes). The rest of the electorate did not vote for them and did not want them. Thus, many Egyptians found themselves forced to choose between two options they did not want or like. This led to several calls to boycott the second round of elections or to form a revolutionary coalition until the launch of what was known as the 'squeezing the lime' campaign. This urged Egyptians to squeeze the lime and elect Morsi as a punishment for the old regime and to prevent it from coming back. Many figures and revolutionary forces joined the campaign despite disagreeing with Morsi ideologically and politically. A lot of claims were made at that time such as the blood of the revolution's martyrs is an obstacle between them and the old regime, and that the Muslim Brotherhood was present with the revolutionary forces in Tahrir Square at the 25 January Revolution against the old regime. The revolutionary forces' support for Morsi culminated in front of the public after the polls closed in the Fairmount meeting where Morsi promised inclusive rule along with other guarantees for the democratic rule required by the revolutionary forces.

On the other hand, those who were more afraid of the creation of an Islamic state than their fear of the old regime campaigned and voted for Shafiq just to punish Morsi and prevent him from ruling them.

This extensive polarisation led to the rise of voters' participation from 46% in the first round to 51% in the second round. It also led to the rise of the number of votes for both candidates: Morsi got 13,230,131 votes and Shafiq got 12,347,380 votes, giving Morsi a narrow victory, only 3.46% over his opponent Shafiq.[18]

Thus, although campaign professionalism was the main factor that determined their winning in the first round of elections, the decisive factor in the second round of elections was the effect of the punitive voting Egyptians resorted to.

4.5   Conclusion

Widespread analysis[19] attributed Moussa's and Shafiq's success in the first round of elections to several factors such as the Muslim Brotherhood's organisational ability (Al-Saadawy 2012; Trager 2016), patronage and ideology (Al-Ississi and Attah 2014), deep state[20] (Shehata et al. 2012; Clevers and Nimeh 2015), the divided and disorganised opposition in the case of the other candidates (Ottaway 2013), and the role of businessmen and clientelism (El Tarouty 2015). In contrast to these analyses which did not put enough weight on the role of candidates' campaigns, this chapter infers that the professionalism of both Morsi's and Shafiq's campaigns played a role in the result of the first round of elections which made them the two front runners competing again in the second round. The chapter concluded this by applying the professionalisation index (Tenscher et al. 2012) which assesses the campaigns' professionalism by breaking it into two parts: structure (hardware) and strategies (software). Breaking the campaigns into two components helped in providing a thorough understanding of the overall strategy and tactics and how they were implemented.

While applying the professionalisation index, slightly cosmetic amendments were implemented which was mainly adding some components that are deduced from the same indicators in the index, such as adding debates, the internet, and social media in the strategy indices to better explain the actual strategies adopted in the case of the 2012 Egyptian elections as explained previously.

While assessing how the structures and strategies are prioritised is useful and can be a determinant for measuring how professional a campaign is and whether this correlates with the outcome, it may not explain everything. As proved in this chapter, professionalism appeared to correlate with a functionalist approach with candidates being willing to do or say anything in order to win. Thus, according to the way professionalism was applied in this election, it perhaps appears that a form of professionalism that highlights branding more is better for democracy, especially for a country in its transitional period trying to build a democracy such as Egypt.

The index proved that in the first round of elections, Morsi's campaign was the most professionalised followed by Shafiq's campaign. The index also proved the other three campaigns tended to invest more in their strategies; yet it was not always in their favour such as the decision by both Moussa and Aboul Fotouh to participate in the debate. Another obstacle that faced them in developing their strategies was sticking to the brand they created in opposition to Moussa and Shafiq who were ready to do anything to win.

The chapter also explained the tendency of Moussa and Shafiq to resort to professionalism by applying the party-centred theory criteria as both candidates were reacting to internal and external factors, including changing electoral circumstances and the situation in Egypt in general. For the first time since its establishment in 1928, the Muslim Brotherhood found an opportunity to rule Egypt. And for the NDP, it was the first time since its establishment in 1978 to be out of power. This might give a reason for the fierce competition.

However, in the second round of elections, professionalism was not the crucial factor. There were other influential factors that determined elections' results in the second round such as the punitive voting Egyptians resorted to.

The importance of applying professionalism and the professionalisation index is that it gives a more comprehensive understanding of how the campaigns were working more than other framework or theories that concentrate on only one aspect. For instance, those studies concentrating on the importance of patronage or organisational strength can still be fitted in the index to be studied with other components. For example, the organisational strength can be assessed in the structure indices. The patronage can be assessed under audience targeting. Other analyses that only studied the image or the mass media can be still fitted into the professionalisation index in the strategy indices. This is why the professionalisation index gives a better understanding of the campaigns since its components reflect a wider aspect of study and analysis rather than analysing only one component or one criterion.

This difference in analysis (i.e. whether it is professionalisation or other factors such as the deep state and organisational strength) is often ascribed to the way different schools study campaigns and elections. As Strömbäck et al. (2013: 46) explain, different schools give different weight to what matters the most when studying and explaining elections. For example, scholars in political campaigning and marketing stress the importance of campaigns' strategies and tactics; whereas scholars in political science concentrate more on the importance of political substance, political programme, and other political factors taking place at the time of elections. Other scholars stress the importance of the candidate himself (Strömbäck et al. 2013: 46).

Nevertheless, although this research stressed the importance of campaigning in this election, it did not neglect other factors that different schools study, especially when it came to the second round of elections, which adds credibility to the findings.

Despite the effort made to guarantee the credibility of the findings, the research should highlight its exploratory nature. It is still the first attempt to study campaign professionalism in Egypt and thus the 2012 Egyptian election campaigns.

Although the data collected is not limited, future studies assessing other Egyptian elections should take into consideration the political environment in which the 2012 elections were taking place.

Future studies can also offer more in-depth analysis in studying the professionalisation of the 2012 presidential elections by studying each campaign separately through interviewing all the campaigns' key staff. This should give a more in-depth understanding and analysis of all that was happening in the campaign, which was not possible in this study.

Future studies can also concentrate on studying the effect of each component studied in the index on both the overall campaign, and on voting behaviour. This would result in better understanding the weight of each of the components and might lead to amending the components of the structure and/or the strategy indices to better reflect the indicators they are measuring and assessing in the Egyptian context.

Further longitudinal studies on future Egyptian elections covering the topics above are needed on both theoretical and practical levels. At the theoretical level, these studies would help academics to understand and explain the campaigns' professionalism patterns and their effect on the election process and voters' behaviour. At the practical level, it would help candidates and campaign managers to develop their strategies and tactics to maximise the returns.

NOTES

1. This is interview with Mohamed Al-Shahawy. Aboul Foutouh's campaign manager.
2. Egypt is divided, for administrative purposes, into 27 governorates. These governorates are either fully 'urban' or else a mixture of 'urban' and 'rural', depending on its second tier division whether it's divided to Markaz and Qesm or Qesm and districts.
3. Interview with Yara Khalaf, Amr Moussa's campaign, Campaign's media team.

4. Interview with Hossam Moeness. Sabahy's campaign manager.
5. Public opinion polls were another main feature of this election. Several centres were keen to conduct public opinion polls. Some were conducted by governmental centres such as the information and decision support centre, others were conducted by research centres affiliated with state-owned newspapers such as Al-Ahram Centre for Political and Strategic Studies (ACPSS), others were conducted by partnership between independent newspapers and independent research centres such as those conducted by Baseera centre and Al-Masry Al-Youm newspapers.

   Most of these polls put Amr Moussa and Abdel Moneim Aboul Fotouh as the front-running candidates. It also reported accelerated progress in the popularity of other candidates such as Morsi and Shafiq over time. However, these polls were not proven to be accurate in comparison to the election results. For example, Moussa, who was reported as the top candidate, came fifth in the election results. And Morsi, who was not a top candidate in these polls, came as a top candidate in the results.

   These inaccurate results led some to accuse the polls of bias or being pseudo polls, to the extent that some presidential candidates such as Abdul Ezz Al-Hariri, Hamdeen Sabahi, and Hisham Bastawisi filed lawsuit against the head of the Shura Council, head of press supreme council and chairman of newspapers and poll centres that conducted polls accusing polls of directing the voters to vote for specific candidates (Ahram gate 27/5/2012).

   Several reasons were given to explain the polls' inaccuracy such as ignoring some segments in the Egyptian societies such as housewives, illiterate citizens, and some border governorates. Majed Othman, head of Baseera, argued that this inaccuracy was mainly because of undecided voters, as 33% of the sample had not decided yet at the time of polls (Aswat Masryia 24/5/2014). In addition was the difficulty of getting the governmental permissions required to conduct face-to-face polls, which make some centres conduct telephone interviews, which lead to inaccuracy as it depends on mobile phones, making verifying identities and details very difficult. But others argued that this inaccuracy was mainly due to a lack of experience, lack of access to lower classes, and lack of access to remote locations (Al-Fagr 22/5/2012).
6. In 2012, one GDP was equal to approximately 10 LE.
7. PEC website
8. Interview with Mohamed Aboul Gheit, Aboul Foutouh campaign's in Asyout governorate.
9. El-Khoreiby's study was conducted a sample of 228 respondents. Only 126 of them responded to the second phase of questions. Phillips's study was conducted on a sample of 393 respondents. Thus, both were very limited to represent the 50,403,717 registered voters.

10. Mahmoud Ibrahim, Internet and Social Media Manager in Shafiq's campaign.
11. Interview with Yehia Hamed, Morsi's campaign spokesperson and former investment minister during Morsi's term in presidency.
12. Interview conducted with Abdel-Galil El-Sharnoby in October 2016. El-Sharnoby held several official positions in the Muslim Brotherhood such as: Head of media unit which was responsible for all the governorates, deputy head of the Brotherhood's media unit, member of the weekly newsletter committee, ex editor in chief of Ikhwan online website.
13. According to the theory, ideologically right-wing parties are supposed to be more professional. Right wing refers to the conservative or reactionary section of a political party or system. In the Egyptian case, conservative and not right wing best describe both the Muslim Brotherhood and the dismantled NDP, since they are not reactionary.
14. For full results in each governorate, see HEC website on: http://pres2012.elections.eg/round1-results.
15. People's assembly elections were conducted on three stages from 28 November 2011 till 11 January 2012. First parliamentary session started on 23 January 2012.
16. Average voter turnout in governorates was 47%. In some governorates, such as Port Said, voter turnout was 60%.
17. The five governorates are Dakahlia, Mounifia, Sharqia, Gharbia, and Qalyubia.
18. Number of void votes was 843,257 votes. The number was nearly equal to the difference of votes between Morsi and Shafiq which was 882,751 votes.
19. During Mubarak's era, arguments explaining winning in parliamentary elections were almost the same, revolving around patronage, clientelism, organisational strength and ideology. For a detailed review on elections during this era and its implications on the nature of future elections, see Blaydes 2001. For a detailed analysis of all arguments explaining Brotherhood victories in the past 30 years, see Masoud 2014. For a detailed analysis of the role of clientelism during Mubarak's era, see El Tarouty 2015.
20. The idea of the 'deep state' was first used to describe the political structure of Turkey, which has a democratic government, but also a powerful military that has the authority to intervene. It was used during the Egyptian transitional period to refer to a set of institutions and bodies believed to be involved in running the country either in the form of secret manipulation or in having control of government policy. These include bureaucratic institutions, intelligence service, military, judiciary institution, and the media. Due to the long period of their existence, they develop patterns of behaviour and rules in the administration that cannot be easily changed even after revolution (for more, see Abdel Meguid 2014).

REFERENCES

Abdel Meguid, W., 2014. What does the term 'deep state' in Egypt mean? *Al-Arabyia* [online], 10 January 2014. Available from: https://www.alarabiya. net/ar/arab-and-world/egypt/2014/01/10/؟ماذا-تعنى-الدولة-العميقة-فى-مصر. html [Accessed 28 January 2016].

Abelson, R. P., Kinder, D. R., Peters, M. D. and Fiske, S. T., 1982. Affective and semantic components in political person perception. *Journal of Personality and Social Psychology*, 42 (4), 619–630.

Ahram Gate, 27/5/2012. Lawsuit in administrative court to stop elections opinion polls, as it influences the public opinion. *Ahram Gate* [online], 27 May 2012. Available from: http://gate.ahram.org.eg/News/213020.aspx [Accessed 28 January 2016].

Al-akhbar, 2012. Interview with Khaled Aly. *Al-akhbar* [online], 17 May 2012. Available from: http://al-akhbar.com/node/64501 [Accessed 18 January 2017].

Al-Arabiya, 29/11/2012. Battles of the constitution in Egypt between the majority and minority. *Al Arabiya* [online], 29 November 2012. Available from: http://www.alarabiya.net/articles/2012/11/29/252554.html [Accessed 1 November 2016].

Al-Fagr, 22/5/2012. Elections polls are incomplete. *Al-Fagr* [online], 22 May 2012. Available from: http://archive.is/FglJ [Accessed 28 January 2016].

Al-Ississ, M. and Attah, S., 2014. Patronage and ideology in electoral behavior: evidence from Egypt's first presidential elections. *European Journal of Political Economy*, 37 (2015), 241–248.

Al-Saadawy, A., 2012. *What the brotherhood lost* [online], 12 July 2012. Washington, DC: Carnegie Endowment for International Peace. Available from: http://carnegieendowment.org/sada/?fa=48833&lang=ar [Accessed 18 January 2017].

Aswat Masriya, 24/5/2014. Challenging facing opinion polls in Egypt. *Aswat Masriya* [online], 25 May 2014. Available from: http://aswatmasriya.com/voters/view.aspx?id=6f533b8e-a070-4cfe-981d-8240210c6616 [Accessed 28 January 2016].

Bass, B., 2011. Advantages & disadvantages of vertical organizational design. *Small Business Chron* [online], 16 August 2011. Available from: http://smallbusiness.chron.com/advantages-disadvantages-vertical-organizational-design-19024.html [Accessed 1 January 2017].

Benoit, W. L., 1999. Let's put 'debate' into presidential debates. *Rostrum*, 74 (9), 21–24.

Benoit, W. L., 2001. The functional approach to presidential television spots: acclaiming, attacking, defending 1952–2000. *Communication Studies*, 52 (2), 109.

Benoit, W. L., 2002. *The primary decision: a functional analysis of debates in presidential primaries*. Westport: Greenwood Press.

Benoit, W. L., 2007. *Communication in political campaigns*. New York: Peter Lang.

Bienkov, A., 2012. Astroturfing: what is it and why does it matter? *The Guardian* [online], 8 February 2012. Available from: https://www.theguardian.com/ commentisfree/2012/feb/08/what-is-astroturfing [Accessed 1 November 2016].

Blaydes, L., 2001. *Elections and distributive politics in Mubarak's Egypt.* New York: Cambridge University Press.

Boorstin, D. J., 1961. *The image: a guide to pseudo-events in America.* New York: Vintage Books.

Burton, M. J. and Shea, D. M., 2015. *Campaign craft: the strategies, tactics, and art of political campaign management.* 5th edition. Westport: Praeger.

Chadwick, A., 2011. The political information cycle in a hybrid news system: the British prime minister and the 'Bullygate' affair. *The International Journal of Press/Politics*, 16 (1), 3–29.

Chaffee, S. H. and Rimal, R. N., 1996. *Political persuasion and attitude change.* Ann Arbor: University of Michigan Press.

Clevers, M. and Nimeh, Z., 2015. *Pharaohs of the deep state: social capital in an obstinate regime* [online]. The Netherlands: Maastricht Economic and Social Research Institute on Innovation and Technology, UNU-MERIT. Working paper #2015-056. Available from: www.merit.unu.edu/publications/ wppdf/2015/wp2015-056.pdf [Accessed 1 January 2017].

Coleman, S., 2000. *Televised election debates: international perspectives.* London: Macmillan.

Converse, P., 1964. The nature of belief systems in mass politics. *In:* Apter, D., ed. *Ideology and discontent.* New York: Free Press, 206–261.

Cwalina, W., Falkowski, A. and Kaid, L. L., 2000. Role of advertising in forming the image of politicians, comparative analysis of Poland, France, and Germany. *Media Psychology*, 2 (2), 119–146.

Cwalina, W., Falkowski, A. and Newman, B., 2011. *Political marketing: theoretical and strategic foundations.* Armonk: M. E. Sharpe.

El Tarouty, S., 2015. *Businessmen, clientelism, and authoritarianism in Egypt.* London: Palgrave Macmillan.

El-Khoreiby, I., 2013. Towards the development of the voter's choice behaviour model: analysis of the Egyptian 2012 presidential elections. *Journal of Arab and Muslim Media Research*, 6 (2/3), 177–199.

Elsebahy, N., 2013. *The impact of social media outlets on the presidential elections: a case study on Egypt's 2012 presidential elections.* Thesis (MA). American University, Cairo, Egypt.

Elsheikh, D., 2011. *New form of opposition in Egypt ... from movements to revolution.* Thesis (MA). SOAS, University of London, England.

Esser, F. and Strömbäck, J., 2012. Comparing election campaign communication. *In:* Esser, F. and Hanitzsch, T., eds. *The handbook of comparative communication research.* New York: Routledge, 289–307.

Ezzabawy, Y., 2013. Funding elections campaigns in presidential elections 2012. *In:* Rabeea, A. H., ed. *Presidential election 2012.* Cairo: Al-Ahram Centre for Political and Strategic Studies, 171–204.

Farrag, D., 2013. Brand image in politics: a case study of the 2012 Egyptian presidential election. *International Journal of Teaching and Case Studies*, 4 (4), 296–312.

Garzia, D., 2011. The personalization of politics in Western democracies: causes and consequences on leader–follower relationships. *Leadership Quarterly*, 22 (4), 697–709.

Gibson, R. and Römmele, A., 2001. Changing campaign communications: a party-centered theory of professionalized campaigning. *Harvard International Journal of Press/Politics*, 6 (4), 31–43.

Gibson, R. and Römmele, A., 2009. Measuring the professionalization of political campaigning. *Party Politics*, 15 (3), 321–339.

Glass, D., 1985. Evaluating presidential candidates: Who focuses on their personal attributes? *Public Opinion Quarterly*, 49, 517–534.

Green, D. and Gerber, A., 2008. *Get out the vote: how to increase voter turnout.* Washington, DC: Brookings Institution Press.

Griffin, D., 2010. Tall vs. flat organizational structure. *Small Business Chron* [online], 6 March 2010. Available from: http://smallbusiness.chron.com/tall-vs-flat-organizational-structure-283.html [Accessed 1 January 2017].

Hill, B., 2011. The importance of a good organizational structure. *Small Business Chron* [online], 28 February 2011. Available from: http://smallbusiness.chron.com/importance-good-organizational-structure-3792.html [Accessed 1 January 2017].

Huebsch, R., 2010. The vertical structure vs. the horizontal structure in an organization. *Small Business Chron* [online], 9 August 2010. Available from: http://smallbusiness.chron.com/vertical-structure-vs-horizontal-structure-organization-4904.html [Accessed 1 January 2017].

Ingram, D., 2011. Why is organizational structure important? *Small Business Chron* [online], 2 August 2011. Available from: http://smallbusiness.chron.com/organizational-structure-important-3793.html [Accessed 1 January 2017].

Isotalus, P., 2011. Analyzing presidential debates: Functional theory and Finnish political communication culture. *Nordicom Review*, 32 (1), 31–43.

Isotalus, P. and Aarnio, E., 2006. A model of televised election discussion: the Finnish multi-party system perspective. *Javnost – The Public*, 13 (1), 61–71.

Johnson, D. W., 2001. *No place for amateurs: how political consultants are reshaping American democracy.* New York: Routledge.

Joseph, C., 2017. Advantages & disadvantages of a vertical & horizontal organization. *Small Business Chron* [online]. Available from: http://smallbusiness.chron.com/advantages-disadvantages-vertical-horizontal-organization-24212.html [Accessed 1 January 2017].

Karvonen, L., 2010. *The personalization of politics: a study of parliamentary democracies.* Colchester: ECPR Press.

Khamis, S. and Mahmoud, A., 2013. Facebooking the Egyptian elections: framing the 2012 presidential race. *Journal of Arab and Muslim Media Research*, 6 (2,3), 134–155.

Kriesi, H., 2012. Personalization of national election campaigns. *Party Politics*, 18 (6), 825–844.

Lees-Marshment, J., 2001. *Political marketing and British political parties: the party's just begun.* Manchester University Press.

Lisi, M., 2013. The professionalization of campaigns in recent democracies: the Portuguese case. *European Journal of Communication*, 28 (3), 259–276.

Maarek, P. J., 2011. *Campaign communication and political marketing / Philippe J. Maarek*, n.p.: Chichester, West Sussex; Malden, MA: Wiley-Blackwell, 2011.

Masoud, T., 2014. *Counting Islam: religion, class, and elections in Egypt.* Cambridge University Press.

McAllister, I., 2007. The personalization of politics. *In:* Dalton, R. J. and Klingemann, H. D., eds. *The Oxford handbooks of political science: the Oxford handbook of political behavior.* Oxford University Press, 571–588.

Monbiot, G., 2011. The need to protect the internet from 'astroturfing' grows ever more urgent. *The Guardian* [online]. Available from: https://www.theguardian.com/environment/georgemonbiot/2011/feb/23/need-to-protect-internet-from-astroturfing [Accessed 1 November 2016].

Mykkänen, J. and Tenscher, J., 2014. Adding or weighting? Alternatives to measure parties' campaign professionalism [online]. *European Consortium for Political Research General Conference*, Glasgow 5 September 2014. Available from: https://ecpr.eu/Filestore/PaperProposal/7582fc4f-5b0a-48f8-83dc-5204237a7d16.pdf [Accessed 1 June 2016].

Norris, P., 2000. *A virtuous circle: political communications in postindustrial societies.* Cambridge University Press.

Ostroff, F., 1999. *The horizontal organization: what the organization of the future actually looks like and how it delivers value to customers: what the organization of … like and how it delivers value to customers.* Oxford University Press.

Ottaway, M., 2013. The unfinished Egyptian transition. *The National Interest* [online], 25 January 2013. Available from: http://nationalinterest.org/commentary/egypts-immature-revolution-8013 [Accessed 1 January 2017].

Paletz, D. L., 2002. *The media in American politics: contents and consequences.* New York: Longman.

Phillips, N. V., 2013. *The impact of mass media uses and gratifications on voters: case of Egypt 2012 presidential elections.* Thesis (MA). Center for Migration and Refugee Studies, American University in Cairo, Egypt.

Rabeea, A. H., 2013. Constitutional and legal environment to 2012 presidential elections. *In:* Rabeea, A. H., ed. *Presidential election 2012.* Cairo: Al-Ahram Centre for Political and Strategic Studies, 11–48.

Rahat, G. and Sheafer, T., 2007. The personalization(s) of politics: Israel, 1949–2003. *Political Communication*, 41 (1), 65–80.

Scammell, M., 1998. The wisdom of the war room: US campaigning and Americanization. *Media, Culture and Society*, 20 (2), 251–275.

Scammell, M., 1999. Political marketing: lessons for political science. *Political Studies*, 47 (4), 718–739.

Shehata, S., Hanna, M., Ottaway, M. and Slavin, B., 2012. *Egyptian elections, round one* [online]. Washington, DC: Carnegie Endowment for International Peace. Available from: http://carnegieendowment.org/2012/05/31/egyptian-elections-round-one/av10 [Accessed 1 January 2017].

Shoman, M. and Saleh, A., 2013. Campaigns' strategies & tactics in 2012 presidential elections. *In:* Rabeea, A. H., ed. *Presidential election 2012.* Cairo: Al Ahram Centre for Political and Strategic Studies, 205–239.

Shukr, A., 2013. Elections results. *In:* Rabeea, A. H., ed. *2012 presidential elections.* Cairo: Al Ahram Centre for Political and Strategic Studies, 281–301.

Sides, J., Shaw, D., Grossmann, M. and Lipsitz, K., 2012. *Campaigns & elections: rules, reality, strategy, choice.* New York: W.W. Norton and Company.

Smith, G. and French, A., 2009. The political brand: a consumer perspective. *Marketing Theory,* 9 (2), 209–226.

Chaffee, S. H., and Choe, S. Y., 1980. Time of decision and media use during the Ford-Carter Campaign. *The Public Opinion Quarterly,* 1, p. 53, JSTOR Journals.

Strömbäck, J., 2007. Political marketing and professionalized campaigning. A conceptual analysis. *Journal of Political Marketing,* 6 (2–3), 49–67.

Strömbäck, J., 2008. Four phases of mediatization: an analysis of the mediatization of politics. *International Journal of Press/Politics,* 13 (3), 228–246.

Strömbäck, J., 2009. Selective professionalisation of political campaigning. A test of the party-centered theory of professionalised campaigning in the context of the 2006 Swedish election. *Political Studies,* 57 (1), 95–116.

Strömbäck, J., Grandien, C., and Falasca, K., 2013. Do campaign strategies and tactics matter? Exploring party elite perceptions of what matters when explaining election outcomes. *Journal of Public Affairs,* 13 (1), 41–52.

Sullivan, J., 2010. Four basic elements of organizational structure. *Small Business Chron* [online], 6 April 2010. Available from: http://smallbusiness.chron.com/four-basic-elements-organizational-structure-288.html   [Accessed   1 January 2017].

Tenscher, J., 2013. First- and second-order campaigning: evidence from Germany. *European Journal of Communication,* 28 (3), 241–258.

Tenscher, J., Mykkänen, J., and Moring, T., 2012. Modes of professional campaigning: A four-country comparison in the European parliamentary elections, 2009. *The International Journal of Press/Politics,* 17 (2), 145–168.

Trager, E., 2016. *Arab Fall, how the Muslim Brotherhood won and lost Egypt in 891 days.* Washington, DC: Georgetown University Press.

Van Aelst, P., Sheafer, T. and Stanyer, J., 2012. The personalization of mediated political communication: a review of concepts, operationalizations and key findings. *Journalism,* 13 (2), 203–220.

Wattenberg, M. P., 1987. The hollow realignment: Partisan change in a candidate-centered era. *Public Opinion Quarterly,* 51 (1), 58–74.

Wisconsin Advertising Project, 2017. *An overview of the Wisconsin advertising project* [online]. University of Wisconsin-Madison. Available from: http://wiscadproject.wisc.edu [Accessed 1 January 2017].

CHAPTER 5

Conclusion: The Impact of Campaigns' Professionalism on the Democratisation Process in Egypt

This book indicates the levels of professionalism adopted by the candidates in the 2012 presidential elections in Egypt may have impacted upon the outcome. Previous chapters explained how the readiness of both Morsi and Shafiq to adopt some 'professionalised' techniques was behind their success in the first round of elections, with Morsi's campaign proving to be the most 'professional', helping him in securing his path towards Egypt's presidency, to be the first elected president after the 25 January Revolution and the first elected president in a very unpredictable first multi-candidate election in Egyptian history. This chapter aims to conclude the study by discussing the implications of the levels of campaign professionalism on the democratisation process in Egypt. The chapter concludes that professionalism—as applied by Morsi's campaign—had a negative impact on Egypt's democratic transition in general, as it led Egypt to be stuck in its transitional period, rather than moving to a functional emerging thin democracy. The chapter argues that this was mainly due to Morsi's performance once elected. The chapter also provides an evaluation of the application of the professionalisation index in order to understand campaigns in nascent democracies.

© The Author(s) 2018   229
D. Elsheikh, *Campaign Professionalism during Egypt's 2012 Presidential Election*, Political Campaigning and Communication,
https://doi.org/10.1007/978-3-319-75954-8_5

5.1   Professionalisation and Democracy

Literature on professionalisation can be divided into three main sections: (a) studies devoted to defining professionalisation, its emergence, and how to measure it (Lilleker and Negrine 2002; Tenscher et al. 2012; Gibson and Römmele 2001, 2009), (b) studies discussing the relationship between professionalisation and electoral outcomes (Herrnson 1992; Medvic and Lenart 1997), (c) and studies discussing the positive and negative impact of professionalisation on the quality of democracy (Koch 2011; Norris 2004a, b; Hamelink 2007). Studies analysing the impact of professionalisation on the democratic process can be divided into two main trends (Rayner 2014). The first trend believes that professionalisation enhances democracy by allowing better engagement with voters and thus better voter participation. Pippa Norris found that there is a positive relationship between voters' attention to campaigns' messages and activities and the levels of 'civic knowledge, political efficacy and voting participation' in the United States, Britain, and other countries (Norris 1996, 1997, 2004a, b). Norris also argues that those who follow more media outlets and campaigns' activities are more 'knowledgeable, trusting of government and participatory' (Norris 2000, 2004a, b). The second trend, which depends on theories of media malaise and video malaise, argues that professionalisation depends too much on communication and marketing techniques which manipulate voters to win, creating a cynical society, civic disengagement, and perhaps a polarised society due to polarised messages it used (see Koch 2011; Norris 2004a, b; Johnson 2001; Magleby et al. 2000). Hamelink (2007) explains the difference between the two trends by arguing that the professionalisation strengthens thin[1] democracies but 'does little to assist the development of strong, participatory, deliberative democracy' (Hamelink 2007: 185).

While Hamelink's conclusion might be theoretically logical, it does not help in explaining the impact of using professionalism on the democratic process in Egypt as there is a difference between applying professionalism in an already functioning democracy (whether thin or thick) and in applying it in a country which is still in a transitional phase. When professionalisation occurs within developed democracies, there are usually higher levels of civic education and a more developed critical media and public sphere. The absence of these checks and balances in a state such as Egypt—which we cannot call a democracy yet as it is still in its transitional period—can be argued to make the effect of professionalisation damaging to the democratic process, especially when it is only victory focused, ready to do or say anything for the sake of winning.

In 2012, Egypt was neither a thin democracy nor a strong thick one. It was not a democracy at all. On the contrary, Egypt was in a transitional period trying to build the basis of a democracy. It was trying to build a thin democracy. In this transitional process, Egypt was still trying to build its democratic institutions (new constitution, new parliament, new president) after which it would start its democratisation process. After starting the democratisation process, a country—Egypt in this case—can be transformed into a thin democracy, then to a strong democracy. In each of these stages (removing a regime through a revolution, then the transitional stage, then a thin democracy, then a consolidated or thick democracy), the process could fail and there could be a reverse (see Fig. 5.1).

When the campaigns were launched in Egypt, Egypt did not have any prerequisite that allows it to be considered a democracy, even a weak democracy. As it did not have any of the prerequisite democratic institutions, it did not have an elected president, or elected parliament, or a constitution. In 2012, campaigns took place in a transitional period characterised by liquidity, polarisation, emergence of new political forces not known before, floundering in polices and in coalition with different forces.

Thus, Hamelink's argument on thin democracies cannot be applied to Egypt as Egypt had not reached the level of thin democracy at that time. Hamelink's ideas might be applied in a country that had already moved from the transitional period to be a new functioning, emerging thin democracy, on the contrary to what this chapter argues. In the case of Egypt, in that transitional state, the main two winning campaigns—Morsi and Shafiq—adhered closely to a model of professionalisation that compares well to that of many established democracies such as the United States or the United Kingdom. While adhering to this model of

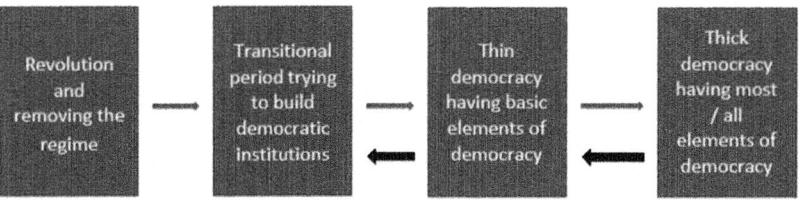

Fig. 5.1 Democratisation cycle

campaigning, they followed a 'do anything to win' approach. This approach affected the process of democratisation negatively and perhaps hindered the process of transition to a new emerging democracy. In other words, the use of professionalism by the campaigns of Morsi and Shafiq in the 2012 election had a negative impact on the democratisation process Egypt was trying to start, leaving it stuck in the transitional period. Having said that, the chapter is not arguing that professionalisation in itself has been in tension with democratisation, as the media malaise model suggests. Instead, the chapter is arguing that because it helped Morsi win, it has facilitated all the anti-democratic moves which this chapter will describe. Thus, the chapter supports neither the virtuous circle nor media malaise assessments of professionalisation: it shows that what matters is who uses it effectively to win.

The next section will highlight some of the negative consequences of Morsi's application of professionalisation during the transitional period. The reason for choosing Morsi's campaign to highlight these negative implications can be summarised in the following reasons: (a) Morsi was the winner and became the new president of Egypt. (b) Previous chapters proved how professionalism helped him in winning, thus it is important to know whether he would continue using the same professionalised methods after winning. (c) His campaign practices, policies, and promises were rediscovered during his era, especially when he did not fulfil them, creating more polarisation in the society. (d) Practices used by his campaign during his campaign time still had influence and consequences during his ruling era. (e) Shafiq's exit from the Egyptian political scene is the reason why this chapter concentrates on assessing the impact of using professionalism through Morsi's campaign. This does not deny the role Shafiq's campaign also played in creating polarisation as proven in previous chapters.

5.2   NEGATIVE IMPACT OF PROFESSIONALISATION DURING MORSI'S PRESIDENCY

5.2.1   *Manipulating and Deceiving Voters Through Fake Projects and Fake Promises*

The content of Morsi's campaign was built on his election programme which was called the Nahda project or 'the renaissance project'. It was reflected as well in the campaign's slogans, 'Renaissance is the will of the people' and 'we hold the good for Egypt'. It was also reflected in the campaign symbol which was in the shape of a bird, known as the 'Renaissance bird'.

Newspapers and different media outlets—including official Muslim Brotherhood media outlets—loaded with stories about this project and how it would bring good fortune and prosperity for Egyptians. The programme was distributed in various media outlets and published by almost all newspapers (shorouknews 10/5/2012). It was also uploaded onto the campaign official website (Al-Masry 25/6/2012). The project consisted of seven axes that cover several aspects of the Renaissance of Egypt, which all gave various promises to Egyptians. For example, according to the project, Morsi promised to launch 100 national projects to be distributed in each governorate so that each governorate could become a leader in a field, that is, agricultural, industrial, tourism, and so on (Alarabiya net 21/5/2012). The cost of each project was to exceed one billion dollars (Al-Masry 25/6/2012).

Ikhwan web, the Muslim Brotherhood official English website, also stressed the importance of the project. A sample of these would appear in the following stories which were all published on their English official website.[2]

- On 27 April 2012, the website published a story quoting sentences from the Khairat Al-Shater interview. During an interview with the Al-Haqiqa programme on the Dream Two TV channel talking about the project and saying that 'establishing a democratic system and strong political institutions is the actual beginning of the launch of the Renaissance Project'.

- On 29 April 2012, the website published a story saying that 'Dr. Mohamed Morsi revealed that the Nahda Project has 20 billion Egyptian Pounds (US$3.33 billion) to be spent on the reconstruction of the Sinai during the first 5 years of implementing the project'.

- On 7 May 2012, the website published a quotation from Mohamed Gouda, prominent economist and member of the Freedom and Justice Party (FJP) saying that the Nahda project was prepared and had 'a large number of Egyptian experts and scientists'.

- On 7 May 2012, the website published a story quoting Ayman Al-Zahayri, FJP Secretary in South Sinai: "The renaissance train has already left the station, and will bring good fortunes to the Egyptian people. Dr. Morsi has a wealth of experience in economy, politics and democracy. He is also a scientist who has submitted scientific researches to NASA. We are confident Egypt will be all the greater with Dr. Morsi as president".

- On 16 May 2012, the website published a story that FJP's Nahda project team organised a conference about Renaissance experiences around the world and that it would be attended by former Malaysian PM Mahathir Mohamad to speak about the Malaysian Renaissance model.

- On 20 May 2012, the website published a story saying that 'Dr. Morsi assures businessmen that the scientific committee in charge of his Nahda (Renaissance) Project comprises 10 specialized experts, that Egyptian markets will be open to foreign investors, and that $20 billion will be invested in tourism'.

The extensive stress on the Nahda project from the Muslim Brotherhood, FJP members, campaigns' members, Morsi and Al-Shater themselves made Morsi's name synonymous with the word Nahda. When Morsi was elected as president, Egyptians were waiting for him to start fulfilling promises in the Al-Nahda project. Some activists even launched a website called 'Morsi Meter' to measure what he would fulfil from his promises mainly in the first 100 days. According to the website, Morsi made 64 promises during his election campaign, and the website wanted to check what he fulfilled and what he did not.

However, when Morsi came to power, the surprise that shocked Egyptians was that there was nothing called Al-Nahda project. The Muslim Brotherhood leader started denying that they had launched a detailed project called Al-Nahda, saying that it was only a vision and that Egyptian media got it wrong. Khairat Al-Shater himself said on 14 August 2012 after his meeting with revolutionary forces that the media dealt with the project incorrectly and that the Brotherhood does not have a clear programme or final schedule for it to implement and that it was just a 'preliminary proposal' (Alarabiya net 29/8/2012). In another speech by him broadcast on the Al Jazeera live channel, Al-Shater said that implementing Al-Nahda project needs qualified and enthusiastic citizens

(Al-Masry alyoum 12/9/2012). The latter statement provoked anger as it made it appear as if the problem was with the Egyptian people—as they did not have the degree of awareness needed for the project—but not in the project itself (Gad 2014: 275)

From the above overview, it appears that Morsi's campaign was able to convey professionalised campaign messages for a main core project of its campaign that did not exist. It was able to deceive voters without any ethical rules and without being afraid of becoming accountable. The discovery of the non-existence of the project also led to a state of distrust and cynicism towards any future Muslim Brotherhood promises. It made it very difficult to believe in them again, creating an early perception that what is built on falsehood is false in itself. It even created a platform for sarcasm and jokes.

The manipulation was not limited to the electoral programme or the Al-Nahda project only. It also appeared in how Morsi's presented himself as a NASA scientist—which was proven to be false as explained in previous chapters—trying to give himself extra credit and qualifications, to create a specific leadership image that did not exist, for the sake of getting more votes.

5.2.2   Manipulating Other Egyptian Political Forces

The manipulation was not limited to the general voters but extended to other political forces in Egypt including the Muslim Brotherhood's own allies such as Salafists represented in Al-Nour Salafists party.

Between the two rounds of elections, exactly on 22 June 2012, Morsi had a meeting with some of the revolutionary forces, along with other non-Islamist public figures. The result of this meeting was what was known as the Fairmount agreement. According to this agreement, Morsi promised inclusive rule. He promised that the next prime minster would be an independent national figure and that the government majority would not be from the Muslim Brotherhood (Al-Masry 23/6/2012). He also promised not to appoint a vice president from the Muslim Brotherhood, promising to consider appointing four vice presidents to include a woman, a Copt, and a youth figure. He also promised to ensure the independence of the judicial and legislative power (Gad 2014: 17).

However, after Morsi won the election and became the new president, another surprise appeared. Morsi did not fulfil his promise of pluralism and inclusive rule. On the contrary, he started what was known as the

Brotherhoodisation—*akhwanat al-dawla*—of the Egyptian state. The term refers to appointing Brotherhood members or Brotherhood sympathisers to top official jobs in each and all governmental institutions and public bodies. The problem with this Brotherhoodisation of the state is that it was not limited to the governmental posts or ministerial appointments but was extended to every public institution in the state, giving the Muslim Brotherhood a monopoly of control over all areas of Egyptian life (El-Din 2012).

In other words, these appointments meant changing the structure of the Egyptian state and the identity of future generations. For example, when they control the Ministry of Education from inside and have the upper hand in forcing and changing education curricula, this means changing the identity and culture of future generations. When they control the Ministry of Endowment, this would mean that they would have full control over what is said in mosques as they would have the upper and only hand in appointing Imam to mosques. When they implant their members in the governorates and councils, this would mean that all these appointed members would act as their 'field co-coordinators' in future elections. This action increased speculation and raised fears that they were not planning to stop ruling the country at any stage.[3]

These acts of state Brotherhoodisation even excluded other Islamic allies to the Muslim Brotherhood such as the Salafists. In a televised on-air meeting between Morsi and different political forces, the leader of the Nour party complained about Morsi installing officials from only one party—referring to the Freedom and Justice Party, the political arm of the Muslim Brotherhood in influential executive positions. He gave a list of these appointed Brotherhood members in 13 governorates to President Morsi.[4]

Again, Morsi's use of tactics consistent with professionalisation in the campaigning period helped him to deceive and manipulate other political forces in the country, convincing them of the intention to implement inclusive rule. However, because of the Muslim Brotherhood's ideological orientation, it wanted to have monopoly control over power, not only excluding opponents or civilian forces but also excluding their Islamic allies.

5.2.3 Changing Egypt's Identity and Increasing the Polarisation in the Public Sphere

In a narrowcasting campaigning activity targeting the Islamic voters in Al-Mahala in June 2012, prominent Islamic figure Safwat Hegazy was filmed talking to those attending the event about the Islamic Caliphate State. Hegazy was saying then that it would be called the United Arab States, and its capital would not be Cairo, Makkah, or Madina, but Jerusalem—Al Quds. He then chanted with the audience the slogan 'To Jerusalem, we are going, martyrs in millions'.

The event was filmed and uploaded on YouTube and broadcast later by several private media outlets.[5] The controversy of the event can be summarised twofold. The first is again deceiving and manipulating voters through the narrowcasting events. For the Muslim Brotherhood represented by Morsi, were not going to liberate Jerusalem or unite all Arab and Muslim states under the 'Islamic Caliphate'.

The second issue would be that although this event might have secured the vote of Islamic voters attending, it raised fears among other non-Islamist forces: Is the Muslim Brotherhood aiming to dissolve the Egyptian national identity into an Islamic one? How would they liberate Jerusalem? From where would they bring the weapons? Would they involve the civilian citizens or the army in a war?

Apparently, the event showed a sort of manipulation and was misleading to the voters as Morsi was not going into a war with Israel. On the contrary, he stressed respecting and abiding by all Egypt's international treaties and agreed for Israel to instal cameras on the Israeli-Egyptian borders, something Mubarak never agreed on (Gad 2014: 18).

Although the event is proven to be just 'electoral campaigning', it helped in increasing the trend of polarisation that would take place in Egypt during Morsi's presidency, which all proved part of an attempt to change the identity of Egypt.

Examples of further attempts would be changes taking place in some schools after promoting Muslim Brotherhood members in the Ministry of Education, as some schools were reported separating Muslim and Christian students, each in a separate class (Gad 2014: 291). Another example would be an essay question that came in an Arabic language exam to the first secondary students: The role played by the government, the secular liberal parties, the corrupt media, and the foreign organisations in conspiring against the Egyptian people after the 25 January Revolution (Gad

2014: 291), thus applying negative descriptions to other political forces in the country; media is corrupt, and non-Islamic parties are secular and all conspiring against Egypt! Changes were also clear in appointing a Muslim Brotherhood supporter to the Ministry of Culture, who came with a plan to dismiss non-Islamist figures from the ministry (ElNabawi 2013). The action re-highlighted the issue of attempts to change Egypt's culture, especially as these actions happened amid calls from the Shura Council to ban ballet dancing as it promotes 'indecency' in society (Al-Arabiya 21/6/13).

Changes were not limited to the educational and cultural process only, but there was an attempt to implement projects that would affect every day Egyptian lives. By the end of 2011, Egyptians found two pages on Facebook announcing the establishment of what was called an Egyptian Committee for the Promotion of Virtue and the Prevention of Vice (BBC Arabic 28/12/2011). The group made it clear that it would not force Egyptians to do anything by coercion. However, this was not done practically. During Morsi's presidency, the media reported stories that were attributed to the committee such as in Luxor, a teacher cut the hair of two girls in the preparatory schools as they did not wear the Hijab (Al-Watan 21/10/12). A woman wearing Niqab in the tube cut the hair of a 13-year-old girl because she was not wearing Hijab (Youm7 8/11/2012). A journalist receiving a threatening message signed by the Committee for the Promotion of Virtue and the Prevention of Vice, asking her to stop her husband—who is journalist as well—from criticising Islamic rule (Suleiman 2013). In Suez, a young man—a student in Engineering—was killed in the street by two men who claimed he was performing an obscene act in the street (Omran 2012). The committee also published an advertisement looking for a thousand youth volunteers to work with it, with a weekly reward of 500 LE, and that they would be provided with 1000 electro-shock weapons (Suleiman 2013).

The hate crimes did not stop at this level. It was crowned by a shocking incident towards the end of Morsi's rule in June 2013—by the lynching of four Shias—including a sheikh, by a mob in the village of Abu Musallam in Giza (EIPR 2013). The event was explained by the Human Rights watch as due to 'months of hate speech' (HRW 2013).

All these incidents raised the fear of non-Islamist Egyptians and increased the polarisation of Egyptian society and the anger against Morsi's rule. As explained by Hillal in an interview, Egyptians were not angry towards Morsi because of his failure in running the country but because of their fear of their Egyptian identity (Al-Wafd 25/1/2017).

5.2.4 Using Technology and Mass Media Outlets to Destroy and Distort Opponents

On 4 June 2012, the presidency invited party leaders and public figures to meet with President Morsi to discuss a report about the implications of Ethiopia's diversion of one of the Nile's tributaries as part of their construction of the Nahda Dam. The meeting was converted into a comic movie or a circus. Those who attended the meeting thought that it was a confidential secret meeting with the president. No one told them that the meeting was being broadcast live on-air. Morsi rarely spoke and left the platform to the leaders. They started offering strange solutions, unaware that citizens at home—even Ethiopian leaders—were viewing them live. They offered solutions suggesting the involvement of the Egyptian intelligence service to destroy any dam Ethiopia built, leaking false information to the Ethiopian government, and supporting ethnic liberation movements in Ethiopia against the government (Al-Masry 4/6/13). The meeting continued like this until one of the attendees asked all in attendance to vow not to leak anything of what was mentioned in the meeting outside the room. He was then handed a note informing them that they were on-air, and Morsi finally revealed that the meeting was broadcast live (Stack 2013).

The meeting provided fertile material for sarcasm and jokes between Egyptians. It was even the main topic in one episode of Bassem Youssef's satirical show[6] giving it the title 'looking for a scandal'. However, for Morsi, the meeting had its role as it highlighted the political weaknesses of the political forces that attended the meeting, as if Morsi wanted to tell Egyptians, are these the political forces you want me to include in the political process.

The above example is not the only instance where Morsi used media outlets to undermine his opponents. The role of the electronic committees continued in Morsi's era, but instead of campaigning for him, the new role included opening Facebook pages criticising Morsi's rule to control the amount of disapproval, highlight topics they can defend or divert criticism away from certain issues as explained by Abdel Galil El-sharonoby in a personal interview. It also used to comment on online articles that contained any criticism of Morsi or the Muslim Brotherhood by accusing the writer of treason, anti-Islamic tendencies or receiving funds from abroad to criticise the regime (Gad 2014: 284). The role of the electronic committees was extended to even include creating a database for non-Islamist public figures and sending them threatening SMS messages or calling them all night and threatening them in person (Gad 2014: 284). As explained by those who received these calls and messages, when they reported the phone number to the police, they discovered that the numbers were not registered in the communication ministry, thus no one could obtain them (Gad 2014: 285). This suggests the argument highlighted in previous chapters about the Muslim Brotherhood's IT department that helps the electronic committees with technical issues.

5.2.5   The 'Do Everything to Win' Approach

During the campaign, Morsi was able to secure his path towards the presidency by doing everything in order to win. After proven to be an effective approach during his campaign, he resorted to it again during his presidency. Although Morsi won the elections, he mainly won as Egyptians resorted to punitive voting. In other words, the majority of Egyptians were against him. This could be the reason why Morsi was trying to have full power and full control over all the institutions in the country and the Egyptian public sphere as well in order to secure his presidency. This was mainly applied through two ways. The first was through the Brotherhoodisation process. The second was by entering a direct confrontation with the institution he was not able to Brotherhoodise, again in order to control it and secure his presidency. These institutions that he confronted included the Judiciary, the army, the church, the media and, more importantly, the ordinary Egyptian people who were part of each of these confrontations.

5.2.5.1 The Judiciary

Morsi's tense relationship with the Judiciary and the rule of the law appeared from day one. For him the judges were those who dissolved the Islamic dominated parliament and the constitution assembly that were formed in the transitional period as elaborated in previous chapters. He perceived they could 'conspire' against him again and threaten his legitimacy as a president. Since the Brotherhoodisation of the Judiciary system was difficult due to laws organising presidential interference and since any judge need to come from the Judiciary cadre, confrontation was the solution.

The confrontation with the Judiciary started on the same day of announcing Morsi as the president: his campaign stated that he would not swear the presidential oath in front of the SCC in accordance with the SCAF June constitution declaration, but in front of the people's assembly which was already dissolved after it was proven unconstitutional as mentioned in previous chapters. This act created polarisation in the public sphere (CNN 25/7/2012). To end the polarisation, Morsi swore the oath in three places: SCC, Tahrir Square, and Cairo University; an indication that the SCC is not the main legitimate place and one that can be considered as an early confrontation with SCAF and with Egyptian judges in general.

While saying the oath in Tahrir Square, another clash with the rule of law took place. Some supporters of Omar Abdel Rahman, the Islamic leader in Al-Gama'a Al-Islamiyya, who was spending his life term sentence in the United States in relation to the New York attacks in 1993, were holding his photo and asking President Morsi to release him (Trager 2016). Morsi replied that he would do his best. This act raised many critical questions in the Egyptian media: Did Morsi just promise to release a terrorist who is spending his sentence after trial in US prisons? (Al-Watan 29/6/12; Awsat 30/6/12).

Disrespect for the rule of law and challenging the Judiciary was also apparent in Morsi's surprising controversial decree in July ordering the currently dissolved parliament to reconvene.[7] A decree that forced the SCC to issue a statement halting the presidential decree as the parliament was already proven unconstitutional (The Guardian 10/7/2012). The issue caused polarisation and protests in the street. In the end, Morsi suspended his decree.

Another clash with the rule of the law and with the Egyptian Judiciary happened in October when Morsi attempted—against Egyptian law[8]—to remove the current Attorney General by making him an Ambassador to the Vatican, a move that caused fierce anger from all political forces.

The major clash with the rule of law happened in November and December 2012, when Morsi issued a constitutional declaration giving himself ultimate power and when he helped in passing a constitution which non-Islamic forces did not agree on.

This constitutional crisis started on 22 November 2012 when Morsi issued his most controversial decree which granted him full power.[9]

According to it, all his decisions are 'final and binding and cannot be appealed by any way or to any entity'. He gave himself the right to appoint a new Attorney General for four years in opposition to Egyptian law and immunised the constitution Assembly and Shura Council from potential dissolution by court order (Ahram online 22/11/2012).

The declaration was condemned by non-Islamic political forces and sparked violent protests in Tahrir Square and at the presidential palace in Cairo leading to hundreds of injuries and several deaths. In the end, Morsi agreed to limit its scope to 'sovereign matters' but insisted on keeping his right to protect the constitution assembly from dissolution (BBC News 24/12/12).

Morsi's declaration of 22 November gave the constitutional assembly until January to complete drafting the constitution. However, members of the constitution assembly met overnight to finish the constitution draft, an act that was described by the BBC as 'a marathon overnight session of voting on a rushed draft' (BBC News 24/12/12); and an act that was taken when the SCC announced that it would rule on whether the constitution should be dissolved (BBC News 29/11/12). The constitution was approved by the panel and sent to Morsi who called for a referendum on 15 December, refusing to postpone it as requested by the opposition forces. This was an action that caused outrage protests and discontent.

The conflict between Morsi and the judges reached its peak when Morsi's supporters surrounded the court building intimidating the judges in order to prevent them from reviewing the constitution assembly. This action was inspired by his campaign's activities, where his supporters used to show their numerical power by participating in protest or by forming long human chains. The action of surrounding the court this time led the court to suspend its work indefinitely. In a statement, the Supreme Constitutional Court (SCC) called it a 'dark day' in the history of the judiciary and expressed sadness at the 'psychological assassination' of the court (The Guardian 2/12/2016).

Amid all this outrage, the rule of the law was once again broken when Morsi's supporters entered the area around the presidential palace known as Ittihadiyah Palace, where anti-Morsi peaceful protests were taking place and took control of the area. Muslim Brotherhood supporters also captured anti-Morsi protestors and tortured them.[10] Videos of tortures along with videos of severely injured victims speaking of what happened were uploaded on social media and private TV channels sparking another wave of anger and polarisation in the Egyptian public sphere.

5.2.5.2 *The Army*

The confrontation with the army also started from the time of campaigning and continued during Morsi's presidency. After closing the polls in the second round of elections, Morsi's campaign claimed that he was the winner before any official results were announced, an action that was described as an attempt from Morsi to 'control the narrative' (Trager 2016: 141). His campaign also leaked messages that the army was conspiring with Shafiq to change the election results to favour Shafiq. Moreover, the Muslim Brotherhood members came from all governorates for a sit-in protest in Tahrir Square, threating to use violence if Shafiq was announced as winner. This action caused severe tension, fear, and polarisation in the Egyptian public sphere and more importantly sent a direct message to the army to fear Morsi's failure in this election.[11]

The confrontation with the army did not stop after announcing Morsi as the new president. Although the details of this confrontation are not available to the public, there are some incidents that can clarify the degree of confrontation or how Morsi was trying to gain control. The most prominent incident was replacing the military chiefs after less than two months into his presidency, an action that was described by the Washington Post as a 'bid to consolidate power' (Londoño 2012).

However, the confrontation between the presidency and the army was not always that clear. It appeared to the public mainly through Morsi's speeches. Morsi made several statements that were understood to provoke both the army and the Egyptian people as well. Morsi's speeches used to be improvisatory, exceeding the length of two hours and sometimes more, making them very difficult to follow or to cut for a news clip, which allowed him many opportunities to make controversial, problematic statements. Some of these problematic statements were directed or referred to the army.

Four main examples can be recalled regarding this issue. The first example would be during the 6 October anniversary which celebrates Egypt's victory over Israel in 1973. The commemoration took place in Cairo Stadium. Egyptians were surprised to see Tarek al-Zumar, the leader in Al-Gama'a Al-Islamiyya, who spent 30 years in prison as a punishment for his role in assassinating President Anwar Al-Sadat, who led the victory of the event back in 1973. This act was considered offensive by the army, Sadat's family, and the Egyptian people (Elaph 8/10/12).

A second famous example would be the incident of kidnapping seven security officers in Sinai on 16 May. In this incident, Morsi commented that the efforts made to release them should 'preserve the lives of everyone, whether the kidnapped or the kidnappers' (Al-Masry 17/5/13). His statement raised a state of anger among the Egyptian people and hidden anger among the army of course. The Egyptian people, the non-Islamists, already feared extremism and terrorist attacks, but now their president was equating a terrorist who kidnapped an officer with the kidnapped officer. Although the statement raised fear among Egyptians, it also became one of the satirical statements often associated with Morsi.[12] For the army, the degree of anger was understood when they issued a statement after releasing the soldiers thanking the Army intelligence and Sinai tribes, without thanking the president (Trager 2011).

Nonetheless, the situation between Morsi and the army was not limited to some hyperbole or bullshit statement (Belfiore 2009). On 10 June, Morsi spoke about the Ethiopian dam project saying that 'all options are open' referring to a possibility of military action, involving the army and the Egyptian people in unnecessary confrontation and war. The turning point in the relationship between Morsi and the army—as described by Reuters—was the 'Syria support conference', where Morsi blessed Egyptians to go for Jihad to Syria and moreover hinting at Egypt's military intervention in Syria (Reuters Arabic 2/7/13). This action forced army leaders to break their silence and refute Morsi's statements (Al-Masry 17/6/13).

The above examples show the amount of 'unprofessionalism' from Morsi's side. As a president, it would have been assumed that he would act more professionally with the army but, apparently, he used to resort to professionalism only for the sake of getting votes. After winning, he was not applying the same methods while dealing with the various institutions. One would assume that he would hire an expert to help him write his speeches, rather than being improvisational every time and creating unnecessary tension every time he spoke. However, it appears that these sorts of professional methods and techniques were not a priority for him during his presidency. The priorities were the methods and techniques he was depending on during and after the campaign, such as depending on the everything to win approach and on the organisational weight of the Muslim Brotherhood that can mobilise people in the street to surround a court or to protest in the streets, just to consolidate power and secure his presidency, without paying attention to the division and polarisation his actions caused in the Egyptian public sphere.

5.2.5.3 The Church and Christians

Morsi's relation with the Egyptian Christians was another extension of his campaign. Of course, he could not Brotherhoodise the Church or Christians, thus confrontation through the 'everything in order to win' approach was the solution.

During the start of campaign, Morsi gave Christians many assurances that they would be protected in his era. He repeatedly said that their protection was his own personal responsibility (Gad 2014: 74), but this reassuring speech changed as soon as the result of the first round of elections appeared as many incidents took place that would fan the flames of sectarian strife. For example, immediately after announcing the results of the first round of elections, the Muslim Brotherhood started saying that Shafiq won because of Christians' votes.[13] Tarek al-Zumar, the leader in Al-Gama'a Al-Islamiyya, asked Christians to apologise to the Egyptian people (Gad 2014: 103). Moreover, Al-Gama'a Al-Islamiyya issued a press release saying that Shafiq won due to what they called the 'sectarian voting' that took place in the first round of elections (Gad 2014: 103). This was a continuance of the deceptive and manipulating techniques for both media and ordinary voters to secure the Islamic vote in the second round of elections.

The same approach of confrontation continued during Morsi's presidency. The confrontation reached its peak during the constitutional crisis and the demonstration that took place around the Ittihadiyah Palace, as Freedom and Justice leaders,[14] along with other Islamist figures, claimed that 80% of those protesting at the palace were Christians and that the Church was the one mobilising them (Gad 2014: 78), again creating unnecessary polarisation in the society, but this time between their Islamist supporters from one side and Christians and the Church in general from the other side.

5.2.5.4 Confrontation with the Media

Public media was also affected by the Brotherhoodisation. The Islamist-dominated Shura Council appointed a new Supreme Council for the press making sure it was also Islamist-dominated. The new council replaced editors in all state-owned publications to ensure they are either Islamists or Muslim Brotherhood sympathisers. A new Minister of Information—Salah Abdel Maqsoud—was also appointed from the Muslim Brotherhood. Soon after these appointments, Egyptian editors and writers left their columns blank to protest against decisions taken to control the media.

The problems were not only limited to Brotherhoodisation. According to the Arabic Network for Human Rights, during the first 200 days of Morsi's presidency, the authorities were investigating 24 cases where journalists were accused of insulting the president, in comparison to only 14 cases during the past 115 years (Al-Masry 20/1/13). There were also 600 complaints filed to the police against some journalists (Al-Arabiya net 3/4/13).

The real conflict with the media appeared when Islamist supporters gathered in a sit-in protest surrounding the media production zone in Cairo, blocking access to it and preventing presenters and those working inside from entering or going out. They were protesting against what they called media bias against the ruling Islamist President Mohamed Morsi (Al-Arabiya net 25/3/13), repeating the previous situation of surrounding the SCC court and repeating a technique that was proven successful in their campaign. The extent of the problem also appeared when the Muslim Brotherhood's general guide blamed the media as the main cause for problems between the Muslim Brotherhood group and the Egyptian political forces (Gad 2014: 280).

5.3   The Lost Hope

It was assumed that having an elected president would eliminate the problems Egypt was facing. It was also assumed that the newly elected president would end the state of polarisation and increase trust and transparency, in order to build the required dream of democracy. Conversely, what happened in reality is that the campaigns had already increased the polarisation in the society as explained in previous chapters. When Morsi was elected as president, he did not try to end this polarisation. On the contrary, he continued the 'everything in order to win' approach to consolidate power to protect his presidency. This approach Morsi resorted to made him re-enforce polarisation in the society, reinforce the distrust issue, and reinforce the non-abidance of the rule of law. More importantly, he created other forms of new problems such as the confrontation with the state's institutions and trying to change Egyptian identity in favour of an Islamic—perhaps extremist identity. All these factors had a negative impact on the democratisation process of Egypt. It made Egypt go back again to square one and remain in the transitional period once more.

5.4   MORSI'S 'DEMOCRACY'

Dahl (1998: 37–38) highlights five criteria for a democratic process:

(1) Effective participation: all members must have equal and effective opportunities for making their views known.
(2) Voting equality: each member should have equal opportunity to express his vote.
(3) Inclusion of all adults: all adults must have their full rights of citizenship.
(4) Enlightened understanding: each member must have equal and effective opportunities to learn about relevant policy alternatives and their consequences.
(5) Control of the agenda: members must have exclusive opportunities to decide which subjects are placed on the agenda.

By applying these criteria to Morsi's era,[15] it can be easily concluded from the examples mentioned in this chapter that Morsi's rule did not fulfil them. For the first criterion, the effective participation, Egyptians did not have equal and effective opportunities for making their views known. There was an attack on every outlet that can fulfil this criterion. There was an attack on private media which was playing that role. Public media was already Brotherhoodised. There was an attack on opposition forces and opposition leaders and even journalists who criticised the Muslim Brotherhood or Morsi. The inclusion of all adults' criterion was also not fulfilled due to the exclusion of any other force rather than the Brotherhood and the phenomenon known as the Brotherhoodisation of the state. There was no enlightened understanding: Egyptians were manipulated and deceived and were not allowed to have real opportunities to learn about the real policies the Muslim Brotherhood was implementing, which appeared to be only in favour of the Islamic forces. In addition to this, Egyptians did not have any opportunity to decide the subjects placed on the agenda; the easiest thing was to spread accusations about all those who tried to express a subject or an idea that opposes the Muslim Brotherhood's plans to the extent that some Egyptians were tortured by the Brotherhood members for stating their views as in what happened in Ittihadiyah incident. Perhaps the only criterion fulfilled from Dahl's five criteria was voting equality as Egyptians had equal opportunities to express their votes. Nonetheless, the process was still faulty as they were not allowed to express or to decide topics placed on the agenda of voting from the beginning. An example of this would be the constitution referendum Morsi pushed for, which was passed although the voting turnout was only 33%, an alarming turnout that showed an indication of their distrust in the process and anger at the same time, as all their efforts and protests requesting a more representative constitution were not listened to.

The failing path towards democracy was clear by the mid of Morsi's rule, as he entered into clashes, confrontations, and conflicts with almost all sectors in Egypt including non-Islamists Muslims, Christians, judges, media, and various state institutions, in order to protect his presidency. Although logically one might assume that he would resort to what we described as 'professionalism' again during his ruling period, he did not do so. As described in previous chapters, Morsi resorted to professional experts to help him with his campaign. They helped him with the programme, with the feedback, with the media, and so on. They were all from the Muslim Brotherhood, but they did the role requested from them at that time. When Morsi became president, it seemed that he did not resort to professionals to advise. It was assumed that he would resort to experts from all political forces to manage the country 'professionally' and democratically, but he did not. On the contrary, he was concentrating on installing his Brothers into top governmental positions and excluding anyone else, even other Islamic forces. He appeared to be a president to what he called in his speeches 'my family and my clan' and not to all Egyptians as he promised to be. When Egyptians started protesting against what was happening, and later started asking him to leave, he did not take it seriously. On the contrary, he claimed that those who opposed him were either Christians from the old regime or against the revolution. By the end of his rule, he had entered into conflict with everyone. In short, Morsi continued all the undemocratic policies he was elected to change. It was clear that Egypt's path towards democratisation was entering a cul-de-sac, making it very difficult to solve these clashes through normal traditional methods.

This is why the Tamarod movement—a grassroots movement meaning "revolt" in Arabic—started a petition asking Morsi to step down and to allow early presidential elections.[16] Tamarod said it was able to collect more than 22 million signatures from Egyptians with their ID numbers, a much bigger number than those who elected Morsi. Egyptians also went onto the streets protesting in many governorates, and their numbers were estimated to be bigger than the number of those who protested on 25 January asking Mubarak to step down.

Although a professionalised campaign helped Morsi in securing his way towards the presidential palace, it did not help Egyptians in having democratic rule. It helped Morsi to conceal his real ideology and plans. Professionalisation helped him to make cosmetic exterior practical changes, but not real ideological ones. The professionalism allowed the Muslim Brotherhood represented by Morsi to hide their real ideological thoughts and present themselves as a democratic entity that advocated freedom and pluralism, which was proven not to be true.

However, professionalism cannot be blamed for this. Professionalism does not ask politicians or candidates to manipulate and deceive voters. It depends on who utilises it and how it is utilised. It is a double-edged sword. In order for it to strengthen democracy, it needs to be coupled with the more cultural and ethical aspects of democracy which restrain tendencies towards more partisan and oppressive actions which some election winners might have. For example, if a more progressive and democratic politician had run a more professionalised campaign and won, Egypt's situation might have been different.

In addition to this, professionalisation is a process and method of implementing things that requires continuity, a continuous process that is not limited to campaign time only. The same methods and techniques applied by a candidate during a campaign could be applied by him after his winning. It is an indication that his way of campaigning and influencing people was effective and should be continued to secure his rule and power. However, a candidate has to develop his methods and techniques during the term of his rule. During the campaign, public attention is distributed among all candidates, but after the election, public attention is focused on the elected candidate. Thus, if the candidate did not develop the methods that helped him in winning, he could be easily uncovered, mainly by the media, other competitors, and more importantly the public, as happened in the case of Morsi when both the 'electronic committees' and some of his 'contradicted' speeches were discovered after being elected. The newly elected candidate should also be aware that he is not the most 'professional' any more as there are also other entities or politicians who are developing their methods and ways and who may become more professional than him. This is why it is important for the newly elected candidate not only to continue with his methods and techniques that helped him in winning, but also to develop them to match and follow political and social developments taking place.

In the case of Morsi, his main mistake was that he did not develop the methods and techniques used during his campaign period to match the new era. During the campaign period, he was in an 'armed race' focusing too much on destroying the other candidates, mainly Shafiq, in order to win. During this race, both candidates ignored the wider implications for them if elected and for the democracy process in general. After Morsi won, he continued with the same negative undemocratic practices he used to resort to in his campaign. However, during his campaign period, the attention was distributed on all candidates. Nobody was aware of or had enough evidence to know, for example, about his campaign resorting to astroturfing or how it works. When he became the president, he was under the spotlight and he was the focus of the public sphere's attention which is why it was a big mistake for him not to develop his methods and techniques and to continue with the same practices his campaign was depending on.

For example, he could have developed the use of experts and professionals to include those from outside the Brotherhood or to limit the role of his 'electronic committees' to positively campaign for him instead of targeting opposition or even to continue using the Muslim Brotherhood affiliated public opinion polls used by his campaign to get a sense of Egyptian's discontent towards his rule and how to fix it. Conversely, what Morsi did was completely the opposite: instead of trying to gain the actual support of the majority of Egyptians, he participated in increasing the polarisation through trying to have consolidated control over all and every institution in the state. This attempt to consolidate control and overall power can be understood as an extension of the campaigns. In the end, he won and became the president with a marginal victory, a victory that came through a majority that voted for him, not because they were convinced but only voted for him to preclude Shafiq through punitive voting as explained in previous chapters, a marginal victory that gave him an excuse to 'do anything' to protect his presidency by applying the same 'anything to win' approach he was applying during his campaigning period. The same result is almost concluded by Trager (2016: 181) who argues that Morsi's electoral victory 'gave him the legitimacy to do whatever was needed to advance his agenda and protect his presidency'. Moreover, Trager explains this by referring to what he called a 'Brotherhood's paranoia'. A paranoia that resulted from its historical experience, making them fear that those who put them in prison in the past, could put them again in prison if they got the chance (Trager 2016: 182). This again would explain why the Brotherhood was doing everything and anything it could to protect its presidency and why it continued focusing on its 'doing anything to win' approach rather than developing its approaches, methods, and strategies to keep pace with the new era. This is why studying and analysing the presidential campaigns not only offered insights into how campaigns were managed and operated but also helped in offering an analysis of Morsi's policies after winning the elections, which was an extension of his campaign's logic.

5.5   AMERICANISATION OR PROFESSIONALISATION

This study showed how adopting an Americanesque professionalised campaigns strategy, where candidates are ready to do or say anything in order to win was inappropriate in the case of Egypt. The study also inferred that the case would be the same in other nascent democracies. The reason for this can be rooted in the different political and cultural context between the United States and other nascent democracies. The United States has a history of elections and campaigning that has been developing over a long period of time. This history provided a learning environment for campaigns, media, and, more importantly, citizens. This history and long experience in campaigning and elections also made American citizens and the media more critical and politically literate, making them aware of the rules of the game—to an extent more advanced than Egyptians. Conversely, Egyptians—and citizens of other nascent democracies—do not have this long experience of national election campaigning enabling the same literacy present in the United States or other consolidated democracies, so the tactics of the highly professional campaigns are alien to them.

Professionalisation, as discussed here, is a catch-all term to describe adapting professionalised strategies and professionalised structures to implement professional—hopefully successful—campaigns, campaigns that can win elections but are not necessarily an asset for democracy. Professionalisation is also used as an umbrella term for many other labels such as Americanisation and Westernisation, where campaigns resort to techniques developed and used mainly in the United States or Western developed countries.

In general, the 'ubiquity' of the term (Tenscher et al. 2016) and vagueness of a clear solid definition have been acknowledged by many scholars

(Tenscher et al. 2016; Lilleker and Negrine 2002). The reason for this is that there is a wide range of competing explanatory theories that can be summarised as follows: (a) Adoption model (Plasser and Plasser 2002), where the US campaigning model is exported to and implemented in other countries exactly as it is, leading to the transformation of campaigns and standarisation of campaign practices, where country-specific traditional campaigning practices withdraw gradually and become substituted by US practices (Plasser and Plasser 2002: 19). (b) Shopping model (Plasser and Plasser 2002), or adaptation mode (Lees-Marshment and Lilleker 2012), where certain structures and strategies are imported from the United States and modified to suit the context in the country that will apply them, leading to the professionalisation of political campaigns outside the United States and the hybridisation of campaign practices (Plasser and Plasser 2002: 19). Lees-Marshment and Lilleker (2012) even extend the scope of the adaptation model to involve other Western countries, not only the United States.

The effect of these two trends—adoption or shopping and adaptation—on other countries has been also studied extensively (Norris 2004a, b; Plasser and Plasser 2002; Tenscher et al. 2016). They can be summarised as follows: (1) Studies concentrating on the importance of the local context and denying a duplicate influence of US campaigns stating that 'innovations emerge locally and simultaneous to developments in the United States' (Tenscher et al. 2016: 3). (2) Studies arguing that campaigns in other countries imitate the US campaigns (Baines and Egan 2001; Negrine et al. 2007). (3) Studies arguing that many of the US campaign practices are 'exported' to a diverse range of countries such as Israel, Russia, and Mexico (Norris 2004a, b; Swanson and Mancini 1996). (4) Studies highlighting that there are culture limitations to the application of the Americanisation thesis, which can make it vary from one country to another such as the regulatory framework, the party system, the media system, and the electorate (Norris 2000; Plasser and Plasser 2002).

While taking this debate into consideration, along with its different accounts, and despite the cultural limitations (Norris 2000; Plasser and Plasser 2002), there is some evidence to suggest that American campaigns in particular—and Western campaigns in general—can be considered as a role model (Scammell 1998) for many of the Egyptian campaigns that were working during the 2012 presidential elections. This can be attributed to two main reasons: (1) some key figures in the campaigns saw the United States as their role model; differences were whether to fully abide by US model of campaigning or to adapt it locally. (2) Some key figures also studied campaigning in the United States, either academically by taking or applying for an academic degree or through practical professional campaigning courses studying the US campaigning model.

An example for this would be Yara Khalaf from Moussa's campaign. Khalaf mentioned clearly that they were adapting the Obama campaign model and that their aim was to run the Moussa campaign in Egypt as the equivalent of the Obama campaign. At the end of the campaign, Khalaf also took her master's degree at the ESLSCA business school in International Business Administration. Her research project focused on studying the position in political campaigns where she compared the Obama campaign with Moussa's campaign applying the Western model of political marketing positioning on both of them. The same applies for General Said Zaatar from Moussa's campaign who was also keen on taking courses in US election campaigning between 1990 and 2002. The case did not differ in the Aboul Fotouh campaign, as El-Shahawy, his campaign manager, was keen on studying the Western model of marketing techniques as well. He gained his Master's degree in International Business administration in 2008 from the ESLSCA business school. And at the end of 2011, when he was campaigning for Aboul Fotouh, he applied for the DBA doctorate of business administration with the Maastricht School of Management. His thesis subject was political marketing in Egypt. However, he dropped out after one year as he had to leave Egypt. The case was almost the same in Shafiq's campaign: Mahmoud Ibrahim, his campaign's social media manager, presented himself as an expert in US elections. Before the campaign he took some courses on US elections in the period between 2005 and 2010 with the International Republican Institute and the National Democratic Institute. After the election, he gained an internship with the help of the US embassy in Cairo to go and work as an intern in Mitt Romney's presidential election campaign. He also travels to the United States whenever there is an election to follow the campaign work there. Ibrahim also stated that some of the field coordinators they resorted to from the dismantled NDP were sent during Mubarak's era to the United Kingdom to learn from both the Conservative and Labour parties' campaigning experience.

Although the above may not act as proof that the campaigns are Americanised, or that the Egyptian campaigns fully adhere to Americanised techniques, it acts as evidence of what the campaign staff wanted their campaigns to look like; they wanted it to look like a professional campaign like those in the United States. For the majority of them, American campaigns were the ideal. Some of them—such as Mahmoud Ibrahim from Shafiq's campaign—highlighted that the differences are only cultural ones, such as the ways of mobilising voters. As he explained, in the United States, they could mobilise voters by emails or SMS. Conversely, in Egypt, they have to go and knock on the door. That is why Ibrahim explained that in many cases they would take the main idea, theme, or strategy from the US or Western model but adapt it locally to be effective in the Egyptian local context. Morsi's campaign also followed an American model, although agreeing not to abide by anything that would not allow them to get more votes or that might suggest that they would lose votes such as the debate. This highlights that they pick, choose, and then adapt locally to suit the Egyptian context (Lees-Marshment and Lilleker 2012).

The effect of the US model even appeared before the campaigning period: rumours spread that some of the potential candidates at that time were bringing American campaign experts and companies to help them with the campaigns—a claim that was proven untrue but showed how the public sphere (not only campaign officials) were thinking of US campaigns. For them, campaigns are an American invention and the best campaigns are in the United States.

From the above, it is clear that the Egyptian campaigns followed an adaptation (Lees-Marshment and Lilleker 2012) or shopping model (Plasser and Plasser 2002), where they adapted certain Americanised and Westernised strategies and techniques, modified them, and applied them according to their cultural and political context in Egypt. As Plasser and Plasser (2002: 39) explained it:

> American campaign techniques represent a giant political supermarket for foreign clients offering a variety of items, practices and techniques.

This idea of shopping in a supermarket (Plasser and Plasser 2002), where you have the luxury to pick and choose according to your needs and resources and then adapt what you bought according to the local context (Lees-Marshment and Lilleker 2012), taking into consideration the cultural, political, media, and legal local factors (Norris 2000; Plasser and Plasser 2002), is clear in how Morsi's and Shafiq's campaigns refused to adapt some strategies such as the debate and preferred a functional approach over a branding one. This again is nearly the same as Mahmoud Ibrahim from Shafiq's campaign also mentioned that they sometimes just get the idea or the main concept from the US campaigns but adjusted it while applying it according to what he described as 'the Egyptian style'. A style that reflects the political and cultural context.

This conclusion correlates with Plasser and Plasser's findings (2002: 38) while studying campaigning in 52 electoral democracies. They found that different countries apply the shopping model while adapting Americanised campaigns by choosing to adapt specific features more than others. For example, Western campaigns' experts are concentrating on the use of electronic mass media. South African experts are keener on the strategic use of political research techniques as a way of developing their strategies. While Ukrainian experts are more interested on the campaign management process and the use of electronic mass media. On the other hand, Latin American campaigns' experts concentrate more on media and PR strategies along with public opinion polls. As the largest electoral democracy in the world where eligible voters exceed 600 million (Plasser and Plasser 2002), Indian campaigners are interested more in computerised campaign techniques and depending on digital software that can help them in the counting of votes (Plasser and Plasser 2002: 38). This also correlates with Mancini's conclusion (1999: 243) that 'Professionalism seems to develop differently in different electorate and political systems and political cultures'.

As in the case of Egypt, the use of professionalisation—as used by Morsi and Shafiq—was not helpful to the wider process of democracy in some of these states. An example of this would be the Russian Republic and previous states of the Soviet Union due to the lack of democratic traditions and party structures (Plasser and Plasser 2002: 44). Plasser and Plasser (2002: 45) also concluded that adopting professionalised Americanised techniques does not always favour some countries, mainly emerging democracies, due to practices like political corruption, electoral fraud, and votes purchase. As they stated:

> the consequences of the proliferation or imitation of US – American campaign techniques in the emerging democracies in Africa and Asia arouse even more pessimistic feelings. (Plasser and Plasser: 45)

These 'pessimistic feelings' were proven to be true in the Egyptian case, mainly with those that chose to adopt a functional negative approach to their campaigns, ready to do anything in order to win as highlighted in previous chapters, which had negative implication on the process of democracy. This again correlates with Hamelink's conclusion that a professionalised campaign 'does little to assist the development of strong, participatory, deliberative democracy' (Hamelink 2007: 185).

Despite the history of elections in Egypt, which almost started in 1866,[17] the 2012 presidential elections were a totally different case. One can argue that Egypt passed by the pre-modern and modern campaign era in its long history of parliamentary elections along with trade union elections, but the case was totally different in terms of the presidential elections. One can also argue that both the 2005 and 2012 presidential election campaigns jumped directly to the postmodern campaign era without passing through the other two phases, pre-modern and modern campaigns: the presidential election campaigns were already born in the postmodern era, and those working on the presidential campaign did not witness the other two eras and did not necessarily build upon these two phases. Some of those working were even not born in this postmodern era. Thanks to the age of globalisation, changes in media environments, and electoral markets (Plasser and Plasser 2002), along with the social, political, and technological developments that are coined with the postindustrial era (Tenscher et al. 2016).

5.6   APPLYING THE PROFESSIONALISATION INDEX IN NASCENT DEMOCRACIES

Despite the moral shortage, the professionalisation index still offers a comprehensive way of studying campaigns in nascent democracies. It is flexible enough to amend the components that reflect the criteria it measures. As explained, in the case of Egypt, there was a necessity to add social media and debates as independent criteria. In the Egyptian case, they did not aim to be biased towards new technologies. On the contrary, they reflected the real logic behind the campaign strategies. This indicates that other components can be added or deleted when applying the index to other countries, depending on the context the campaigns were working in and the methods they were using, which will differ from one country to another. This context could be the regulatory framework, the party system, the media system, and the electorate (Norris 2000) or extend to include institutional and cultural limits (Plasser and Plasser 2002).

Future academics studying future campaigns in similar transitional environments should take into consideration the possibility of transferring the index into a qualitative method while studying single countries, rather than the quantitative method the index was already designed for. The qualitative use of the index offers the opportunity to learn all aspects of the campaign as well as reflecting on some of the potential impacts.

The reason for this is that while studying completely new election campaigns, the quantitative method would be useless in describing the mechanisms and logic of the campaign. It will just give numbers and comparisons without real insight into what happened, how it happened, and why it happened. Having said that, the quantitative method would still be useful if doing a comparative study between several countries (Tenscher et al. 2016) or doing longitudinal analysis on several campaigns over a long period of time, where quantitative data is already present. Academics should always assess the benefits and disadvantages of each approach while taking into account what is the real aim of their study. Is it longitudinal study of the level of professionalisation in various countries or the level of professionalism in a specific country at a specific point where extensive data is not available?

Another element that would help future academics is to add weight to each of the components, which was one of the limitations of the index in general and one of the limitations of this study specifically due to time and resource constraints. Adding weight to the variables by studying the effect they had on voting behaviour would add significantly to the index itself and would help in better analysis of the studied campaign, especially in nascent democracies. More importantly, the index will benefit more from adding criteria and components that can measure and assess the democratic values in order to study and analyse the wider implications of the campaigns, not only who won and who lost or which campaign was more 'professional' than the other. Adding such criteria would be essential, especially in nascent democracies due to the absence or the non-embeddedness of the democratic culture and values in these societies.

5.7   An Index for Campaign Practitioners

As discussed before, the importance of the professionalisation index could extend to benefit practitioners. It can still be used as a practical guide mainly in nascent democracies. A campaign can resort to it as a step-by-step guide or as a checklist especially if they are starting from scratch, with no previous experience in national or presidential elections.

There are several questions a new campaign needs to ask itself before starting. The most important has to do it with its logic: to what extent they are willing to go negatively or positively? If they go positively, do they have a plan to counter attacks? Are they going to resort to astroturfing? If they resort to it, will they use it negatively or positively? If they will not resort to it, do they have the strategy and resources required to counter astroturfing undertaken by other campaigns? And more importantly, if they decide to go negatively and perhaps follow the path of doing any and everything in order to win, do they have a plan to eliminate the damage of their approach when they get elected to office so as not to repeat the Egyptian experience? A campaign needs to ask itself these sorts of questions in order to develop a structure and a strategy that could help them to establish their campaign mainly in nascent democracies. Below are some of the main themes a campaign needs to think about from the first moment their candidate starts thinking about running for office, before the actual commencement of their campaign.

Some of these themes raise serious concerns about the ethics and morality of the campaign. It will be fully up to the campaign to decide whether it will adopt an ethical and positive approach or whether it is ready to commit to non-ethical and immoral things and adopt manipulative methods in order to win. In the case of deciding to be manipulative and not to abide by ethics and morals, it has to bear in mind the consequences of this approach when their candidates get elected to office, by having a strategy for solving problems that are most likely to erupt from their campaign's unethical logic and affect their ruling period and the general idea of a democratic system, due to their unethical manipulation of voters. That is why it is necessary for the campaign to think about all these issues before developing their campaign.

5.7.1   Campaign Structure

5.7.1.1   Campaign Staff
As discussed in Chap. 4, there are two major posts a campaign needs to pay extra attention to. The first is the campaign manager. Is the campaign manager trustworthy, capable of hiring and managing other members of the campaigns including outside agencies and volunteers?

The second post is the field coordinator. Does the campaign have an active well-connected field coordinator(s) who can mobilise voters? How can they reach them, especially if the country is new to elections? Perhaps the campaign should think about influential reference groups in various constituencies or field coordinators who used to work in other sorts of elections before? The campaign has to be aware of the vital role of this post, as it appeared from the Egyptian experience that voters will not go to the polling station alone without being mobilised, and the importance of the field coordinator post comes in here.

A third post the campaign should also think about is the need for a professional media department that can direct the media by feeding stories and adapting to the media logic from one side and on the other side shaping the public sphere debate by positioning the candidate as a front runner.

5.7.1.2 Management Style
A campaign should adapt a centralised hierarchal structure at the top managerial level in order to be able to impose the changes and strategies it needs. Underneath the candidate, along with the top posts, a campaign can resort to a horizontal level management as it will be more efficient in the daily work.

5.7.1.3 Campaign Premises
Although some candidates may resort to public places such as a mosque to manage the campaign from, there is a great need to have separate private premises for the campaigns. Chapter 4 highlighted the importance of having separate campaign premises as a headquarters in the capital and national branches along the country and highlighted examples of locations.

Since this process can be an expensive task, especially with limited resources for an independent campaign that does not have a political party to support, the campaign should think out of the box and create alternative ways to obtain these offices. This could include getting the endorsement of a political party, where this party can give its offices to the campaign to use, or building a base of volunteers and supporters who can then volunteer places for the campaign to use. Having said this, the campaign should have the upper hand in managing these offices and ensure that they abide by the campaign logic, strategies, and policies.

5.7.1.4 Degree of Externalisation
The degree of externalisation can be considered as an extension to the campaign staff. The campaign will not fulfil all its requirements internally. It will need to resort to professional experts and companies that will be

dedicated to work on the campaign on a temporary basis. However, this may be different to an extent in nascent democracies as all the campaigns are temporary. In other words, the dedicated external staff will be working for the duration of the campaign. The type of expertise needed can differ from one country to another. However, in general, the main external experts that a campaign will need should include media professionals, marketing professionals, experts to work on the candidate's programme, and experts to help developing ways to monitor and get feedback.

5.7.1.5 *Internal Campaign Communication Structures*

A campaign should make sure that members of the campaign are communicating effectively and that there are ways to avoid miscommunication between staff. Means of communication can vary from one campaign to another and can be a mixture of face-to-face communication, phone calls, messages, and emails. Perhaps the most two important criteria a campaign should take into its consideration is that members of the campaign, along with volunteers, can use the method of communication chosen effectively. For example, a campaign should not use text messages with a volunteer who cannot read or write, or emails if the receiver does not have good internet coverage, or high technological means if the receiver is technology illiterate. The second important item is that the campaign needs to secure its internal communication methods to avoid security breaches such as, but not limited to, leaking data and hacking.

5.7.1.6 *Feedback*

Chapter 4 highlighted the importance of having a separate department and dedicated staff to monitor feedback and communicate it effectively to the campaign manager, candidate, and other related departments.

Effective feedback can be gathered through public opinion polls and focus groups. However, in nascent democracies, it may be difficult to have efficient public opinion polls available. Thus, there is the need for the campaign to think again outside the box and develop its own ways of getting feedback away from media manipulation. This could include having its own public opinion poll with the help of the business sector, conducting focus group sessions in various cities in the country, and making use of the field coordinators to get them to obtain feedback from various places they are working in. The campaign could also get feedback from media outlets including social media, but they have to take into consideration that it could be manipulative and does not represent the actual sentiments of voters. They can only use it as an indication and a way of monitoring negative aspects highlighted about their campaign and their candidate.

5.7.1.7 Opposition Research

A campaign should have a dedicated unit and dedicated staff to conduct research on other campaigns and other candidates. This could include background research on all opposing candidates; media monitoring of candidate appearance; content analysis of candidate media appearance, use of social media and websites; and monitoring candidate's promises and programmes. Although not ethical, a campaign may also extend to involve sending unknown staff from the campaign to attend the opposing candidates' public events, or perhaps if the campaign decided to go negative, penetrating other campaigns, although this will not be useful if discovered, and if the candidate was elected, as it will not be helpful for the wider democratic process since it will be discovered sooner or later.

5.7.1.8 Campaign Duration

Campaign duration laws vary from one country to another in nascent democracies or in countries where high levels of negativity and attacks are adopted. As explained in Chap. 4, long campaign durations do not always favour the candidate, especially when candidates do not enter the election race at the same time or when the interval between various candidates entering the election race exceeds a year, such as the Egyptian case. In such a case, it may be better that the candidate starts introducing themselves without announcing their real intention to be candidate. In other words, as soon as the candidate decides that he will enter the race, he should begin finding a place for himself in the public sphere. This could happen by engaging in the debates taking place in the public sphere or by engaging in some projects that interest the public in his country. The main aim of these activities would be to make himself known to and trusted by the public and present himself as an authentic person without making the public think that he is doing this in order to enter the election. At this stage, opposing candidates and media will not be concentrating on destroying him as he is not a potential candidate and all the attention will be focused on real candidates. After successfully creating this image away from elections, he should then find supporters who are urging him to put himself forward and represent them, which would be a chance for him to announce that he will run for election.

5.7.1.9 Campaign Budget

Campaigns budgets and spending differs from country to country based on the laws organising them. In terms of budget, the campaign usually suffers from two things: from where to get the money and what if they exceeded the amount the law states?

That is why it is always preferable that candidates and campaigns try to influence the law through members of the parliament and institutions managing the election process to raise the amount of campaign spending by comparing the overall expenditures of each candidate's campaign per eligible voter … that is, to have an adequate amount of money per eligible voter.

Chapter 4 also highlighted other ways the campaign could overcome the limit of spending such as depending on in-kind contributions that are not calculated in the official documents of the campaign's spending. In other words, although highly unethical, the campaign could always find ways—if it wants—to circumvent the law in terms of its spending by asking volunteers or candidates' friends to pay themselves for items needed for the campaign (even if the campaign is the one actually giving them the money) and consider it as in-kind donations that will not be calculated in the official documents.

5.7.2   Campaign Strategies

5.7.2.1 Voting Targeting

As explained in Chap. 4, campaigns should be aware that they will not reach or appeal to all voters. Thus is the necessity of dividing voters into segments that can easily be reached and developing a secure base of voters. In order to do this, the campaign will need to locate these targets which again could be a difficult process especially with the absence of data mainly in nascent democracies.

That is why campaigns should again think outside the box to find other alternatives. This could include studying different cities' voting patterns in previous elections and trying to influence lawmakers to make a voter database available for campaigns. Campaigns could also try to build their own voter database by other means—which is usually easy in nascent democracies either due to the absence of regulating laws or not having the culture of abiding by the law if it existed or simply by accepting bribes or the so-called facilitation fees. These other ways of building data could include having membership lists of clubs, trades unions, schools' students to access parents, university students, or even banks' clients or mobile phones' customers. A campaign could also agree with places that their targeted voters may be going to join a subscription list which can be passed to the campaign later. In other words, if the campaign targets middle-class youth, it could agree with some cafes and restaurants to make these clients add their contact details for future promotions and offers, which will be passed later to the campaigns ... and suchlike methods.

5.7.2.2 Narrowcasting Activities

After deciding who the targeted voters are, the campaign should start reaching them through narrowcasting activities. These narrowcasting activities can include specific tailored messages or secret promises or general explanations about the candidate and his promises. A campaign should always take care that what happens in a narrowcasting activity could be leaked to the media even if the media was not invited thanks to modern technologies, especially smartphones. That is why a campaign should always be keen on not providing contradictory messages through these narrowcasting activities. A good narrowcasting activity should personalise the campaigns' messages and the importance of the voters' vote through GOTV (Green and Gerber 2008). A sample of narrowcasting activities could include designated SMS messages that are sent to specific places. For example, if your targeted audience is of a specific religion, you could send SMS messages to mobile phones in the area of their place of worship at the time of prayers. Or if you have a specific programme for school education, a campaign could send messages or go and meet parents when they are collecting their children from schools, and so on.

5.7.2.3 Free Media

Media outlets play an important role in the election period as candidates will mainly reach the wider voters through mass media channels. Unknown candidates might have problems gaining access to the mass media if they are not considering them as front runners, and here is the importance of having an active media department that can force the candidate onto the media agenda. A successful media strategy would include feeding the media with stories in order to stabilise the media agenda setting. Feeding journalists indirectly with stories and creating events and stories that media would be interested in covering might reduce the chances of journalists digging for stories about the candidate themselves and moving the election debate towards totally new issues the candidate might not be good at. At the end of the day, journalists need items to produce and stories to publish with media outlets becoming 24 hours a day; they will need stories to fill their outputs. That is why campaigns should not take what media presents as a real reflection of voters' behaviour, especially in nascent democracies due to the absence of critical media and aware voters. The absence of these checks and balances necessitates that the campaign investigates what is mentioned in media without neglecting it but yet again without exaggerating its role regarding voters' expected decisions as it can simply get it wrong.

5.7.2.4 *Paid Media*

The Egyptian campaign study provided some ideas to use paid media without actually paying. These ideas could mainly help small campaigns that do not have enough resources and money or campaigns that are not supported by parties. From these ideas, in terms of production, a campaign could include volunteers from big advertising companies or famous cinema or TV directors and crew who can do advertisements, whether TV, radio, or online, without getting paid by the campaign. In terms of broadcasting, a campaign can strike a deal with TV channels that their candidate appears on the channel without being paid, in return for which the channel plays their advertisement. Such ideas should limit the cost of paying for paid media.

5.7.2.5 *Debates*

Some might argue that the lesson learned from the Egyptian case is not to participate in debates. However, this would be not applicable in all contexts and might bring attacks on the candidate who refuses, especially if there are other candidates participating. Further, it might not be good for the wider implications of the campaign, such as the negative media coverage and online backlash against Theresa May after she refused to participate in televised debates in which other candidates participated (Coleman 2017).

There are some ideas that a campaign can take into consideration if they decided to go for debates. These include participating in debates only if all candidates are in it, rather than choosing only two candidates to participate; agreeing with other candidates on a positive approach in the debates putting attacks and negativity aside; choosing a professional impartial presenter who is aware of the wider implications the debate might have on the election process; the campaign having its own producer and director who work closely with the channel hosting the debate; it may be applicable for the campaigns to have the questions beforehand, especially in a nascent democracy where media roles are not critical. However, the last option is not advisable as it will transfer the debate into a pre-recorded show and will not achieve the aim from it, especially as sooner or later the audience will know that the candidates had the questions beforehand.

5.7.2.6 Internet and Social Media
A campaign should have a separate team for internet and social media. The team should be following what other campaigns and candidates are saying on social media, that is, working closely with both feedback and opposition research teams. It should also rebroadcast the campaign's and candidate's messages on the campaign's internet and social media outlets, besides creating specific content for the online, rather than only depending on what is broadcasted on other outlets. A campaign should also have dedicated persons to reply and engage with social media audiences as some other campaigns might be deliberately trying to consume the team's time. Thus, the need is to divide the work without consuming all the team time. The main question, however, is the campaign's need to address whether it is going to resort to astroturfing or not and how it will counter astroturfing campaigns that already exist.

5.7.2.7 Campaign Activities
A campaign should be keen on media coverage by creating events mainly aimed at media coverage known as pseudo-events. This could include a variety of events depending on the context in each country. Although these activities are mainly designed for media, it will help the campaign in reinforcing its image and messages and will give extra credit to the campaign as voters will see the media attracted to cover the candidate and campaign's activities. These activities could range from double-decker buses to press conferences to launching events for the campaign and the programme.

5.7.2.8 Degree of Personalisation
A campaign should be keen on developing messages that show the personal character of their candidate and make him appear to the public as an authentic character. It may be wise for the campaign to do this by appearing in various media outlets through indirect political broadcasts, infotainment

broadcasts, or pure entertainment programmes. This will depend on the media environment the campaign is working in. It will also differ depending on other issues such as whether the candidate is known to the public or not, as candidates who are not known to the public will have to focus first on introducing themselves to the voters. The campaign media team may also provide media outlets about personal stories and personal trusted contacts who are close to the candidate who can help in creating personal stories about the campaign.

5.8   CONCLUSION

Some of the ideas presented in this study are that the 'do anything to win approach' can lead to unethical manipulation of voters which would have a negative impact on democracy. That is why the study suggested the importance of developing an index that can be converted to a practical guide that can have ethical and democratic components and at the same time guarantee winning. For these reasons, some might argue that the unethical tactical advice given to campaigns' practitioners may contradict the study's aspirations. However, in the absence of an index that can stop manipulation and ensure winning, and with practitioners still eager to manipulate and do everything in order to win, and not paying attention to the wider implications, the researcher finds it wise to highlight the unethical practical advice—alongside the ethical—that can also be learned from the Egyptian experience. This leaves it to campaigners to use their own moral compass when developing a campaign by deciding which approach they want to adapt and implement according to their own local context. Ethics and democratic values cannot be imposed on those who do not believe in them, especially with the absence of clear legislation, the absence of the rule of law, and more importantly the absence of citizens and media systems that condemn these unethical practices. In a country where even ordinary citizens and media compete in manipulating the laws and manipulating each other's, ethical tactics might not be appealing until citizens themselves believe in them before campaigners, which will not happen in one day.

The academic and practical ideas presented in this chapter are purely a result of the study of the 2012 Egyptian elections. Future studies of elections in other countries should investigate the extent to which these ideas can be applied in other countries' contexts, taking into consideration ethical, institutional, cultural, and electoral differences, along with differences in the media and legal system. Future studies about other Egyptian elections should also take into consideration changing the political, cultural, and social environments the campaign will be working in. As explained in this study, the 2012 Egyptian election took place in an extraordinary situation as it happened directly after a revolution and was almost the first multi-candidate election where the winner was not previously known, situations that would not exist in every election.

Professionalisation, as discussed in this study, is just a process and an academic framework that is used to understand how campaigns are conducted. Although Egyptian candidates along with their campaigns' managers might not be aware of it, they still resort to it by adopting techniques used by other countries. They also resort to it by adopting techniques written in books they read or subjects they studied, as some of the campaigns' staff had already studied subjects like marketing and political communications. They also follow campaign activities in other countries such as the United States. However, as this chapter proved, fully adopting the techniques of a professional campaign, in the way they were implemented, was inappropriate to use in a country like Egypt due to the negative impact it had on its democratisation process. In the case of Egypt, the lack of experience for both candidates and citizens, the way the campaigning system was working in terms of doing anything to win, then fully consolidating power, and the lack of both critical objective media and educated citizens since both were easy to manipulate, all meant that democracy does not automatically become embedded in the country as when candidates import the full modes of campaigning utilised in more advanced democracies; which is why adopting the full techniques of a professional campaign, as conducted in fully consolidated democracies, might not be appropriate for a transitional country, nascent or emergent democracies.

Studying the professionalism of the Egyptian campaigns by applying the professionalisation index offered insight to the campaigns and its implications on the democratisation process under the rule of Morsi, the winning president. However, the greater emphasis on resources and sophisticated strategies of the professionalisation index make it an incomplete index to be applied to the Egyptian campaigns, campaigns that are taking place in a country that is still in its transitional phase. This is because the index does not include necessary criteria for the democratic process: items like ethics, transparency, participation, enlightened understanding, and suchlike criteria that are necessary if we need to consider the wider implications of the campaigns, not just who won and who lost. This is why there is a great need for a professionalisation framework or index that does not depend only on resources, sophistications that might extend to involve an 'anything to win approach'; a framework that can also be converted later into a model or a guide to be followed by campaigns, especially for those who have real sincere democratic efforts so that they can inform and engage voters, not manipulate them, and at the same time guarantee winning. Perhaps future research could be able to develop both a professionalisation framework and a model for campaigns to follow, a framework and a model that can guarantee winning but at the same time guarantee enhancing the democratic values, which were missing in the case of Egypt.

NOTES

1. Thin democracies can be defined according to the minimalist definition of democracy which is 'free competition for a free vote' (Schumpeter 1943: 271). This was not the case of Egypt in the transitional period, as there was no 'free competition for a free vote'. In the transitional period, there was no elected president or elected representatives in parliament or even a constitution. For more information on different types of democracies and wider definitions, see Chap. 2.
2. Stories on the project in Muslim Brotherhood media outlets were much more plentiful. However, it was difficult to find them on their Arabic website now. The author is not sure if it is a technical problem or if they were removed deliberately. However, stories about the Nahda project are still available on their English outlets.
3. For a list of Muslim Brotherhood appointed officials in various institutions, see Al-Masry Al-Youm investigative report on 14 February 2013. The report shows with names the Muslim Brotherhood monopoly over various institutions including 19 governorates, ministries, unions, various councils, and public bodies. http://www.almasryalyoum.com/news/details/286656.
4. Part of the broadcast meeting where Al-Nour's leader mentioned his concerns: https://www.youtube.com/watch?v=LncLJYV8AyQ https://www.youtube.com/watch?v=xOfHPdyLVBQ.
5. For example, Nas Book programme on Rotana Masriya channel uploaded on YouTube on 10 June 2012 available from: https://www.youtube.com/watch?v=tHDCugwhWhg and Al-Sada Al-Mohtaramon programme on OnTV channel, uploaded on YouTube on 18 March 2013 available from: https://youtu.be/o1Lz7ylfA28.
6. Bassem Youssef hosted the Al Bernameg (Show), a satirical news programme, considered to be the Egyptian version of the American pro-

gramme 'Daily Show' by Jon Stewart. Part of the episode commenting on the meeting discussed can be viewed on: https://www.youtube.com/watch?v=_yxVREd4nn8.

7. The parliament already reconvened but the session did not exceed 12 minutes. See Al-Masry 11 July 2012.

8. According to Egyptian law, the attorney general/general prosecutor cannot be removed by the president.

9. For more details, see the constitutional declaration in Ahram Online 22/11/2012. And for more explanation on the crisis, see BBC News 24 December 2012.

10. For more details about the torturing process, see Al-Masry Al-Youm Newspaper special coverage on 7 December 2012 which is also available on its English version website 'Egypt Independent' on 7 December 2012.

11. For a detailed description for these incidents, see Trager 2016: 137–144.

12. There is a list of similar controversial statements and nonunderstandable statements said by Morsi, Egyptians often recall to make jokes of.

13. Gad (2014) disapproved this argument by comparing the number of votes with Christians registered in these areas. For more information, see Gad 2014: 102–109.

14. Mohammed al-Beltagi, the Secretary General of the Freedom and Justice Party, the political arm of the Muslim Brotherhood group, said that 60% of those protesting at Ittihadiyah are Christians. Safwat Hegazy, the Salafist Islamic figure, said they were 80%. For more info, see Gad 2014.

15. For chronological order of full events during Morsi's era, see Jadaliyya 22 July 13. For detailed analysis of these events and their role in ending Morsi's rule, see Trager 2016.

16. For more info, see BBC News 1/7/13.

17. Egypt witnessed a sort of elections in miniature amid the French Expedition in 1798. In this period, Napoleon Bonaparte tried to play the role of the Saviour who can save Egyptians from their bad conditions under the rule of the Ottoman Empire. He formed two general assemblies whose members could be elected only via indirect elections by another committee formed of 14 members. In Ismail's pasha era, mainly in 1866, Egypt witnessed its first parliamentary elections, where Egyptians were able to vote through direct elections. However, it limited the right to run for elections to the elite only.

References

Ahram Online, 22/11/2012. English text of Morsi's constitutional declaration. *Ahram Online* [online], 22 November 2012. Available from: http://english.ahram.org.eg/News/58947.aspx [Accessed 1 February 2017].

Al Arabiya, 21/5/2012. Mohamed Morsi, raises 100 national project for the advancement of Egypt. *Al Arabiya* [online], 21 May 2012. Available from: https://www.alarabiya.net/articles/2012/05/21/215498.html   [Accessed 28 January 2017].

Al Arabiya, 21/6/2013. 'Indecent' ballet? Egyptian Islamist lawmaker angers dancers. *Al Arabiya* [online], 21 June 2013. Available from: http://english.alarabiya.net/en/life-style/art-and-culture/2013/06/01/Egypt-s-Islamist-lawmaker-says-ballet-is-obscene-artists-angry.html [Accessed 1 February 2017].

Al Arabiya, 25/3/2013. Egypt's Islamists block access to Media Production City. *Al Arabiya* [online], 25 March 2013. Available from: http://english.alarabiya.net/en/News/2013/03/25/Islamists-block-access-to-Egypt-Media-City.html [Accessed 1 February 2017].

Al Arabiya, 29/11/2012. Battles of the constitution in Egypt between the majority and minority. *Al Arabiya* [online], 29 November 2012. Available from: http://www.alarabiya.net/articles/2012/11/29/252554.html [Accessed 1 November 2016].

Al Arabiya, 3/4/2013. Morsi leads Mubarak in the suppression of media freedoms. *Al Arabiya* [online], 2 April 2013. Available from: https://www.alarabiya.net/ar/arab-and-world/egypt/2013/04/03/مرسي-يتفوق-على-مبارك-في-قمع-الحريات-الإعلامية.html [Accessed 1 February 2017].

Al-Arabiya, 29/8/2012. Al-Shatter: Nahda project is just an idea. *Al Arabiya* [online], 29 August 2012. Available from: https://www.alarabiya.net/articles/2012/08/29/234976.html [Accessed 28 January 2017].

Al-Masry, 11/3/2013. In a message to the Muslim Brotherhood, Allam El-din: stop denying the facts. *Al-Masry Al-Youm* [online], 11 March 2013. Available from: http://www.almasryalyoum.com/news/details/294398 [Accessed 1 February 2017].

Al-Masry, 11/7/2012. SCC cancel the president's decision and the Muslim Brotherhood replies by law and in the field. *Al-Masry Al-Youm* [online], 11 July 2012. Available from: http://today.almasryalyoum.com/article2.aspx?ArticleID=346033 [Accessed 1 February 2017].

Al-Masry, 12/9/2012. Al-Shatter: implementing the Nahda project requires qualified and enthusiastic citizens. *Al-Masry Al-Youm* [online], 12 September 2012. Available from: http://www.almasryalyoum.com/news/details/163253 [Accessed 28 January 2017].

Al-Masry, 14/2/2013. *Al-Masry Al-Youm* monitors the state's Brotherhoodisation in the first eight months of Morsi rule. *Al-Masry Al-Youm* [online], 14 February 2012. Available from: http://www.almasryalyoum.com/news/details/286656 [Accessed 28 January 2017].

Al-Masry, 17/5/2013. Alert in the Sinai after the kidnapping of seven soldiers. *Al-Masry Al-Youm* [online], 17 May 2013. Available from: http://today.almasryalyoum.com/article2.aspx?ArticleID=382719 [Accessed 1 February 2017].

Al-Masry, 20/1/2013. The Arabic network: 24 cases of insulting the president in Muri's era, in comparison to 14 cases in 115 years. *Al-Masry Al-Youm* [online], 20 January 2013. Available from: http://www.almasryalyoum.com/news/details/283887 [Accessed 1 February 2017].

Al-Masry, 23/6/2012. Morsi announce the formation of a national front against the Constitutional Declaration and undertake deputies from outside the freedom and justice party. *Al-Masry Al-youm* [online], 23 June 2012. Available from: http://today.almasryalyoum.com/article2.aspx?ArticleID=343813 [Accessed 28 January 2017].

Al-Masry, 25/6/2012. Al-Nahda project: 7 axes and 16 years to fulfil. *Al-Masry Al-youm* [online], 25 June 2012. Available from: http://www.almasryalyoum.com/news/details/188548 [Accessed 28 January 2017].

Al-Masry, 4/6/2013. 'Gossip' on the 'dam'. *Al-Masry Al-Youm* [online], 4 June 2013. Available from: http://today.almasryalyoum.com/article2.aspx?ArticleID=384946 [Accessed 1 February 2017].

Al-Masry, 7/12/2012. A Brotherhood torturing square on Ittihadiyah palace. *Al-Masry Al-Youm* [online], 7 December 2012. Available from: http://today.almasryalyoum.com/article2.aspx?ArticleID=363066 [Accessed 1 February 2017].

Al-Masry, 17/6/2013. The army rejects the covered hall 'trap'. *Al-Masry Al-Youm* [online], 17 June 2013. Available from: http://today.almasryalyoum.com/article2.aspx?ArticleID=386438 [Accessed 1 February 2017].

Al-Sada Al Mohtaramon, Safwat Hijazi: Morsi Hieid, Islamic caliphate, 2013. [television programme, video, online]. OnTV. YouTube, 18 March 2013. Available from: https://www.youtube.com/watch?v=o1Lz7ylfA28&feature=youtu.be [Accessed 1 June 2016].

Al-Wafd, 25/1/2017. Interview with Ali El Din Hilal. *Al-Wafd* [online], 25 January 2017. Available from: http://alwafd.org/ تحقيقات-وحوارات/1448111-د-على-الدين-هلال-يخرج-عن-صمته-ويتحدث-لـ [Accessed 1 February 2017].

Al-Watan News, 21/10/2012. The Attorney General ordered an investigation with teacher accused of the 'hair cut'. *Al-Watan News* [online], 21 October 2012. Available from: http://www.elwatannews.com/news/details/65237 [Accessed 1 February 2017].

Al-Watan News, 29/6/2012. Omar Abdel-Rahman – the Mufti of terrorism – waiting for the rescue of President Morsi. *Al-Watan News* [online], 29 June 2012. Available from: http://www.elwatannews.com/news/details/22001 [Accessed 1 February 2017].

Al-Youm 7, 8/11/2012. The girl who had her hair cut speaks, saying that the women wearing Niqab intimidated her. *Al-Youm Al-Sabea* [online], 8 November 2012. Available from: http://www.youm7.com/story/2012/11/8/840303/ طفلة-قص-الشعر-بالمترو-ل-اليوم-السابع-الست-المنتقبة-هددتنى [Accessed 1 February 2017].

Awsat, 30/6/2012. Morsi saying the presidential oath in Tahir: I will not tolerate my powers and promise to work on releasing Sheikh Omar Abdel-Rahman. *Al-Sharq Al-Awsat* [online], 30 June 2012. Available from: http://archive. aawsat.com/details.asp?section=4&issueno=12268&article=684186#. WJzEQLGcZ-U [Accessed 1 February 2017].

Baines, P. and Egan, J., 2001. Marketing and political campaigning: mutually exclusive or exclusively mutual?. *Qualitative Market Research: An International Journal*, 4 (1), 25–34.

BBC Arabic, 28/12/2011. The Committee for the Promotion of Virtue and the Prevention of Vice launch a war on Facebook. *BBC Arabic* [online], 28 December 2011. Available from: http://www.bbc.com/arabic/middlee-ast/2011/12/111227_egypt_religious_police.shtml [Accessed 1 February 2017].

BBC News, 1/7/2013. Profile: Egypt's Tamarod protest movement. *BBC News* [online], 1 July 2013. Available from: http://www.bbc.co.uk/news/world-middle-east-23131953 [Accessed 1 February 2017].

BBC News, 24/12/2012. Q&A: Egypt constitutional crisis. *BBC News* [online], 24 December 2012. Available from: http://www.bbc.co.uk/news/world-middle-east-20554079 [Accessed 1 February 2017].

BBC News, 29/11/2012. Egypt assembly votes on constitution. *BBC News* [online], 29 November 2012. Available from: http://www.bbc.co.uk/news/world-middle-east-20536323 [Accessed 1 February 2017].

Belfiore, E., 2009. On bullshit in cultural policy practice and research: notes from the British case. *International Journal of Cultural Policy*, 15 (3), 343–359.

CNN Arabic, 25/7/2012. Where will the president Morsi say the oath? *CNN Arabic* [online], 25 July 2012. Available from: http://archive.arabic.cnn. com/2012/egypt.elections/6/25/egypt.morsiOath/ [Accessed 1 February 2017].

Coleman, S., 2017. Ducking the debate. Election analysis. Centre for the study of journalism, culture and community. Bournemouth University, UK. Available from: http://www.electionanalysis.uk/uk-election-analysis-2017/section-3-news-and-journalism/ducking-the-debate/ [Accessed 20 July 2017].

Dahl, R. A., 1998. *Democracy and its critics*. New Haven: Yale University Press.

Egyptian Initiative for Personal Rights, 2013. *Report on 'Shia massacre' in Abu Musallim village in Giza* [online]. Egyptian Initiative for Personal Rights, 26 June 2013. Available from: http://www.eipr.org/press/2013/06/ تقرير-عن-مذبحة-الشيعة-في-زاوية-أبو-مسلم-بالجيزة [Accessed 1 February 2017].

El-Din, G., 2012. *Ahram Online* presents: the idiot's guide to Egypt's presidential elections 2012. *Ahram Online* [online], 23 April 2012. Available from: http:// english.ahram.org.eg/NewsContent/36/0/36418/Presidential-elections-/0/Ahram-Online-presents-The-Idiots-Guide-to-Egypt's-.aspx [Accessed 19 September 2016].

Elaph, 8/10/12. Popular anger because of the presence of the killers of Sadat celebrations of the October War. *Elaph* [online], 8 October 2012. Available from: http://elaph.com/Web/news/2012/10/766452.html [Accessed 1 February 2017].

ElNabawi, M., 2013. Inside the Culture Ministry. *Mada Masr* [online], 28 June 2013. Available from: http://www.madamasr.com/en/2013/06/28/feature/culture/inside-the-culture-ministry/ [Accessed 1 February 2017].

Gad, E., 2014. *For the group but not for Egypt*. Cairo: Al-Dar Al-Masriah Al-Lubnaniah.

Gibson, R. and Römmele, A., 2001. Changing campaign communications: a party-centered theory of professionalized campaigning. *Harvard International Journal of Press/Politics*, 6 (4), 31–43.

Gibson, R. and Römmele, A., 2009. Measuring the professionalization of political campaigning. *Party Politics*, 15 (3), 321–339.

Green, D. and Gerber, A., 2008. *Get out the vote: how to increase voter turnout*. Washington, DC: Brookings Institution Press.

Hamelink, C., 2007. The professionalisation of political communication: democracy at stake? *In*: Negrine, R., Mancini, P., Holtz-Bacha, C. and Pappathanassopoulos eds. *The professionalisation of political communication*. Bristol: Intellect, 179–188.

Herrnson, P. S., 1992. Campaign professionalism and fundraising in congressional elections. *Journal of Politics*, 54, 859–870.

Human Rights Watch, 2013. Egypt: lynching of Shia follows months of hate speech. *Human Rights Watch* [online], 27 June 2013. New York: Human Rights Watch. Available from: https://www.hrw.org/news/2013/06/27/egypt-lynching-shia-follows-months-hate-speech [Accessed 1 February 2017].

Jadaliyya, 22/7/2013. Egypt's president Morsi in power a timeline. *Jadaliyya* [online], 22 July 2013. Available from: http://www.jadaliyya.com/pages/index/13101/egypts-president-morsi-in-power_a-timeline- [Accessed 1 February 2017].

Johnson, D. W., 2001. *No place for amateurs: how political consultants are reshaping American democracy*. New York: Routledge.

Koch, T., 2011. The professionalization of political marketing – a detriment to the democratic process? Department of Media and Communication, University of Leicester. *ResearchGate* [online]. Available from: https://www.researchgate.net/publication/215669646_The_Professionalization_of_Political_Marketing_-_A_Detriment_to_the_Democratic_Process [Accessed 1 June 2016].

Lees-Marshment, J. and Lilleker, D., 2012. Knowledge sharing and lesson learning: consultants' perspectives on the international sharing of political marketing strategy. *Contemporary Politics*, 18 (3), 343–354.

Lilleker, D. G. and Negrine, R., 2002. Professionalization: of what? Since when? By whom? *Harvard International Journal of Press/Politics*, 7 (4), 98–103.

Londoño, E., 2012. Egypt's Morsi replaces military chiefs in bid to consolidate power. *Washington Post* [online], 12 August 2012. Available from: https://wpo.st/QDib2 [Accessed 1 February 2016].

Magleby, D. B., Patterson, K. D. and Thurber, J. A., 2000. Campaign consultants and responsible party government [online]. *Annual Meeting of the American Political Science Association*. Washington, DC, 27 August–3 September 2000. Available from: https://www.researchgate.net/publication/237212017_Campaign_Consultants_and_Responsible_Party_Government [Accessed 1 June 2016].

Mancini, P., 1999. New frontiers in political professionalism. *Political Communication*, 16 (3), 231–245.

Medvic, S. K. and Lenart, S., 1997. The influence of political consultants in the 1992 congressional elections. *Legislative Studies Quarterly*, 22, 61–77.

Negrine, R., Mancini, P., Holtz-Bacha, C. and Pappathanassopoulos eds., 2007. *The professionalisation of political communication*. Bristol: Intellect, 179–188.

Norris, P., 1996. Does television erode social capital? A reply to Putnam. *P.S.: Political Science and Politics*, 29 (3), 474–480. Available from: https://www.hks.harvard.edu/fs/pnorris/Articles/Articles%20published%20in%20journals_files/Does_TV_Erode_Social_Capital_1996.pdf [Accessed 1 June 2016].

Norris, P., 1997. *Electoral change since 1945*. Oxford: Blackwell.

Norris, P., 2000. *A virtuous circle: political communications in postindustrial societies*. Cambridge University Press.

Norris, P., 2004a. The evolution of election campaigns: eroding political engagement? *Conference on Political Communications in the 21st Century*, University of Otago, New Zealand, January 2004. Available from: https://www.hks.harvard.edu/fs/pnorris/Acrobat/Otago%20The%20Evolution%20of%20Election%20Campaigns.pdf [Accessed 1 June 2016].

Norris, P., 2004b. Political communications and democratic politics. *In:* Bartle, J. and Griffiths, D., eds. *Political communication transformed: from Morrison to Mandelson*. Basingstoke: Palgrave Macmillan UK, 163–180.

Omran, I., 2012. After killing the young man in Suez. Muslim scientists: promoting virtue by hand threatens the stability of society. *Ahram Gate* [online], 8 July 2012. Available from: http://www.ahram.org.eg/archive/Religious-thought/News/159244.aspx [Accessed 1 June 2016].

Plasser, F. and Plasser, G., 2002. *Global political campaigning: a worldwide analysis of campaign professionals and their practices*. Westport: Praeger.

Rayner, J., 2014, What about winning? Looking into the blind spot of the theory of campaign professionalization. *Journal of Political Marketing*, 13 (4), 334–354.

Reuters Arabic, 2/7/2013. Sources: The turning point for the army was Morsi's position on Syria during Syria conference. *Reuters Arabic* [online], 2 July 2013. Available from: http://ara.reuters.com/article/topNews/idARACAE9 B20M720130702?sp=true [Accessed 1 February 2017].

Rotana Masriya, 2012. *Nas book* [television programme, video, online]. Rotana Masriya, 10 June 2012. YouTube. Available from: https://www.youtube. com/watch?v=tHDCugwhWhg [Accessed 1 June 2016].

Scammell, M., 1998. The wisdom of the war room: US campaigning and Americanization. *Media, Culture and Society*, 20 (2), 251–275.

Schumpeter, J. A., 1943. *Capitalism, socialism and democracy*. London: George Allen and Unwin.

Shorouk News, 10/5/2012. Publishing the full project of Al-Nahda. *Shourouk News* [online], 10 May 2012. Available from: http://www.shorouknews.com/ news/view.aspx?cdate=10052012&id=6772223f-2ed3-47ab-a105-d3c-55f4a3fdb [Accessed 28 January 2017].

Stack, L., 2013. With cameras rolling, Egyptian politicians threaten Ethiopia over dam. *New York Times* [online], 6 June 2013. Available from: https://thelede. blogs.nytimes.com/2013/06/06/with-cameras-rolling-egyptian-politicians-threaten-ethiopia-over-dam/?_r=0 [Accessed 1 June 2016].

Suleiman, H., 2013. *The Committee for the Promotion of Virtue and the Prevention of Vice, from the Saudi failure to the Egyptian reality* [online]. Giza, Egypt: Arab Center for Research Studies. Available from: http://www.acrseg.org/2298/ bcrawl [Accessed 1 February 2017].

Swanson, D. and Mancini, P., 1996. *Politics, media, and modern democracy: an international study of innovations in electoral campaigning and their consequences*. Westport: Praeger.

Tenscher, J., Koc-Michalska, K., Lilleker, D., Mykkänen, J., Walter, A., Findor, A., Jalali, C. and Róka, J., 2016. The professionals speak: practitioners' perspectives on professional election campaigning. *European Journal of Communication*, 31 (2), 95–119.

Tenscher, J., Mykkänen, J. and Moring, T., 2012. Modes of professional campaigning: a four-country comparison in the European parliamentary elections, 2009. *The International Journal of Press/Politics*, 17 (2), 145–168.

The Guardian, 10/7/2012. Decree to restore Egypt's parliament cancelled. *The Guardian* [online], 10 July 2012. Available from: https://www.theguardian. com/world/2012/jul/10/egypt-parliament-reconvenes-five-minutes [Accessed 1 February 2017].

The Guardian, 2/12/2016. Egypt's top court suspends work after Morsi supporters surround building. *The Guardian* [online], 2 December 2016. Available from: https://www.theguardian.com/world/2012/dec/02/egypt-court-suspends-work-morsi [Accessed 1 February 2017].

The Muslim Brotherhood, 16/5/2013. Freedom and Justice Party receives Mahathir Mohamed in Renaissance Experiences conference. *Ikhwan Web* [online], 16 May 2013. Available from: http://www.ikhwanweb.com/article.php?id=30944 [Accessed 28 January 2017].

The Muslim Brotherhood, 2/5/2012. FJP: Dr. Morsi's Nahda project backed by 80-year experience. *Ikhwan Web* [online], 2 May 2012. Available from: http://www.ikhwanweb.com/article.php?id=29946 [Accessed 28 January 2017].

The Muslim Brotherhood, 20/5/2012. Dr. Morsi to businessmen: we will invest $20 billion in Egyptian tourism industry. *Ikhwan Web* [online], 20 May 2012. Available from: http://www.ikhwanweb.com/article.php?id=30000 [Accessed 28 January 2017].

The Muslim Brotherhood, 22/6/2012. Morsi campaign press conference at Fairmont hotel to discuss latest developments. *Ikhwan Web* [online], 22 June 2012. Available from: http://www.ikhwanweb.com/article.php?id=30125 [Accessed 28 January 2016].

The Muslim Brotherhood, 27/4/2012. Al-Shater: Nahda project starts with building a strong democratic system. *Ikhwan Web* [online], 27 April 2012. Available from: http://www.ikhwanweb.com/article.php?id=29928 [Accessed 28 January 2017].

The Muslim Brotherhood, 28/4/2012. Dr. Morsi's electoral program – general features of Nahda (renaissance) project. *Ikhwan Web* [online], 28 April 2012. Available from: http://www.ikhwanweb.com/article.php?id=29932 [Accessed 28 January 2017].

The Muslim Brotherhood, 29/4/2012a. Dr. Morsi: 20 billion pounds for the reconstruction of Sinai over 5 years. *Ikhwan Web* [online], 29 April 2012. Available from: http://www.ikhwanweb.com/article.php?id=29937 [Accessed 28 January 2017].

The Muslim Brotherhood, 29/4/2012b. Dr. Morsi: Sinai is priority in Nahda (renaissance) project. *Ikhwan Web* [online], 29 April 2012. Available from: http://www.ikhwanweb.com/article.php?id=29936 [Accessed 28 January 2017].

The Muslim Brotherhood, 31/5/2012. Morsi presidential campaign announces new slogan, new spirit for start of new phase. *Ikhwan Web* [online], 31 May 2012. Available from: http://www.ikhwanweb.com/article.php?id=30037 [Accessed 28 January 2017].

The Muslim Brotherhood, 7/5/2012a. Dr. Mohamed Morsi – a brief biography. *Ikhwan Web* [online], 7 May 2012. Available from: http://ikhwanweb.com/article.php?id=29964 [Accessed 3 September 2016].

The Muslim Brotherhood, 7/5/2012b. Dr. Morsi assures tourism has priority in Nahda project. *Ikhwan Web* [online], 7 May 2012. Available from: http://www.ikhwanweb.com/article.php?id=29963 [Accessed 28 January 2017].

The Muslim Brotherhood, 7/5/2012c. Gouda: Brotherhood's Nahda project will uplift Egypt in four years. *Ikhwan Web* [online], 7 May 2012. Available from: http://www.ikhwanweb.com/article.php?id=29966 [Accessed 28 January 2017].

Trager, E., 2011. Unbreakable Muslim Brotherhood: grim prospects for a liberal Egypt. *Foreign Affairs* [online], 90 (5), 114–126. Available from: https://www.foreignaffairs.com/articles/north-africa/2011-09-01/unbreakable-muslim-brotherhood [Accessed 1 January 2017].

Trager, E., 2016. *Arab Fall, how the Muslim Brotherhood won and lost Egypt in 891 days.*

INDEX[1]

[1] Note: Page numbers followed by 'n' refer to notes.

© The Author(s) 2018   279
D. Elsheikh, *Campaign Professionalism during Egypt's 2012
Presidential Election*, Political Campaigning and Communication,
https://doi.org/10.1007/978-3-319-75954-8

Printed by Printforce, the Netherlands